KILLING REAGAN

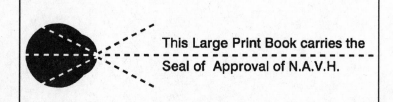

This Large Print Book carries the
Seal of Approval of N.A.V.H.

THE VIOLENT ASSAULT THAT CHANGED A PRESIDENCY

KILLING REAGAN

BILL O'REILLY
AND
MARTIN DUGARD

WHEELER PUBLISHING
A part of Gale, Cengage Learning

GALE
CENGAGE Learning®

Farmington Hills, Mich • San Francisco • New York • Waterville, Maine
Meriden, Conn • Mason, Ohio • Chicago

GALE
CENGAGE Learning®

Copyright © 2015 by Bill O'Reilly and Martin Dugard.
Wheeler Publishing, a part of Gale, Cengage Learning.

ALL RIGHTS RESERVED
Wheeler Publishing Large Print Hardcover.
The text of this Large Print edition is unabridged.
Other aspects of the book may vary from the original edition.
Set in 16 pt. Plantin.

LIBRARY OF CONGRESS CATALOGING-IN-PUBLICATION DATA

O'Reilly, Bill, author.
  Killing Reagan : the violent assault that changed the presidency / by Bill
O'Reilly and Martin Dugard. — Large print edition.
     pages cm — (Wheeler publishing large print hardcover)
  Includes bibliographical references.
  ISBN 978-1-4104-8259-4 (hardcover) — ISBN 1-4104-8259-6 (hardcover)
  1. Reagan, Ronald—Assassination attempt, 1981. 2. United States—Politics
and government—1981-1989. I. Dugard, Martin, author. II. Title.
  E877.3.O74 2015b
  973.927092—dc23   2015031892

Published in 2015 by arrangement with Henry Holt and Company, LLC

Printed in the United States of America
1 2 3 4 5 6 7 19 18 17 16 15

*This book is dedicated to all those
who are caring for an elderly person.
You are noble.*

God had a divine purpose in placing this land between two great oceans to be found by those who had a special love of freedom and courage.

— RONALD REAGAN

PROLOGUE

Reagan Home
Bel-Air, California
June 5, 2004
1:08 P.M.

The man with one minute to live is no longer confused.

Ronald Reagan lapsed into a coma two days ago. His wife, Nancy, sits at the side of the bed, holding the former president's hand. Emotionally and physically exhausted by the ordeal, she quietly sobs as her body rocks in grief. Reagan's breathing has become ragged and inconsistent. After ten long years of slow descent toward the grave due to Alzheimer's disease, a bout of pneumonia brought on by food particles caught in his lungs has delivered the knockout blow. Nancy knows that her beloved Ronnie's time has come.

Counting the former president, six people crowd into the bedroom. There is his physician, Dr. Terry Schaack; and Laura, the Irish nurse whose soft brogue the president is known to find soothing. Two of his grown children stand at the bedside. Ron, forty-six, and Patti, fifty-one, have been holding vigil with their mother for days. They have a reputation for conflict with their parents, but on this day those quarrels have vanished as they lend their mother emotional support. An adopted son from Reagan's first marriage, Michael, has also been summoned, but he is caught in Los Angeles traffic and will miss the president's final breath.

Outside the single-story, three-bedroom house, the foggy Pacific marine layer has burned off, replaced by a warm summer sun. The hydrangea and white camellia bushes are in full bloom. A media horde has gathered on St. Cloud Road in Reagan's posh Bel-Air neighborhood,* waiting with

* A group of Reagan's friends bought the house for $2.5 million while he was still in office and leased it to him with an option to buy — which Reagan did, in December 1989, for $3.0 million. The 7,192-square-foot home sits on a 1.29-acre lot and features a swimming pool, three bedrooms, and six bathrooms. Next door is the former Kirkeby Estate, which served as the setting for the *Beverly Hillbillies* television show. Despite the price

10

their cameras and news trucks for the inevitable moment when the fortieth president of the United States passes away. The former actor and college football player is ninety-three. Even into his seventies, he was so vigorous that he rode the hills of his Santa Barbara ranch on horseback for hours and cleared acres of thick hillside brush all by himself.

But years ago his mind betrayed him. Reagan slowly lapsed into a dementia so severe that it has been a decade since he appeared in public. The root cause could have been genetic, for his mother was not lucid in her final days. Or it might have been the result of a near-death experience caused by a gunman's bullet twenty-three years ago. Whatever the reason, Reagan's decline has been dramatic. Over the past ten years, he has spent most days sleeping or looking out at the sweeping view of Los Angeles from his flagstone veranda. His smile is warm, but his mind is vacant. Eventually, he lost the ability even to recognize family and friends. When Reagan's oldest child from his first marriage, Maureen, was dying of

---

of Reagan's home, one real estate agent noted that "it's a very ordinary house — Reagan must be the poorest man in Bel-Air."

melanoma in a Santa Monica hospital in 2001, the former president was in the same hospital being treated for a broken hip — yet was too confused to see her.

So now, the man who lies at home in a hospital bed, clad in comfortable pajamas, is a shell of his former self. His blue eyes, the last time he opened them, were dense, the color of chalk. His voice, which once lent itself to great oration, is silent.

Another breath, this one more jagged than the last. Nancy's tears fall onto the bedsheets at the onset of the death rattle.

Suddenly, Ronald Reagan opens his eyes. He stares intently at Nancy. "They weren't chalky or vague," Patti Davis will later write of her father's eyes. "They were clear and blue and full of love."

The room hushes.

Closing his eyes, Reagan takes his final breath.

The former leader of the free world, the man who defeated Soviet communism and ended the Cold War, is dead.

1

Convention Center Music Hall
Cleveland, Ohio
October 28, 1980
9:30 P.M.

The man with twenty-four years to live steps onstage.

Polite applause washes over Ronald Reagan as he strides to his lectern for the 1980 presidential debate.* The former movie star and two-term governor of California is striving to become president of the United States at the relatively advanced age of sixty-nine. His jet-black pompadour, which he

---

* There were supposed to be three debates in the 1980 campaign, due to the presence of third-party candidate John Anderson, a Republican congressman from Illinois who ran as an independent. President Carter refused to debate Anderson, giving Reagan and Carter the chance to go head-to-head.

swears he does not dye, is held in place by a dab of Brylcreem.* His high cheeks are noticeably rosy, as if they have been rouged — although the color may also have come from the glass of wine he had with dinner. At six foot one and 190 pounds, Reagan stands tall and straight, but his appearance does not intimidate: rather, he looks to be approachable and kind.

The governor's opponent is incumbent president Jimmy Carter. At five nine and 155 pounds, the slender Carter has the build of a man who ran cross-country in college. In fact, the president still makes time for four miles a day. Carter is a political junkie, immersing himself in every last nuance of a campaign. He has made a huge surge in the polls over the last two months. Carter knows that with one week until Election Day, the race is almost dead even. The winner of this debate will most likely win the presidency, and if it is Carter, his comeback will be one of the greatest in modern history.† In another reality, a Car-

---

* Reagan's hair was actually brown, but the wet look of his hairstyling made it appear black.

† One reason Jimmy Carter is behind is that CBS News anchor Walter Cronkite's nightly tally of the number of days the American hostages had been

ter loss would make him the first president in nearly fifty years to be voted out of office after just one full term. Still boyish at fifty-six, but with a face lined by the rigors of the presidency, he now stands opposite Reagan, a man he loathes.

The feeling is mutual. Reagan privately refers to the current president of the United States as "a little shit."

As President Carter stands behind the pale-blue lectern, he makes a sly sideward glance at his opponent. Carter is all business and believes that Ronald Reagan is not his intellectual equal. He has publicly stated that Reagan is "untruthful and dangerous" and "different than me in almost every basic element of commitment and experience and promise to the American people."

At his acceptance speech at the August 1980 Democratic National Convention, Carter made it clear that the upcoming election would be "a stark choice between two men, two parties, two sharply different pictures of what America is and the world is."

The president concluded by adding, "It's

---

held in Iran helped lower voter confidence in Carter.

Jimmy Carter and Ronald Reagan shake hands as they greet each other before their 1980 presidential debate in Cleveland, Ohio.

a choice between two futures."

Indeed, Carter appears to be the smarter man. He graduated fifty-ninth in a class of 820 from the U.S. Naval Academy and spent his military career onboard nuclear submarines. The Georgia native with the toothy smile possesses an easy command of facts and figures. He has hands-on experience in foreign and domestic policy and often speaks in soothing intellectual sound bites.

In 1976, Carter defeated his Republican

opponent, Gerald R. Ford, in their three debates, and he is sure he will do the same tonight. Political pollster Pat Caddell, the nation's leading authority on presidential elections and a member of the Carter campaign, predicts that Carter will clinch the election with a decisive debate victory.

Two months ago, Reagan's lead in the polls was sixteen points. But if the election were held today, polls indicate Carter would garner 41 percent of the vote and Reagan 40. However, Caddell has strongly warned Carter against debating Reagan. The biggest knock against Reagan politically is the perception that he is a warmonger. Caddell believes that a debate would allow Reagan to counter those fears by appearing warm and collected rather than half-cocked. Once it became clear that Carter was intent on a public debate, his advisers pressed for the long, ninety-minute format that will be used tonight, hoping that Reagan will wear down and say something stupid.

That would hardly be a first. Ronald Reagan is so prone to saying the wrong thing at the wrong time that his campaign staff has been known to call him "old foot-in-the-mouth." Perhaps the worst public gaffe of his career will occur in Brazil. Speaking at a dinner in that nation's capital city of

Brasilia, Reagan will hoist his glass, proposing a toast to the people of *Bolivia.**

But Reagan is no fool and is much more incisive than Carter about the Soviet Union's Communist regime. He despises it. But he has no foreign policy experience to refer to. Reagan memorizes speeches and phrases, rather than immersing himself in heavy study or specific details. While this might not be a problem at most campaign events, where Reagan can read from a prepared speech, it could be trouble here in Cleveland: the rules of the debate stipulate that neither candidate is allowed to bring notes to the stage.

Yet Reagan will not admit to being at a disadvantage. He believes his communications skills will make up for his lesser book smarts. Reagan, in fact, is far different from

* He immediately attempted to cover the slip by adding, "That's where I'm going," referring to his four-nation swing through South America. In fact, he was not going to Bolivia. His next stop was Colombia, whose capital city is Bogotá. Officials tried to cover for Reagan by changing the transcript of the speech to read "Bogota." When asked why, they replied that it was what Reagan intended to say and refused to alter their correction.

how most people perceive him. He has an army of close acquaintances but few friends. He freely offers his opinions about public policy but rarely shares deep personal thoughts. Some who work for him think Reagan is distant and lazy, as he so often lets others make tough decisions for him. Others, however, find his manner warm, friendly, and endearing and his hands-off management style liberating.

Reagan does not really care what other people think. He confidently marches ahead, rarely showing any self-doubt.

To bring him luck in the debate, Reagan traveled to his native state of Illinois and visited the tomb of Abraham Lincoln this past week. He actually rubbed his nose on the statue of the great political debater, hoping some of Lincoln's brilliance would rub off on him.

Not that Reagan is intimidated. Of Carter he has said condescendingly, "He knows he can't win a debate if it were held in the Rose Garden before an audience of Administration officials, with the questions being asked by Jody Powell," referencing the president's hard-living press secretary.

The truth is that Reagan's campaign has lost whatever momentum it once possessed. "Ronald Reagan's presidential campaign may be running out of steam," wrote the *Wall Street Journal* on October 16.

"I think Reagan is slipping everywhere," one of his top aides told reporters in an off-the-record conversation. "If he doesn't do something dramatic he is going to lose."*

Meanwhile, Carter's aides are almost giddy in their optimism. "The pieces are in place for us to win," they tell *Newsweek* magazine.

At the stroke of 9:30, the debate begins.

Ruth Hinerfeld of the League of Women Voters opens the proceedings with a short speech. She speaks her few careful lines in a hesitant tone before handing the proceedings over to the evening's moderator, veteran journalist Howard K. Smith of ABC News. Smith sits at a desk to the front of the stage, his tie loose and his jacket unbuttoned.

"Thank you, Mrs. Hinerfeld," he says before introducing the four journalists who

---

* While this remark is still unclaimed, those within the Reagan and Carter circles believe they were the words of the late Lyn Nofziger (1924–2006), a political veteran who was known for his candor with the press.

will launch questions at the two candidates.* The chatter and applause that filled the room just moments ago have been replaced by palpable nervous tension. There is a sensation that tonight may change the course of U.S. history.

As both Reagan and Carter well know, the 1970s have been a brutal time for America. In 1974, President Richard Nixon resigned under threat of impeachment after the Watergate affair. The unchecked growth of the Soviet Union's war machine and the American failure to win the Vietnam War have tilted the global balance of power. At home, inflation, interest rates, and unemployment rates are sky-high. Gasoline shortages have led to mile-long lines at the pumps. Worst of all, there is the ongoing humiliation that came about when Iranian radicals stormed the American embassy in Tehran in 1979 and took almost the entire staff hostage. Nearly six months later, a rescue attempt failed miserably, resulting in the deaths of eight American servicemen.

* Barbara Walters, ABC News; William Hilliard, Portland *Oregonian;* Marvin L. Stone, *U.S. News & World Report;* and Harry Ellis, *Christian Science Monitor.*

One week from today, when Americans go to the polls to pick a U.S. president, the fifty-two hostages will have spent exactly one year in captivity.

The United States of America is still very much a superpower, but an air of defeat, not hope, now defines its national outlook.

The small theater in which the debate will unfold was built shortly after World War I, at a time when America had flexed its muscle on the world stage and first assumed global prominence. But tonight, there is a single question on the minds of many watching this debate:* can America be fixed?

Or, more to the point, are the best days of the United States of America in the past?

"Governor," asks panelist Marvin Stone, editor of the magazine *U.S. News & World Report,* "you have been criticized for being all too quick to advocate the use of lots of muscle, military action, to deal with foreign crises. Specifically, what are the differences between the two of you on the uses of American military power?"

Reagan's career as a Hollywood actor has

---

* Three thousand in the auditorium and 80.6 million watching at home on television.

seen him through a number of personal highs and lows. He has experienced failure and divorce, and endured the humiliation of acting in films that made him look ridiculous. But he has also learned poise under fire and the art of delivering a line. Now, as Stone zeroes in on what some see as a glaring weakness in Reagan's résumé, those communication skills desert him. He fumbles for words. Eloquence is replaced by odd pauses. "I believe with all my heart," Reagan says slowly, as if he has forgotten the question completely, "that our first priority must be world peace."

Offstage, in the Carter campaign's greenroom, the president's staff roars with laughter as they watch an uncomfortable Reagan on a television monitor.

There is more to Reagan's answer, but it is clear that he is searching for a way to leave the moment behind and revert to the well-rehearsed lines he has prepared for tonight. "I'm a father of sons," Reagan finally says, finding a way to use one of those scripted answers. "I have a grandson. I don't ever want to see another generation of young Americans bleed their lives into sandy beachheads in the Pacific, or rice paddies and jungles in Asia, or the muddy, bloody battlefields of Europe."

About ten feet away, Carter grips his lectern as if standing at a church pulpit. His eyes are tired and his face pinched.* Naturally peevish, he is tired from staying up late trying to negotiate the release of the American hostages in Iran. The talks are at a delicate point, and he knows that his electoral victory is assured if he succeeds. Carter is so preoccupied with these talks that he initially refused to spend time prepping for the debate. The lack of sleep has made him short-tempered, tense, and difficult to be around. This fatigue also makes it difficult for Carter to hide his utter contempt for Reagan as they share the stage.

When it comes his turn to field the same question, the president speaks in simple declarative sentences, reminding the audience and the millions watching on television that he is committed to a strong national defense. He mentions the American journalist H. L. Mencken by name and quotes him on the nature of problem solving. It is a

* The Reagan campaign argued that the lecterns should be side by side, which would accentuate Reagan's height. The Carter campaign refused. On the night of the debate, as one observer noted, the lecterns were "as far as possible apart, without actually going off the stage."

literary allusion meant to remind the audience of Carter's intellect, but it is a misstep — Mencken is against religion, suspicious of democracy, and elitist. Carter's mentioning him is a thinly veiled attempt to rally the more left-leaning aspects of the Democratic Party. But the American public, Democrat and Republican alike, is in a patriotic mood. They long for a return to simple, straightforward American values. The words of H. L. Mencken only succeed in making Carter look out of touch.

Stone pounces. The balding editor leans into his microphone. He speaks to the president of the United States as if he were lecturing a cub reporter. "Under what circumstances would you use military forces to deal with, for example, a shutoff of Persian Gulf oil, if that should occur, or to counter Russian expansion beyond Afghanistan into either Iran or Pakistan? I ask this question in view of charges that we are woefully unprepared to project sustained — and I emphasize the word *sustained* — power in that part of the world."

Carter will reach for his water glass eleven times tonight. It is his tell, as gamblers call a nervous tic. Another tell is that Carter blinks constantly when ill at ease.

"We have made sure that we address this

question peacefully, not injecting American military forces into combat but letting the strength of our nation be felt in a beneficial way," he answers, eyelids fluttering as if he were staring into the sun. "This, I believe, has assured that our interests will be protected in the Persian Gulf region, as we've done in the Middle East and throughout the world."

This is not an answer. It is an evasion. And while Carter is hoping to appear presidential and above the fray, the fact is that he looks indecisive and somewhat weak.

When it comes Reagan's turn to field the same question, he stumbles again — though only for an instant. His thought process seems to be clearing. Reagan has rehearsed this debate with adviser David Stockman, whose sharp intellect rivals that of Carter. That practice now shows in Reagan's new confidence. Statistics suddenly roll off his tongue. He rattles off the 38 percent reduction in America's military force under the Carter administration, the refusal to build sixty ships that the navy deems necessary to fulfilling its global mission, and Carter's insistence that programs to build new American bombers, missiles, and submarines be either stalled or halted altogether.

The outrage in Reagan's voice will connect to those viewers sick and tired of America's descent into global impotency.

Jimmy Carter reaches for his water glass.

More than one thousand miles west, in the city of Evergreen, Colorado, a twenty-five-year-old drifter pays little attention to the debate. Instead, John Hinckley Jr. fixates on schemes to impress Jodie Foster, the young actress who starred opposite Robert De Niro in the 1976 movie *Taxi Driver* — a film Hinckley has seen more than fifteen times. Even though he has never met her, Hinckley considers Jodie the love of his life and is determined to win her hand.

Hinckley's obsession with the eighteen-year-old actress is so complete that he temporarily moved to New Haven, Connecticut, to stalk her while she attended Yale University. Hinckley is a college dropout, unable to focus on his own studies, yet he had little problem sitting in on Foster's classes. In New Haven, he slid love notes under the door of her dorm room, found her phone number, and, in a brazen move, called Foster and asked her out to dinner. Shocked, she refused. So stunned was Foster by Hinckley's advances and subsequent actions that she will not speak

27

of them for years to come.

Now, nearly penniless and having moved back in with his parents, John Hinckley ruminates over how to make Jodie Foster change her mind. His plans are grandiose and bizarre. Hinckley has contemplated killing himself right before Foster's very eyes, or perhaps hijacking an airliner.

He has even plotted the assassination of President Jimmy Carter.

The pudgy Hinckley, who wears his shaggy hair in bangs, has yet to see a psychiatrist for the schizophrenia that is slowly taking control of his brain. That appointment is still one week away. But no amount of therapy will ever stop him from thinking about Jodie Foster — and the lengths to which he must go to earn her love. Now, sitting in a small basement bedroom, Hinckley considers suicide.

Bottles of prescription pills cover his nightstand. It will take a few more days to summon his courage, but Hinckley will soon reach for the container labeled "Valium" and gobble a deadly dosage.

Once again, John Hinckley will fail.

He will wake up nauseated but alive, vowing to find some new way to impress Jodie Foster.

Killing himself is not the answer. Clearly, someone else must die.

About halfway through the ninety-four-minute debate, Ronald Reagan gets personal. "I talked to a man just briefly there who asked me one simple question," Reagan says gravely. " 'Do I have reason to hope that I can someday take care of my family again?' "

Watching from the side of the stage, Nancy Reagan can see that her husband is gaining confidence with every question. This gives her solace, for Nancy was so afraid that her Ronnie would say something foolish that she initially opposed the debate. More than that of any of his advisers, it is Nancy's opinion that matters most to Reagan. They have been married twenty-eight years, and she has been a driving force behind his run for the presidency. Throughout their marriage he has chosen to address her as Mommy, a term of endearment mocked by some journalists covering Reagan.

Nancy Reagan wears a size four dress and has thin legs and thick ankles. Her mother was an actress, her adoptive father an esteemed surgeon, and she grew up determined to find fame.* She relies on sleeping pills and tranquilizers, and sometimes bursts into tears from stress, but there is steel in her voice when she corrects her husband or sees to it that one of the campaign staff is disciplined. Nancy Reagan professes shock when the press portrays her as the conniving Lady Macbeth, but the description isn't entirely off the mark. She is by far the more grating half of the Reagan marriage, and she is determined that this election be won at all costs.

Cheating is not out of the question. Although he does not yet know it, Jimmy Carter's briefing notes for this debate were recently stolen from the White House and

---

* Nancy Reagan was born in New York City on July 6, 1921, as Anne Frances Robbins. Her mother was an actress and her father a used-car salesman. The two split up when the girl who had earned the nickname Nancy was just six. She was sent to live with family in Maryland. Her mother remarried, to a Chicago neurosurgeon named Loyal Davis, who adopted Nancy and gave her his surname. In 1949, after working for a time as a sales clerk, she traveled to Hollywood to pursue her dream of becoming an actress. During that time she dated several prominent names in Hollywood, among them Clark Gable.

secretly handed over to the Reagan campaign. This, of course, has allowed Reagan to know in advance how Carter will respond to every question. Certainly, no one is pointing to Nancy Reagan as having engineered the theft — indeed, reports of the act will not be leaked to the public for three more years, and the real culprit remains in question.* Yet it is well known that, with so much at stake, she doesn't play

* As noted in Craig Shirley's *Rendezvous with Destiny,* the late Paul Corbin, an influential Democrat and friend of the Kennedy family who was bitter about Ted Kennedy losing to Jimmy Carter in the 1980 Democratic primary race, admitted to stealing the playbook shortly after copies were assembled in the White House on the night of October 23. The book was then given to William Casey, the former World War II OSS spy who led the Reagan campaign. Finally, on October 25, the Carter book was handed to the three key players in Reagan's debate prep: James Baker III, David Gergen, and David Stockman. Three years later, when word about the theft was leaked, a ten-month congressional and FBI investigation ensued. Corbin never surfaced as the culprit, and the truth did not come out about his involvement until after his death in 1990. Pat Caddell, when interviewed for this book, said he believes Corbin

nice. To Nancy, gaining access to Carter's playbook is a windfall to the Reagan campaign, not a crime.

As the debate continues, Jimmy Carter is not doing himself any favors onstage. "I had a discussion with my daughter, Amy," Carter says, referring to his thirteen-year-old, "to ask her what the most important issue was. She said she thought nuclear weaponry and the control of nuclear arms."

In the greenroom, Carter's campaign staff is distraught. While prepping for the debate, Carter told them he planned to use his daughter to make a point. His staff strongly urged him not to.

"In the end," Pat Caddell will later recall, "it came down to 'I'm the president. Fuck you.'"

It is a huge mistake. That the president of the United States is allowing a teenager to decide what matters most to America in a time of such great crisis is laughable. One journalist will later write that the statement was "Carter at his worst: Weak and silly."

But Jimmy Carter does not have that sense. "In the debate itself, it was hard to judge the general demeanor that was

---

was given the book by a member of the National Security Council serving in Carter's White House.

32

projected to the viewers," Carter will write in his diary tonight. "He [Reagan] has his memorized tapes. He pushes a button, and they come out."*

Carter's statement is true. Like all veteran actors, Reagan has mastered the art of memorization. Also, while there are a great number of scripted lines that he has written himself or with his speechwriters to help him score points, Reagan has concocted a simple statement to deride Carter. After the president launches into a detailed and very dry explanation about Reagan's opposition to national health care, Reagan pauses at his lectern. It is obvious that Carter is showing off his intellect in a way that is meant to make Reagan look old, slow, and out of touch. The president's words were specifically chosen to ensure that Reagan's scripted lines could not rescue him and to make it obvious to one and all that Jimmy Carter is the more intelligent of the two.

What follows is Reagan at his best. In four simple words that will be remembered for decades, he succeeds in making President

* Just moments after the debate ended, a group of journalists came to Jimmy Carter before he could leave the stage. "Are you prepared to claim victory? Did you win it?" Carter refused to answer.

Carter look foolish. They are words that Reagan came up with during the long hours of practice debates but which he has kept to himself, knowing that for maximum effectiveness the line must sound completely spontaneous.

Slowly shaking his head, Reagan turns to Carter and says, "There you go again."

The auditorium erupts in laughter. Reagan's tone is that of a disappointed parent, saddened by a child who has failed to live up to expectations. The words mean nothing and everything. One short sentence captures the mood of a nation that no longer wants detailed policy explanations as to why the economy has collapsed and Americans are being held hostage in a foreign country.

The time for words has passed. Now is the time for action.

The election may be seven days away, but for James Earl "Jimmy" Carter Jr. of Plains, Georgia, it is over. The only man who does not know that is Carter himself. "Both sides felt good about the debate. We'll see whose basic strategy is best when the returns come in next Tuesday," he will write in his diary.

Reagan finishes the debate with a flourish. "Are you better off than you were four years

34

ago?" he says earnestly into the television camera, wrapping up with an emotional appeal to the American people. "Is it easier for you to go and buy things in the stores than it was four years ago? Is there more or less unemployment in the country than there was four years ago? Is America as respected throughout the world as it was? Do you feel that our security is as safe, that we're as strong as we were four years ago? And if you answer all of those questions yes, why then, I think your choice is very obvious as to who you'll vote for."

So obvious, in fact, that the election is a landslide. Ronald Reagan receives 489 electoral votes; Jimmy Carter receives just 49.*

On January 20, 1981, Ronald Reagan is sworn in as the fortieth president of the United States.

John Hinckley Jr. has a new target.

* Carter won his home state of Georgia, plus Minnesota, the home state of running mate Walter Mondale. The Carter-Mondale ticket also captured Hawaii, Rhode Island, West Virginia, Maryland, and the District of Columbia.

2

Universal Studios
Hollywood, California
September 1950
Daytime

The chimpanzee wears a white jumpsuit as she climbs high into the branches of a eucalyptus tree in the front yard of 712 Colonial Street.* "Peggy" is five years old. She was born in the jungles of Liberia and lured into captivity with a bundle of bananas. Since coming to Hollywood, Peggy has been taught to understand 502 voice commands, ride a tricycle, do backflips on cue, and put on a necktie. She has become one of the motion picture industry's top

* Not an actual street, but a movie set at Universal Studios. Similar homes on the back lot would be used for many productions in the years to come, including the hit television series *Desperate Housewives.*

Ronald Reagan and Peggy the chimp on the set of Bedtime for Bonzo, *1950*

animal performers, commanding a thousand dollars per week in salary. Now, as the cameras roll, she is starring in her first title role. The film is a screwball comedy entitled *Bedtime for Bonzo.*

"Action!" cries director Fred de Cordova.★ Peggy instantly obeys trainer Henry

★ Fred de Cordova, a graduate of Harvard Law School, will go on to become Johnny Carson's longtime producer on *The Tonight Show.* In that

Craig's instruction to do what comes naturally for her: climb a tree.

One would think the act will not be quite as easy for her costar. Thirty-nine-year-old Ronald Reagan balances precariously on the top step of an eight-foot ladder leaning against the tree trunk. In his slick-soled shoes, dress shirt, and tie, he is hardly dressed for climbing. His trademark pompadour, meantime, is carefully Brylcreem'd into place. There is no safety rope to halt his fall should Reagan lose his balance, but that is not a problem. Nearly twenty years after his college football career ended, the rugged actor is still lean and athletic. Reagan pulls himself up into the tree with ease, with not so much as a hair out of place.

Just a few years earlier, it would have been ludicrous to imagine Ronald Reagan acting opposite a chimpanzee. He was a star contract player for the Warner Bros. film studio, well on his way to becoming the sort of lead actor who could command any role he wished, like his friends Cary Grant and Errol Flynn.

In every way, Ronald Reagan's life in the

---

time, Carson will make several comedic jabs at *Bedtime for Bonzo*.

early 1940s could not have been better.

But that was then.

Ronald Reagan is twenty-six when he steps off the electric trolley at the Republic Pictures stop in Hollywood. The year is 1937. A torrential April rain drenches the young baseball announcer as he strides quickly along Radford Avenue to the studio gate. If Reagan were to lift his head, he would see the legendary "HOLLYWOOD-LAND" sign just miles above him in the hills, but he keeps his head low, the collar of his raincoat cinched tightly around his throat.

Dutch, as Reagan is known to family and friends, works for radio station WHO in Des Moines, Iowa, covering sports. He has come west to visit the Chicago Cubs spring training camp on nearby Catalina Island, twenty miles off the California coast.* But the storm has shut down the ferries and seaplane service to Catalina, giving Reagan a free day in Los Angeles. Cowboy singing sensation Gene Autry is filming a new Western called *Rootin' Tootin' Rhythm,* and a

* The Wrigley family, who owned the Cubs at the time, also owned a controlling interest in the island, which is why the Cubs trained there.

few of Reagan's friends from back home are playing the roles of Singing Cowhands.* Reagan, who has long fantasized about being a movie star, has come to offer moral support to his pals.

Reagan will later write that "hundreds of young people — from Iowa, Illinois, and just about every other state" — shared his fantasy. They "stepped off a train at Union Station in Los Angeles . . . they got no closer to realizing it than a studio front gate."

But thanks to his pals, Reagan makes it through the gate and hustles to Autry's soundstage. He enters the cavernous building with klieg lights hanging from high wooden beams. He is immediately intoxicated by the sight of the actors, cameras, lights, and everything else that goes into making a movie. All is quiet as filming begins. Gene Autry himself, dressed in the knee-high boots and gun belt of a cowboy, strums a guitar and sings a lament about life on the prairie. The set is made to

* They were members of a band called the Oklahoma Outlaws, which had a big following in the Midwest. Autry, who was looking for ways to broaden his national audience, had arranged to bring them to Hollywood.

look like the parlor of an ornate home. Autry is surrounded by musicians and actors clutching fiddles and guitars, all dressed as cowboys.

"Cut," yells director Mack Wright as the song winds down. Autry stops. Everyone relaxes on the set. A few minutes later, as Wright calls for "action," the scene is repeated.

"I was starry-eyed," Reagan admits to a friend that night. His friend's name is Joy Hodges, and she and her band are performing at the stately Biltmore Hotel in downtown LA. Joy knew Reagan back in Des Moines, and they now enjoy a quiet dinner between sets. The walls are lined with oak, and a marble fountain gurgles in the background. Reagan tells her his dreams of becoming a movie star and how he wishes he could find a way to break into the business.

Joy Hodges, a pretty, raven-haired lady, finds Reagan intriguing.

"Take off your glasses," she commands.

He removes them, and Joy instantly becomes a blur to Reagan.

Hodges, on the other hand, can see him quite clearly — and she likes what she sees. "Studios don't make passes at actors who wear glasses," she warns him before going back onstage for her second set.

Thus, the fairy tale begins. By ten the next morning, Reagan is meeting with Joy's agent, who arranges a screen test for the handsome young man. The test eventually makes its way to Jack Warner, the powerful head of Warner Bros. Pictures. He also likes what he sees and offers Reagan a seven-year contract at two hundred dollars a week — almost three times what he makes at WHO. A hairstylist transforms Reagan's center-parted look into the trademark pompadour he will wear the rest of his life. A tailor ingeniously alters the taper of his collar to create the optical illusion that Reagan's neck is not so thick. Finally, after some deliberation, the publicity department declares that he can keep his real name on-screen.

So it is that by June 1937, just two months after stepping out of the rain at Republic Pictures, Ronald Reagan is acting in his first motion picture. The movie is called *Love Is on the Air.* Appropriately enough, Reagan plays a radio announcer.

Sarah Jane Mayfield — or Jane Wyman, as she is known in Hollywood — knows a thing or two about love. It is early in 1938 as she arrives on the set of the film *Brother Rat.* At

42

Up-and-coming movie star Ronald Reagan, 1939

the age of twenty-one, she is already married. Her current husband is dress manufacturer Myron Futterman, whom she wed in New Orleans six months ago. Small, with bangs worn high on her forehead and a husky voice that will one day become her trademark, Wyman has struggled to break into Hollywood since coming west from Missouri. But now she finally has gotten her foot in the door through a series of small roles in B movies and is determined to become a star. Her weakness is being impulsive when it comes to love, and she separates from Futterman almost as quickly as she married him.

As Ronald Reagan begins his tenth film in less than a year,[*] there is no hiding the fact that his *Brother Rat* costar has quickly become infatuated with him. By December 1938, Jane Wyman officially divorces Myron Futterman and takes up with Reagan.

They soon become Hollywood's golden couple, "wholesome and happy and utterly completely American," in the words of gossip columnist Louella Parsons, who, knowing that nothing in Hollywood lasts forever, nevertheless predicts that their union will last thirty years. Wyman and Reagan are married in January 1940, shortly before Reagan begins filming *Knute Rockne All American* with Pat O'Brien. He plays the role of legendary Notre Dame running back George Gipp, uttering the immortal line

---

[*] Such a pace will be unheard of in years to come, but in an era before television, studios produce hundreds of films each year, and for an actor to go from one picture to another is as simple as walking from one soundstage to a different one next door.

Ronald Reagan and Jane Wyman with baby Maureen

"Ask 'em to go in there with all they've got, win just one for the Gipper," before dying on-screen. It is his first A film and is soon followed by a costarring role alongside the swashbuckling womanizer Errol Flynn in *Santa Fe Trail.* Just four short years after breaking into Hollywood, Ronald Reagan is now a major star. He and Wyman are soon building a massive new house and spending their evenings at the best Hollywood nightclubs.

In 1941, Wyman gives birth to a beautiful daughter whom they name Maureen.

World War II is raging. But Ronald Reagan's poor eyesight exempts him from fighting overseas. He stays in California but is eager to contribute to the war effort. Long before moving to Los Angeles, Reagan had joined Iowa's Army Reserve, serving in the cavalry. In May 1937, before making his first motion picture, he was offered a commission as a second lieutenant in the U.S. Cavalry Officer Reserve Corps.

He begins active duty as a second lieutenant in the U.S. Army in April 1942, assigned to making training films and selling war bonds. He secures a top secret clearance, meaning he is often privy to classified information about upcoming American bombing raids. In the process, he learns how such attacks are planned and conducted. Reagan's career up until now has seen him in a series of jobs that do not require leadership or organization. But the army teaches him about taking charge and motivating the men he commands. These are lessons he will use for the rest of his life.

The duties of Reagan's U.S. Army First Motion Picture Unit shift in the waning days of the war. In June 1945, he sends a photographer to a local aircraft factory to take pictures of women working in war production. Pvt. David Conover shoots using color film, a rarity at the time, snapping the indelible image of an eighteen-year-old brunette holding a small propeller. The wife of a young merchant seaman, the fetching girl earns twenty dollars a week inspecting parachutes at a company named Radioplane, which also makes some of the world's first drone aircraft.* She has a wholesome smile, wears a modest green blouse, and has clipped her factory ID badge to the waistband of her pleated gray skirt. Her name is Norma Jeane Dougherty, and these photographs will soon open the doors of Hollywood to her. Eventually, Norma Jeane will divorce her sailor husband and change

* Code-named Operation Aphrodite, the drone program featured radio-controlled B-24 bombers that were packed with explosives and flown into position by pilots, who would then bail out as the planes flew on to their targets, guided from afar by a "mother ship." Sometimes, however, the explosives detonated long before the pilots were able to eject. One such fatality was Lt. Joseph P. Kennedy Jr., older brother of future U.S. president John F. Kennedy, who died in a similar naval program known as Operation Anvil.

her name, as she becomes one of the most famous women in the world. As his own career is on the verge of combusting, Ronald Reagan is directly responsible for initiating the fame of Marilyn Monroe.

At war's end, Reagan makes a triumphant return to Hollywood. Warner Bros. gives him a new long-term contract worth a million dollars, with a guarantee of fifty-two thousand dollars per movie. Reagan and the petite Wyman live in a five-thousand-square-foot custom home on a knoll overlooking Los Angeles. He spends his off time playing golf with comedians Jack Benny and George Burns, and enjoys steak dinners with Wyman at the exclusive Beverly Club. Also in 1945, Reagan and Jane Wyman adopt a baby boy, whom they name Michael.

Reagan's first movie of the new contract is *Stallion Road,* in which he plays a horseback-riding veterinarian. Reagan's on-screen mount is a midnight black thoroughbred mare named Tar Baby. Reagan likes "Baby" so much that he buys her before filming is completed. To give her a place to gallop, he fulfills a lifelong dream and buys a small ranch in the San Fernando Valley, which he will keep for a couple of years before buying a larger property in Malibu.

Then tragedy strikes. In June 1947, Jane Wyman gives birth prematurely to a young daughter. Reagan is ill in the hospital with pneumonia at the time and cannot be at Wyman's side when Christine Reagan comes into the world. She lives just nine hours. The loss deeply affects his marriage to Wyman.*

Trying to put their lives back together, Ronald Reagan and Jane Wyman pour themselves into their work. Yet, despite all the trappings of success, Ronald Reagan's glory days in Hollywood are numbered. Warner Bros. soon casts him in a series of forgettable pictures that make little money

* Michael Reagan later wrote of Wyman that the death of Christine was "probably the most painful experience of her life, and I don't think she ever truly recovered from it." Wyman's 1951 movie *The Blue Veil* reopened those wounds, as the protagonist dealt with the matter of premature infant death. Filmed in and around St. Patrick's Cathedral in New York City, the film had a profound impact on Jane Wyman's life. The experience brought about a spiritual transformation; three years later, Wyman was baptized into the Catholic Church.

and are scorned by critics. Reagan is perplexed. His Hollywood fairy tale is in danger of coming to an end — and he is powerless to do anything about it.

Reagan is a hardworking, restless man who craves physical activity. He is the son of an all-too-often-drunk Irish shoe salesman and a Bible-thumping mother. Their parenting methods taught young Ron to avoid extremes in behavior, leading him, at times, to appear clueless and shut off. Also, it is true: Ronald Reagan is not a great intellect, having struggled to maintain a C average in college. Yet he can memorize paragraphs of script with ease and then recite them again and again on cue. Reagan also is a thinker, craving long periods of solitary meditation — preferably on horseback. He believes that "as you rock along a trail to the sound of the hooves and the squeak of the leather, with the sun on your head and the smell of the horse and the saddle and trees around you, things just begin to straighten themselves out."

Reagan first learned to ride while working as a teenage lifeguard back at Lowell Park in Dixon, Illinois, and lives by the saying "Nothing is so good for the inside of a man as the outside of a horse."

But no long gallop aboard Baby can hide

the fact that Ronald Reagan's personal and professional lives are now veering in new and disastrous directions.

Jane Wyman is growing bored with her husband, though he is oblivious to her dissatisfaction. Reagan can often be self-centered and callous. He has a habit of talking down to his wife because he possesses a college degree and she does not. He also likes to be the center of attention; sometimes screening his personal print of the 1942 movie *Kings Row* when guests come over for dinner.*

Jane Wyman is not impressed when friends suggest that Reagan, who is developing a fondness for political activism, run for Congress. "He's very politically minded. I'm not very bright," she answers coolly, when asked if she supports the idea.

* Of the fifty-three films he made in his career, *Kings Row* was Reagan's favorite. He plays the second lead in the picture, a young man whose legs have been amputated by a villainous surgeon. Reagan's key line, which he uttered spontaneously, happens the moment the young man looks down and sees that his legs are gone: "Where's the rest of me?" It later became the title of his 1965 memoir.

Ann Sheridan and Ronald Reagan in Kings Row, *Reagan's personal favorite of all his performances*

Ronald Reagan has also become fond of lecturing. Any topic will do. "Don't ask Ronnie what time it is," Wyman warns fellow actress June Allyson, "because he will tell you how a watch is made."

When a baseball game comes on the radio, Reagan often ignores his wife and children, turning up the volume and drowning out their words by pretending to be the broadcaster and calling the game. In that way, he shuts out his family for hours.

To make matters worse, Reagan resents Wyman's growing level of celebrity. Her movies, such as *The Yearling,* are earning money, critical praise, and Academy Award nominations. No longer the star when the two go out, Reagan must hover at his wife's elbow as *she* basks in the public's applause.

So it is that Ronald Reagan's newfound political activism, his wife's growing fame, and the death of their baby daughter combine to drive a wedge into their marriage. In 1947, Wyman cruelly mocks him during a lengthy speech he delivers before the Screen Actors Guild membership, foreshadowing the marital split that is soon to come. "Oh, for God's sake, Ronnie," she shouts to actress Rosemary DeCamp, "shut up and go shit in your hat."

The end comes while Wyman is filming *Johnny Belinda* on location in Pebble Beach, California. She begins an affair with costar Lew Ayres. In May 1948, Jane Wyman files for divorce from Ronald Reagan, citing mental cruelty.

"I just couldn't stand to watch that damn *Kings Row* one more time," she explains when the marriage is finally over.

The divorce traumatizes Reagan. He is shattered and sometimes weeps openly, telling friends that the end of his marriage has left him "ashamed." He clings to hope that the relationship can one day be salvaged and still drives the green Cadillac convertible Wyman gave him as a gift before the divorce. But when she publicly declares, "Lew Ayres is the love of my life," it becomes clear that there will be no reconciliation.

Embittered, Reagan begins to behave in a callow fashion. He spends lavishly at Hollywood nightclubs such as Ciro's, the Coconut Grove, and Slapsy Maxie's, drinking too much and conducting a series of sexual affairs with women decades younger than he. His actions do not go unnoticed by the press. *Silver Screen* magazine writes, "Never thought we'd come right out and call Ronnie Reagan a wolf, but leave us face it. Suddenly every glamour gal considers him a super-sexy escort for the evening. Even he admits he's missed a lot of fun and frolic and is out to make up for it."

One of Reagan's liaisons is with actress Penny Edwards, who is just twenty, and another is with the twenty-two-year-old actress Patricia Neal. During a memorable one-night stand in his apartment, Reagan takes the virginity of eighteen-year-old Piper Laurie after first barbecuing her a hamburger. Ironically, at the time of their liaison, Reagan was playing the role of Laurie's father in *Louisa*. The actress will later remember Reagan as a "show-off" in the bedroom, a self-absorbed lover who bragged about his sexual stamina during the act and became impatient when she did not climax. "You should have had many orgasms by now," Reagan scolded Laurie after what she claims was about forty minutes of sex. "You've got to see a doctor about your abnormality."*

Reagan reaches bottom when he wakes up one morning at the Garden of Allah Hotel on Sunset Boulevard and does not know the name of the woman lying next to him. After that, he vows to rein in his behavior.

But he does not. Three years after his divorce, when he proposes marriage to twenty-six-year-old actress Christine Larson by offering her a diamond wristwatch, Reagan is also having relationships with six

* Laurie would go on to win Academy Award nominations for *The Hustler, Carrie,* and *Children of a Lesser God*. Patricia Neal would win an Academy Award for Best Actress in 1963 for *Hud,* costarring Paul Newman. Penny Edwards was never nominated but made a name for herself as Roy Rogers's love interest in six Hollywood Westerns.

other women. Larson turns him down.*

Now living on his own in an apartment above the Sunset Strip, Ronald Reagan soon grows apart from his young son and daughter. Three-year-old Michael and seven-year-old Maureen Reagan will long remember their father as loving but also absent from their lives for long periods of time — as was their mother. Both children are sent away to boarding schools by the time they enter the second grade. "There's a distinct difference between the care provided by a parent and the care provided by a paid caretaker," Maureen will say years

* Chief among Larson's reasons for turning him down is her adherence to the Bahá'í Faith, which does not believe in politics. However, that excuse belies the fact that Larson was not in love with Reagan. Among others, she is seeing actors Gary Cooper and Mickey Rooney. She will also go on to have an affair with Lew Ayres, the actor who was involved with Jane Wyman while she and Reagan were still married. In another example of the mattress hopping so common in Hollywood at the time, the legendary lover and Reagan's friend, Gary Cooper, will be rumored to have slept with almost every single leading lady of his lengthy career, including Patricia Neal.

later. "It was simply one of the prices all of us had to pay for their success."

During this playboy period, Reagan's success has flatlined. He is no longer viewed as a bankable star by Hollywood standards. To add insult to injury, as his movie career is clearly in its death throes, Wyman wins her first Academy Award and arrives at the ceremony with Lew Ayres as her date, which only makes Reagan's career seem more marginal.* By 1949, Warner Bros. terminates his long-term contract, leaving him without income to pay the bills for the high-flying Hollywood lifestyle to which he has grown accustomed.

Desperate, Reagan accepts the offer to work on *Bedtime for Bonzo*. Animal movies are all the rage in Hollywood in 1950, thanks to the success of the February release *Francis the Talking Mule*. Jimmy Stewart has just finished *Harvey*, about a man and his invisible rabbit companion, on a set just one block down from where Reagan now films *Bonzo*. *Harvey* will open in October and earn Stewart his fourth

* Wyman won Best Actress for *Johnny Belinda* in 1949. She was also nominated for Best Actress in 1947 (*The Yearling*), 1952 (*The Blue Veil*), and 1955 (*Magnificent Obsession*).

Academy Award nomination.

As Ronald Reagan now clambers up into the tree after the chimp Peggy (Bonzo), he still believes his career will rebound. The film's other star, Diana Lynn, awaits him in the branches, adding to the comedy's madcap narrative. Meanwhile, Bonzo has jumped off a branch and is now inside the house, somehow managing to call the police. Soon there will be cop cars and fire trucks screaming down Colonial Street, all in a scripted attempt to get everyone down from the tree. This is a far cry from Reagan's days making movies such as *Dark Victory* with major stars such as Humphrey Bogart and Bette Davis, or *Sante Fe Trail* with Errol Flynn. In that movie, Reagan played General George Armstrong Custer, whom he considers a great American hero.

Still, Reagan is a professional. He shows up each morning on time, knows his lines, and is pleasant to his coworkers. There are times, however, when he seems distracted. For there are pressing concerns on his mind.

Ronald Reagan is nearly forty years old. His profession is acting, but politics has set a new fire burning in his belly. The newspapers are full of the amazing events going on in the global fight against communism, as President Harry Truman sends U.S.

troops into Korea to stop the Communist advance. Reagan is an ardent supporter of the Democratic president and campaigned for him in 1948. With Truman's time in office due to end if he doesn't run for reelection, Reagan is hoping former army general and World War II hero Dwight Eisenhower will run for president as a Democrat. Even as he deals with Peggy the chimp, Reagan is planning an article for *Fortnight* magazine in which he will explain how to fight communism worldwide. His determination to end the Communist threat is steadfast.

"The real fight with this totalitarianism belongs properly to the forces of liberal democracy, just as did the battle with Hitler's totalitarianism. There really is no difference except in the cast of characters," Reagan will write.

But that is a few months off. For now, Reagan is engaged in far less intellectual fare.

"Cut," director Fred de Cordova yells.

Ronald Reagan climbs down from the tree.

3

Yearling Row Ranch
Santa Monica Mountains, California
December 22, 1951
Morning

Forty-year-old Ronald Reagan gallops Tar Baby over the rolling countryside of his new 270-acre Malibu ranch. He rides English style, wearing skintight jodhpurs and knee-high Dehner riding boots. Christmas is just days away. The air is crisp on this winter morning, the skies clear and blue. Reagan's two children, home on break from Chadwick boarding school, are spending the weekend in the small shingled ranch house back near the barn.

But this weekend is not just a time for a father and his kids. Reagan's latest girlfriend, a thirty-year-old actress named Nancy Davis, has joined them. Though she works very hard to endear herself to his son and daughter, and Maureen and Michael like her very much, Reagan is unsure about this blossoming relationship. He is not ready to be monogamous and is still seeing other women.

Yet Davis is determined to win his heart — by any means necessary. Recently, Davis confessed to Reagan that she might be pregnant. Yet rather than encouraging Reagan to propose marriage, the announcement has the opposite effect. He flees to the home of Christine Larson, the starlet who spurned his offer of marriage earlier this year. Reagan complains to her that he feels trapped by Davis and wonders aloud if she is trying to trick him into marrying her.

But on this day, Reagan does not feel confined. He rides tall and easy in the saddle, feeling the black mare moving beneath him. His connection with Baby is so strong that Reagan now insists upon riding her during on-screen horseback shots. This time last year they were in Tucson, Arizona, filming the Western *The Last Outpost,* which has become a minor success at the box office. The film's horse wranglers warned Reagan that the desert location's heat and dust might prove fatal to the mare. But the actor knows his horse well. Tar Baby survived the grueling shoot without a single problem.

Now, riding on a dirt path lined with sycamores and scrub oak, past Malibou Lake, where he plans to swim in the summer, and the hayfield that parallels distant Mulholland Drive, Reagan finds himself at a curious career crossroads. *Bedtime for Bonzo* was such a box office success that a sequel is in the works. Reagan received mixed notices for his comedic performance, with most reviewers preferring to focus their praise on Peggy the chimp. The *New York Times* called *Bonzo* "a minor bit of fun yielding a respectable amount of laughs, but nothing, actually, over which to wax ecstatic."

Reagan was barely mentioned in the review.

Despite *Bonzo*'s success, he is not offered a role in the sequel.* On top of that, Reagan's tenure as president of the Screen Actors Guild will soon come to an end. It is a time of upheaval and change in Hollywood, and Reagan has been in the thick of the pitched battle between the studios and an

---

* The sequel is titled *Bonzo Goes to College.* It stars Edmund Gwenn, best known for his role as Kris Kringle in the classic *Miracle on 34th Street,* for which he won an Academy Award for Best Supporting Actor.

emerging Communist presence in the show business community.

His "double life," as he calls his now-intersecting twin passions of acting and politics, has consumed him. The ranch has been a tonic in these tough times, his Saturday getaway to clear his head from the strife.

Reagan has been the head of SAG for five years. But no year has been more intense than 1951. In addition to acting in three films and attending the Monday night SAG board meetings, he has also traveled around the country speaking on behalf of an anticommunist group known as Crusade for Freedom. The purpose: to raise money for Radio Free Europe. And though Reagan is still very much a Hollywood actor, the words he scripts for himself are those of a seasoned international politician.

"The battleground of peace today is that strip of strategically located countries stretching from the Baltic to the Black Sea," Reagan says in a recorded speech that is replayed to small groups around America. "They are not big countries geographically, but they contain several million freedom-loving people, our kind of people, who share our culture and have sent millions of their sons and daughters to become part of these

Reagan with Tar Baby

United States. Some call these countries the satellite nations. More accurately, they're the captive nations of Europe."

Reagan is unaware that Crusade for Freedom is secretly backed by the Central Intelligence Agency, although he would likely be delighted if he knew.

Ronald Reagan actually considered joining the Communist Party back in 1938. Many in Hollywood were romanced by the Communists, as Adolf Hitler and his fascist ideology were becoming a threat not just to

Europe but to the entire world. The Communists, with their avowed mission of helping the poor and disenfranchised, seemed poised to thwart Hitler's ambitions. But there was more to Reagan's attraction than mere ideology: as a newcomer to Hollywood, just one year into his studio contract, he saw becoming a Communist as a good way to expand his social circle.

"Reagan got carried away by stories of the Communist Party helping the dispossessed, the unemployed and the homeless," screenwriter Howard Fast will claim years later. "Some of his friends, people he respected, were party members, so he turned to them. Said he wanted to be a Communist . . . said he was determined to join."

But actor Eddie Albert, a costar in *Brother Rat,* was just as determined to talk Reagan out of turning red. Albert's motives were deceptive. He leaned far to the left politically and secretly undertook the discussion at the behest of the American Communist Party leadership, who believed the talkative Reagan was a "flake" and did not want him joining their group.

Albert was successful. Reagan's brief flirtation with communism came to an end. His interest in politics, however, did not cease.

It is August 11, 1941, when Ronald Reagan attends his first meeting of the Screen Actors Guild at the union's headquarters on Hollywood Boulevard. He has been invited to serve as an alternate for actress Heather Angel. The Guild is just eight years old at the time, founded to improve working conditions for actors. Reagan's first meeting is more of a social excursion, as he has little knowledge of the Guild's inner workings. Even when Jane Wyman is elected to the board a year later, Reagan remains distant from SAG, involved as he is with the war effort. But he resumes attending meetings in February 1946 as an alternate for horror-movie actor Boris Karloff. In September of that year he is elected third vice president.

By the end of World War II, with Hitler and the German Third Reich defeated, it is clear that Joseph Stalin and the Communists are just as ruthless and just as intent on global domination as the führer was. The Soviet Union, headquarters of global communism, displaces millions of people across Eastern Europe in order to build an empire even bigger than Hitler's. It is also sending spies out around the world to infiltrate other nations and spread propaganda. Reagan soon sees this played out quite clearly in Hollywood. The actor's union is slowly dividing itself into those, like Reagan, who now consider communism a scourge and those who believe that the political system embraced by the Soviet Union is intellectual and fashionable.

"[T]he important thing is that you should not argue with them. Communism has become an intensely dogmatic and almost mystical religion, and whatever you say, they have ways of twisting it into shapes which put you in some lower category of mankind," wrote novelist and screenwriter F. Scott Fitzgerald, describing the ideological tension in Hollywood.

The illusion that communism is a harmless ideology is shattered on September 27, 1946, when the Confederation of Studio Unions goes on strike. The head of the union is Herb Sorrell, a rough-and-tumble former boxer who is also a longtime member of the Communist Party. The strike is funded by the National Executive Council of the Communist Party. "When it ends up," Sorrell predicted, "there'll be only one man running labor in Hollywood — and that man will be me."

This is not a peaceful protest but a violent and militant attempt by the Communists to begin taking control of every major union in Hollywood — and, by proxy, the motion picture industry itself. In addition to the striking union members, Sorrell has enlisted hired thugs from the San Francisco area to provide menace. Cars are overturned in the streets. Police fire tear gas at the picket lines blocking the entrance to the Warner Bros. studio. Great mobs of strikers attack those attempting to cross the picket lines. Actor Kirk Douglas describes a scene of men armed with "knives, clubs, battery cables, brass knuckles, and chains."

Despite the violence, studio head Jack Warner refuses to buckle. He continues making movies. Actors and employees do not cross picket lines to get to work. Instead, they are smuggled into the studio through a Los Angeles River storm drain. For those preferring not to endure the smells and slime of the subterranean entrance, the other option is riding a bus driven straight through the picket lines at Warner's front gate. Scores of police officers are called in to line the route but cannot prevent the strikers from pelting the vehicles with rocks and bricks. Everyone on board the bus is instructed to lie down on the floor to avoid being hit in the head by broken glass and projectiles.

Ronald Reagan, as vice president of the Screen Actors Guild, considers the storm drain a coward's entrance and refuses to lie down on the floor of the bus. No matter that he has two young children and a pregnant wife at home, Reagan puts himself at risk in order to make a statement: he is not afraid.

Each day, arriving for work on a new film called *Night unto Night,* Reagan is the lone person on the studio bus sitting upright, for all to see. When the strikers later escalate their campaign by forcing the Screen Actors Guild to support the strike, an anonymous caller to Reagan's home threatens that he will be attacked and his face burned with acid if he tries to block SAG's pro-strike involvement.

Furious, Reagan refuses to back down. Instead, he buys a pistol and carries it in a shoulder holster wherever he goes. For the rest of his life, Ronald Reagan will be vehemently anticommunist. For him, it is very personal: he will never forget the threats.

Four weeks into the confrontation, on October 24, 1946, Reagan and strike organizer Herb Sorrell sit down at Hollywood's Knickerbocker Hotel. Sorrell is a powerfully built man, fond of using physical intimidation to achieve his goals. But Reagan is no less strong and is uncowed by Sorrell. He angrily accuses the union boss of being responsible for the threats.

"I have to have guards for my kids because I got telephone calls warning what would happen to me," he seethes, before adding, "You do not want peace in the motion picture industry."

Actor Gene Kelly is also at the meeting as a member of SAG's board of directors. He quickly steps in with a joke to keep the peace: "If Mr. Reagan hits Mr. Sorrell I want it understood that this is not the official feeling of this body."*

Kelly's words have their desired effect.

* Kelly was a man of high ideals who left the Catholic Church when he felt it was not doing enough to halt world hunger, yet donated money to the Provisional Irish Republican Army in its war against Protestants and the British occupation of Northern Ireland. The famous dancer, best known for *Singin' in the Rain,* was once quoted as saying, "I believe in God, the American Way of Life, the freedom of the individual, and everything the Constitution of the United States stands for." To Kelly, this also meant tolerance for the Communists, which made him the perfect middleman for discussions between Reagan and Sorrell.

The meeting calms until it ends at one thirty the following morning, but nothing is resolved.

By December, with the strike in its third month, Reagan is calling a special meeting of SAG's 350 most elite members. Among them is actor Edward G. Robinson, a man known for playing gangsters on-screen. Robinson is also one of Hollywood's most ardent Communists. In a speech that those in attendance will remember for years to come, Reagan assures the membership of his solid standing as a New Deal Democrat and argues that the Guild should maintain a united stand against the strike. Even Robinson marvels "at Reagan's clear and sequential presentation."

Still, the strike drags on.

The duration of the strike angers Reagan. He is appalled by the Communist union leader's zealous desire to take control of Hollywood. What began as a battle of ideologies has now become Reagan's personal mission. He vows to fight communism, wherever it may be.

With Ronald Reagan gaining political confidence, Gene Kelly nominates him for president of the Screen Actors Guild. Veteran actors James Cagney, Robert Montgomery, Harpo Marx, and John Garfield have just stepped down from SAG leadership. Reagan is not present at the time of his nomination, arriving halfway through the meeting to find out that he has won. He is stunned.

The term of office is one year, beginning in 1947. Almost immediately, Reagan is tested by Communist sympathizers attempting to undermine his leadership. "At a mass meeting," Reagan will later write, "I watched rather helplessly as they filibustered, waiting for our majority to leave so they could take control."

A voice in the crowd cries out that the meeting should be adjourned. "I seized on this as a means of ending the attempted takeover. But the other side demanded I identify the one who moved for adjournment."

Reagan is in a bind. While many in the Screen Actors Guild are against the Communists, it is also a career liability to speak out publicly against them. The momentum of the Communist movement is too great, and the possibility of being personally and professionally ostracized from the Hollywood community is very real. Reagan scans the crowd, searching for at least one individual with the backbone to be his ally in this heated moment.

He sees his man. "Why, I believe John Wayne made the motion," Reagan tells the crowd. Wayne is one of Hollywood's best-known tough guys, a former college football player whose starring roles in Westerns and war movies have made him one of the most bankable box office stars in the world. And unlike many Hollywood heroes, who look tall on the screen but are actually diminutive in real life, the gruff Wayne stands at a rugged six foot four.

"I sure as hell did," Wayne roars from the crowd.

The meeting is adjourned.

Finally, after thirteen long months, the strike ends. Yet even as the studios emerge victorious, Hollywood's growing embrace of communism continues unabated, drawing the attention of the feared FBI chief J. Edgar Hoover.

In the waning days of their marriage, Ronald Reagan and Jane Wyman are approached by FBI agents Richard Auerbach and Fred Dupuis, who come to their home uninvited on April 10, 1947. The agents ask the couple to "report secretly to the FBI about people suspected of Communist activity."

Wyman and Reagan quickly offer up six names. This will be the end of Wyman's involvement with the FBI, but Ronald Reagan begins meeting frequently with the bureau to provide more names and information. He is given a code name: T-10. Two of the people he names, actresses Karen Morley and Anne Revere, will not work in Hollywood for the next twenty years.*

Ronald Reagan believes this banishment is just, for he knows the women to be Communists — and thinks the Communist Party is an agent of a foreign power.

Reagan will be damned if he will allow the motion picture industry to undermine the moral fabric of the United States of America.

Ronald Reagan will never waver from the belief that informing for the FBI was the right thing to do; nor will he suffer any repercussions for it. "I talked to Ronnie since," Jack Dales, executive secretary of

* Revere won the Best Supporting Actress award for her role in the movie *National Velvet*. Morley turned to politics after leaving Hollywood, running unsuccessfully for lieutenant governor of New York in 1954. She returned to acting in the 1970s, appearing on television in episodes of *Kojak* and *Kung Fu*.

Reagan testifies before the House Un-American Activities Committee, 1947.

SAG at that time, will comment years from now. "And he has no doubts about the propriety of what we did."

On October 23, 1947, Reagan travels to Washington to appear before the House Un-American Activities Committee, a congressional group trying to root our subversive individuals and practices.* "I believe that,

* Not to be confused with Sen. Joseph McCarthy's Communist investigations, HUAC was originally founded in 1938 to root out Nazi sympathizers. It

as Thomas Jefferson put it, if all the American people know all of the facts they will never make a mistake," said Reagan, responding to questions from HUAC chief investigator Robert Stripling. "Whether the [Communist] party should be outlawed, that is a matter for the government to decide. As a citizen, I would hesitate to see any political party outlawed on the basis of its political ideology. However, if it is proven that an organization is an agent of a foreign power, or in any way not a legitimate political party — and I think the government is capable of proving that — then that is another matter."

Reagan's appearance before the committee is his first visit to Capitol Hill.

It makes a lasting impression on him.

Nearly four years after testifying before Congress, Ronald Reagan guides Tar Baby back to the barn. He hopes soon to add "thoroughbred horse breeder" to the many job titles that currently keep him busy and

---

switched its focus to communism as the Soviet Union rose to power. Thirty-four-year-old Richard Nixon, a newly elected California congressman, was a member of HUAC on the day Reagan testified but was not in attendance.

plans to expand the simple barn into something more elaborate for that purpose.

Reagan leads the mare into her stall and removes her bridle and saddle. Whistling softly to himself, he brushes her torso and flanks. The repetitive movement allows Reagan a contemplative moment.

It is clear that Ronald Reagan needs to make some hard decisions about his future. He gets little respect for his roles as an actor, but he is held in such high esteem for his political activism that when the Friars Club recently honored him they refrained from derogatory jokes and putdowns. Instead, the six hundred members in attendance spent the evening lauding him with sincere speeches about his "stature and dignity," with the legendary singer Al Jolson even going so far as to say that he wished his son would "grow up to be the kind of man Ronnie is."

But with his Guild presidency coming to an end, it seems that Reagan's political days will also cease. All the respect in the world from his Hollywood peers won't pay the bills. He must find a way to revive his career. The mortgage on his ranch alone is eighty-five thousand dollars. Politics doesn't offer that kind of money.

As Reagan steps out of the barn, walking

to where Nancy Davis and his children wait inside the small ranch house, he faces a midlife crisis. Reagan well knows the truth: he is a forty-year-old Hollywood has-been on the verge of losing everything. As he enjoys a brief time of quiet and solitude on this cool December morning, he is unsure of what 1952 has in store for him — hardly aware that it is the year in which he will remarry, father a new child, and vote Republican for the first time in his life.*

* The battle against communism dogged Ronald Reagan right up to the very end of his term as Screen Actors Guild president. On January 16, 1952, during one of Reagan's final SAG meetings, powerful director Stanley Kramer explained to the board that his recent movie, *Death of a Salesman*, was being picketed by pro-Communist groups who were accusing him of discrimination because he refused to employ Communists. In order to prevent the increasing use of this tactic against other filmmakers, Kramer filed a libel lawsuit. Director John Ford, who gained fame making John Wayne Westerns such as *Stagecoach,* stepped forward to say that he would testify on Kramer's behalf. As a result, Reagan and the SAG board issued a formal resolution backing Kramer and repudiating the Communist pressure. Left unsaid was that during his tenure as president of the SAG

board, Reagan had completely shifted the leadership from being sympathetic to communism to openly opposing the ideology and its tactics.

4

Studio City, California
March 4, 1952
5:00 P.M.

"I do," says Ronald Reagan, looking into the large brown eyes of a pregnant Nancy Davis. He is dressed in a black wedding suit with narrow matching tie. Davis, who clutches a fragrant bouquet of orange blossoms and white tulips, does not wear a wedding gown. Instead, she has chosen to wear a gray woolen suit bought off the rack at the I. Magnin department store in Beverly Hills. A single strand of pearls is draped around her neck.

The Rev. John Wells, a Disciples of Christ minister, stands before the small, bare table that represents the altar here at the Little Brown Church. He asks Davis if she, too, agrees to be wed "till death do you part."

"I do," she replies. Nancy Davis has campaigned hard for this moment since setting her sights on Ronald Reagan three years ago. She is undaunted by his flings with other women, accepting his indiscretions while enjoying a few brief affairs of her own.* Davis knows that there are two keys to Reagan's heart: politics and horses. So she has spent hours whitewashing fences at the actor's Malibu ranch and attending the Monday night SAG board meetings to

* Nancy Davis has never been married. She was engaged briefly in 1944 to a young naval officer named J. P. White Jr. but broke it off after just a few months. A series of brief affairs followed. "She was what men at that time thought of as 'available,'" a family friend will later recall. After moving from Chicago to New York in 1945 to pursue a Broadway career, Davis had affairs with actor Alfred Drake and producer Max Allentuck. She moved to California and signed with MGM in 1949, where she earned a reputation for being ambitious and allegedly having a torrid affair with producer Benny Thau, a man well known for using the casting couch to further the careers of young actresses. In 1949 Nancy made a list for herself of show business's most eligible bachelors, with an eye to trying to marry one. Ronald Reagan's name was at the top of the list, beginning the three years of pursuit leading to their marriage.

watch him lead the proceedings. "I loved to listen to him talk," Davis will write of their courtship, "and I let him know it."

Standing in the chapel to Reagan's right is his best man, the hard-drinking actor William Holden. The thirty-three-year-old Academy Award nominee for *Sunset Boulevard* has taken a break from filming the World War II drama *Stalag 17* to be at the ceremony. His wife, Ardis, is serving as Davis's matron of honor. The Holdens have been fighting today and are not on speaking terms. That is not an unusual situation in their eleven-year marriage. The main issue between them is infidelity. Holden underwent a vasectomy after the birth of their second son and is fond of bedding his costars without fear of getting them pregnant, thus leaving his wife in a constant state of jealousy and torment.★

★ Ardis Ankerson is a striking brunette who goes by the stage name of Brenda Marshall. Unlike many actresses, she insists that friends and family use her real name rather than her stage name. She is best known for playing Errol Flynn's love interest in the 1940 pirate film *The Sea Hawk*. She made her last film in 1950, preferring to put her career on hold to raise a family. After a number of separations, William Holden and Ardis Ankerson

Even as Ronald Reagan and Nancy Davis recite their vows, awash in apparent marital bliss, the Holdens sit on opposite sides of the tiny church.

Other than these four, and the gray-haired Reverend Wells, who presides wearing a flowing black robe, there is no one else in attendance for the Reagan-Davis wedding, which makes the Holdens' feud glaringly obvious. The Reagan children, Maureen and Michael, are away at school.

Even though a formal wedding announcement was made on February 21, and gossip writer Louella Parsons spread the word to twenty million people worldwide through her syndicated newspaper column, the ceremony is stunningly casual. There was no limousine to ferry the couple to the church. Instead, Reagan picked Nancy up

---

divorced in 1971. Among Holden's lovers during their marriage were costars Grace Kelly, Audrey Hepburn, Shelley Winters, and the French bombshell Capucine. He also had a torrid week-long affair with Jackie Kennedy in the mid-1950s. Holden, who bragged to a friend that he had played the role of bedroom tutor to the wife of the future American president, commented, "If she goes back to Washington and works her magic with Kennedy he will owe me one."

at her apartment in the Cadillac convertible purchased for him by Jane Wyman.

In addition, there is no formal reception. The group will adjourn to the Holdens' ranch-style home* in nearby Toluca Lake for a quick bite of cake and a splash of champagne before Reagan and Davis drive two hours to Riverside's Mission Inn for their wedding night.

Reagan's initial wedding proposal fell far short of romance. Davis had longed "that Ronnie would take me out in a canoe as the sun was setting and would strum a ukulele as I lay back, trailing my fingers in the water, the way they used to do in the old movies I saw as a little girl."

Instead, Reagan simply pronounced, "Let's get married," over dinner at a Hollywood nightclub shortly after Davis told him she was pregnant. To which she replied, after gazing into his eyes and placing her small hands atop his: "Let's."

Nancy Davis was so eager to marry Ronald Reagan that she willingly accommodated his every wish. If that meant a

---

* Neighbors of the Holdens include Bob Hope, Shemp Howard of the Three Stooges, and Frank Sinatra. The Holden home will one day be owned by actor Denzel Washington.

small ceremony, lacking fanfare or even a hint of the media flashbulbs that might provide a modicum of grandeur — then so be it. Nancy was released from her Metro-Goldwyn-Mayer studio contract just two weeks prior. "I don't want to do anything else except be married. I just want to be Ronnie's wife," she says later.

To Reagan, this anonymous wedding is perfect. His life seems to become more complicated by the day, and he hardly needs a horde of press to remind him that his career is in peril. In addition to dealing with Davis's pregnancy, Reagan was released from his contract with Warner Bros. just five weeks ago. He claims that he wants a small ceremony because the memory of his lavish first wedding to Jane Wyman is still painful. But the truth is that "to even contemplate facing reporters and flashbulbs made me break out in a cold sweat," as Reagan will one day write.

The wedding is so discreet that Reagan has not even invited his mother, Nelle. His father, Jack, died more than a decade ago, but Nelle Reagan now lives nearby, in Southern California. But even though Reagan has a close relationship with his mother, who is a member of the Disciples of Christ denomination, she is not in attendance.

Nancy, on the other hand, has no living relations in Hollywood. Her godmother was Alla Nazimova, the late owner of the legendary Garden of Allah Hotel. Coincidentally, that same den of iniquity was the place where Reagan promised himself that he would stop sleeping around. Thanks to that moment, and to his relationship with Nancy, he is now seen less and less in the nightclubs of Hollywood, preferring to spend weekends at the Malibu ranch.

"It's not that I hunger for somebody to love me," Reagan has confided to Nancy, finally putting the memory of his divorce in the rearview mirror, "as much as I miss having somebody to love."

"I pronounce you man and wife," says Reverend Wells, adjusting his thin wire-frame glasses. Davis is so swept away by the moment that she will not remember saying "I do" or even Ronald Reagan's kiss as their marriage is sealed. Instead, she will recall only the booming voice of Bill Holden as he comes to her side. "Can I kiss the bride?" he asks.

"Not yet," Davis protests. "It's too soon."

But as the svelte Ardis looks on, Holden wraps his arms around Nancy's waist and kisses her passionately on the lips.

Ardis Ankerson has arranged for a photographer to be present at her house as a beaming Nancy Reagan slices wedding cake with her new husband. The three tiers of white frosting, with the small plastic statue of bride and groom perched on top, rests on the Holdens' dining room table. Reagan blinks as the shutter clicks, while Nancy leans in toward the camera with eyes wide open. It is a moment both iconic and timeless, re-created at countless weddings before and since. If not for Ardis possessing the forethought to hire a photographer, there would have been no pictures of this moment.

The resulting images are unassuming. Yet one day they will be considered remarkable, for this evening begins a marriage that will change the world.

It is midnight as the newly married Reagans arrive at the Mission Inn, an elaborate structure built to look like an old Spanish mission, with great stucco walls, exposed beams, and a garden courtyard.* A bouquet

* President Richard Nixon and his wife, Pat, were married at the Mission Inn. A host of other presidents has visited the historic building: Benja-

of red roses waits in their room, compliments of the house.

In Ronald Reagan, Nancy sees a greatness that thus far has eluded him. She will dedicate her life to bringing it forth. Soon, her supplication will vanish and dominance will emerge. Reagan will reluctantly cease his womanizing, although continuing his affair with Christine Larson well past the day his baby daughter, Patti, is born on October 21, 1952.* And while there will be the occasional discreet liaison in the future, Rea-

---

min Harrison, William Howard Taft, William McKinley, Theodore Roosevelt, Herbert Hoover, John F. Kennedy, Gerald Ford, and George W. Bush. Notably, Kennedy is the only Democrat.

* Reagan is not at the hospital the night Patricia Ann Reagan is delivered by caesarean section. He is in the arms of Larson. However, that relationship comes to an end shortly thereafter, when Reagan shows up at Larson's apartment and a French actor wearing just a small towel answers the door. Nancy will never acknowledge that she is aware of the relationship but will later comment, "When I was back in my room and the nurses brought me our baby for the first time, my first thought was that it was sad that Ronnie couldn't be there." Reagan never provided an excuse for his absence; Nancy just accepted that he wasn't there.

Ronald Reagan and Nancy Davis cutting wedding cake with William Holden and his wife, Ardis

gan's days as a playboy are in the past. In time, these affairs will come to haunt him. Not a man normally given to regrets, Reagan will rue his behavior as his love for Nancy grows deeper. "If you want to be a happy man," he will counsel a friend years from now, "just don't ever cheat on your wife."

Nancy Reagan possesses an inner steel

that her husband lacks. This quality will soon make her opinions indispensable. She will become his sounding board, tactician, and adviser, prodding and cajoling him to become the man only she believes he can be.

And while Reagan will always be "Ronnie" to his wife, the power in their marriage will slowly shift until Nancy becomes the matriarch known to her husband as Mommy.

Of such odd synergy are great marriages made.

5

Last Frontier Casino
Las Vegas, Nevada
February 27, 1954
8:55 P.M.

The man with a long fifty years to live is in exile.

Ronald Reagan bounds onstage wearing an apron advertising Pabst Blue Ribbon beer. "Vas vils du haben?" he booms in a thick European accent to Ben Cruz, leader of a slapstick group known as the Continentals.

"Vats zoo got under dere?" Cruz says in a bemused voice, pointing at the hem of Reagan's long apron.

Reagan replies, scratching his groin. "Underwear?"

"Under dere," replies Cruz, pointing at the hem of Reagan's long apron. Then, as the audience bursts out in ribald laughter, Reagan and the Continentals break into song, a well-established vaudeville routine.

Reagan's appearance in Las Vegas is such an oddity that after his first show, the *Las Vegas Sun* wrote, incredulously, that "Ronald Reagan, of all people, opened last night at The Last Frontier." But tonight's audience is learning that Reagan can handle the vaudeville stage and is a master showman. His comedic timing, in particular, is impeccable. The three hundred audience members packed into the Ramona Room roar in laughter at his beer vendor shtick. But Reagan is not finished. Quickly, he switches over to an Irish brogue for a series of scripted one-liners. A wave of deep belly laughs fills the room.

Before the show opened there were widespread fears that the Hollywood actor would bomb in front of a live audience. But Reagan is so spectacular, and the subsequent audiences each night love the show so much, that the Last Frontier wants to book him for another month — if not more.

"Reagan opens with some solid humor and the enthusiastic response loosens him to the point he is grinning all over," the show business newspaper *Variety* wrote in a review. "He shines as a Dutch-jargon bartender in a beer selling bit."

Despite the positive press, Reagan is, in fact, terrified. The Last Frontier is an apt name for the casino, because it might just as well describe the slim territory of celebrity to which Ronald Reagan now clings. He can no longer afford a single miscue. He almost backed out of the Las Vegas gig, knowing all too well that if the show failed, his declining career would be all but over.

Even though the show is a hit, Reagan hopes that this is not his future. Nothing about the remote desert town suits him. He is not a gambler. He reads books in his off time or lounges by the pool with Nancy. Sometimes they take day trips to nearby Lake Mead, to indulge his passion for the outdoors. But Reagan longs to be back in California riding Tar Baby and making movies.

However, that choice is not his to make. He now has a wife and child to support, as well as the two children from his previous marriage. Reagan is paying the mortgage on his Malibu ranch and on the new home he and Nancy recently purchased near the Pacific Palisades. He is thousands of dollars in debt and owes a small fortune in back taxes, yet still he insists on living the life of a major movie star: dining at expensive restaurants such as Chasen's and doing little to curb his personal spending habits. Reagan tells friends he will not accept any part that is not up to his personal standards, when the truth is that quality scripts are no longer being sent his way. Instead, he is being asked to narrate public service documentaries for the grand fee of just $240.

So Vegas it is.

Ronald Reagan performs at 8:30 and 11:30 each night, with an extra 1:30 a.m. show on Saturdays. After the beer garden sketch, Reagan and the Continentals rush offstage for a costume change. Meanwhile, tall and handsome Royce and Ramon Blackburn step onstage to perform their song-and-dance act as the Blackburn Twins. The Honey Brothers trio follows with a slapstick acrobatic comedy routine that often finds them close to flying off the stage. Finally, Reagan closes out the performance standing alone, lit by a single spotlight, reciting a monologue about an actor's life.

It's a grind, but the money is extremely good. Reagan is not the only fading celebrity reduced to playing Las Vegas. At the Sands, a casino just down the Strip from the Last Frontier, former movie star Tallulah Bankhead appears onstage almost naked, also reciting dramatic monologues.

Throughout the show, Nancy Reagan sits alone at a small table nursing an ice water. Nancy, who has never smoked cigarettes, is enveloped by thick clouds of tobacco smoke, making it almost impossible for Reagan to see her from the stage. Yet he knows she is there. Despite the oppressive atmosphere, Nancy attends every show, perched in the same spot every night, surrounded by strangers.

Ronald Reagan's career slide has been hard on the ambitious Nancy. As she watches her husband do underwear jokes, she is determined to live a life of fame and fortune. Nancy Reagan was raised in privilege, but she now finds herself in debt. This is intolerable to her. Nancy's entry into Hollywood was facilitated by her mother's friendships with A-list actors Spencer Tracy and Walter Huston, and there was every expectation that her marriage to Reagan would continue to expand those high-level connections.

But now, nursing her ice water, she well understands that she and Ronnie are no longer welcome at the A-list parties. Despite the raucous crowd packing the cavernous

Ramona Room on this Saturday night, there is abundant evidence that Reagan is finished in Hollywood. Nancy is three hundred miles away from Los Angeles, sitting alone in a gambling establishment designed to look like an Old West outpost. Outside, a cold winter wind blows across the wide-open desert. She and her husband are so far off the Hollywood grid that they might as well be in Siberia.

Yet Nancy Reagan clings to the hope that Las Vegas will soon lead to something better. America is fascinated by a new medium known as television, which beams entertainment directly inside the homes of people everywhere. As a result of its popularity, more than five thousand movie theaters have closed due to declining ticket sales. Ronald Reagan has done a dozen guest appearances on various television shows, but he is reluctant to pursue TV full-time. "The people who owned movie theaters thought that nobody would buy a ticket to see someone they could see at home in their living room for nothing," he will one day write.

Nancy is not as cautious. The Reagans need money. Television is the future. MCA, the talent agency representing Reagan, is pushing him in that direction — and so is his wife. A few months before heading to Las Vegas, Reagan reluctantly agreed to audition to host a show for the CBS television network titled *General Electric Theater.* It will air every Sunday night for a half hour at 9:00 p.m. The pay is $125,000 per year — more than enough to get the Reagans out of debt and keep the couple current on their mortgage payments. There is no assurance Reagan will get the job, as veteran actors Eddie Albert, Walter Pidgeon, and Kirk Douglas have also been approached for the position.

But should Ronald Reagan be offered the GE job, Nancy will make sure he takes it.

The time is now almost ten o'clock on this Saturday night. In a moment, Nancy will duck backstage to be with her husband for a quick bite of dinner between shows. She is determined to return home as soon as possible — and never come back. She cannot imagine a life of sitting alone each night for three hours of vaudeville, losing contact with Hollywood with each passing day, while minor film celebrities such as Lucille Ball are achieving vast fame and fortune on television.

Nancy Reagan stirs her ice water, hearing the cue that signals the end of the performance.

"You see things and say, 'Why?' " Reagan emotes from the stage, quoting the Irish playwright George Bernard Shaw. A single spotlight illuminates him, alone in his tuxedo, speaking to the audience as if each and every member was a personal friend.

"But I dream things that never were and say, 'Why not?' "

The Ramona Room is silent, but only for an instant. Then the audience leaps to their feet in a standing ovation. The showman grins from ear to ear, basking in what has become a nightly occurrence. If Reagan has learned one thing in Las Vegas, it is that he truly loves a live audience, and they love him back.

One week later, on March 5, 1954, Ronald Reagan turns down an offer to extend his run at the Last Frontier.

Television calls.

"I'm Ronald Reagan speaking for General Electric," the actor says into the television microphone. The broadcast is live, taking place on December 12, 1954. "Tonight from Hollywood it is my pleasure to appear in a story entitled 'The Dark, Dark Hours,' " Reagan intones. "Young James Dean, one of the bright new actors in Hollywood, appears with me. And

Constance Ford plays my wife on the *General Electric Theater.*"

The GE theme music comes up as the camera pulls back. Reagan's introduction completed, the scene changes as the camera lens again zeroes in. Now viewers can see that Reagan is in costume. He's wearing pajamas and a bathrobe. In his role as the kindly Doctor Joe, Ronald Reagan answers the door in the middle of the night to find a thuggish James Dean, playing a character named Bud, imploring Doctor Joe to help a friend who has mysteriously suffered a gunshot wound.

Reagan's skepticism about television is clearly gone. His job as host of *GE Theater* gives him the opportunity to be seen in millions of homes each week, talking about the evening's program and sometimes acting in the dramatic presentation. He is lucky to be in the forefront of top motion picture actors who are now crossing over to television. James Dean — or Jimmy, as Reagan refers to him — is making his second appearance on *GE Theater,* just weeks after starring with former child actress Natalie Wood in an adaptation of Sherwood Anderson's short story "I'm a Fool." Neither Dean nor Wood knows they will soon play opposite each other in the landmark motion picture *Rebel*

Without a Cause.

On this night, Reagan plays the hero to Dean's villain, the sort of dashing role that has eluded him for years in motion pictures. By the end of the brief teleplay, Reagan's character has not only wrestled a .32-caliber pistol away from the suicidal Bud but has shown a flash of anger and a knowledge of weaponry that hints at a much darker past. Reagan more than holds his own with Dean, a young actor being hailed as one of the best in Hollywood. The scene concludes with a scowling Reagan shoving a sobbing James Dean, then hugging his family.

Reagan's mastery as a thespian is complete. The viewer is lost in the rage exhibited by his character. The screen goes black. The credits roll.

Then, suddenly, the action shifts to a now-smiling and chipper Ronald Reagan sitting in his dressing room as he once again speaks into the camera. He is still wearing the pajamas and bathrobe, but gone is the brooding and angst so evident just a few seconds ago. Magically, he has returned to a confident, likable persona. "Well," he tells the audience, still winded from his physical interchange with Dean, "I hope you've enjoyed James Dean, Constance Ford, and the rest of us."

In fact, America enjoys *GE Theater* very much — and Ronald Reagan in particular. The show is a smash hit. Reagan's career is back on solid footing, as is his bank account.

But there is more to being the emcee of *GE Theater* than just introducing the night's show and an occasional spot of acting. General Electric is a giant corporation, with plants located in thirty-one states. As part of his contract, Reagan is required to travel to these factories as a goodwill ambassador. It is the thinking of GE's corporate leadership in New York that having the host of their signature television show intermingle with the workers will be good for morale. Afraid of flying, Reagan travels the country by train and then takes time to speak with and listen to each employee he meets.

"At first, all I did was walk the assembly lines at GE plants, or if it didn't interrupt production, I'd speak to them in small groups from a platform set up on the floor of the factories," he will later write.

Reagan is surprised to discover that this clause in his contract is just as fulfilling as his time before the camera. For with every factory he visits, he learns more about the economy and local governments, often accepting invitations to speak to civic groups.

The political passion that has lain dormant since his stepping down as president of the Screen Actors Guild three years ago is now being rekindled. Reagan has come to believe that less governmental interference is the best path for America. The long train rides give him plenty of time to ruminate on this and to write careful speeches on stacks of three-by-five cards. He wraps a rubber band around each stack and saves them. Someday his words will be melded into a spectacular thesis that will become known as "The Speech."

It is "The Speech" that will not only change the course of Ronald Reagan's life but also make him a marked man.

On November 18, 1956, a somber Ronald Reagan opens the latest installment of *GE Theater* wearing a coat and tie. James Dean is dead, killed in a car accident one year ago. Due to popular public demand, *GE Theater* is rebroadcasting the production of "I'm a Fool," starring Dean and his *Rebel Without a Cause* costar Natalie Wood. Reagan speaks fondly of Dean but never flashes a smile or a hint of the trademark warmth that has become synonymous with the host of *GE Theater.* Jimmy Dean, he tells his television audience, was a young actor with unlimited potential.

Reagan's monologue on Dean signals that his years as a lightweight Hollywood actor are coming to an end. He has begun an inexorable journey into ideological warfare and public service that no one, not even Ronald Reagan, could ever have seen coming.

Thus, Reagan's words about James Dean's unlimited potential can also be used to describe him.

6

Ardmore, Oklahoma
May 29, 1955
6:00 A.M.

As a twenty-eight-year-old mother of two is about to give birth to her third child, she and her husband are hoping that it will be a boy. They are affluent people, with a strong belief in the American dream.

If their child is indeed a boy, it will be named after his father, who, in addition to being president of Ardmore's Optimist Club, is a deeply religious and highly prosperous oilman. There will, one day, be whispers that he is connected to the Central Intelligence Agency, whispers that will be scrutinized very closely.

But all this is in the future, as the hoped-for baby boy enters the world.

Two miles across the Oklahoma town, a brand-new and modern Memorial Hospital is opening to the public. The newborn baby boy could very well have earned the honor of being the first child delivered in this state-of-the-art facility. That would be a mark of distinction, if only in Ardmore. But Jo Ann, as the mother is named, has opted to deliver at a hospital known as the Hardy Sanitarium, which will make the birth unique in another way. The opening of the new hospital will mean that Hardy, a two-story brick building that has been a vital part of Ardmore's fabric for forty-four years, will now close for good on this very day. Rather than being the first baby born in the new hospital, Jo Ann's baby will be the last born at Hardy.

So it is that John Warnock Hinckley Jr. is born in an obsolete mental hospital.

At first glance, the baby appears to be completely normal.

7

Los Angeles Memorial Coliseum
July 15, 1960
8:00 P.M.

The man with three years to live is nervous. Sen. John F. Kennedy steps to the podium and gazes out at eighty thousand Democrats, who are on their feet cheering loudly. The forty-three-year-old patrician from Massachusetts is perspiring lightly. His eyes scan the vast outdoor Los Angeles Coliseum, with its vaulting peristyle arches and Olympic cauldron signifying the Olympic Games held there in 1932. This is a spot reserved for conquering heroes, the same lofty perch where Gen. George S. Patton was welcomed on leave from World War II in 1945.

Just two days ago, the wealthy politician with movie star good looks received the necessary votes to secure the Democratic nomination for president. Now, as the national convention comes to a close with his acceptance speech, bedlam fills the Coliseum. Native Americans in full tribal regalia perform ritual dances on the football field, and low-flying TV news helicopters threaten to drown out Kennedy's words.

With many high-ranking Democrats looking on in person, and famous Kennedy celebrity backers such as Henry Fonda and Frank Sinatra joining the festivities, John F. Kennedy begins his speech: "With a deep sense of duty and high resolve, I accept your nomination." Kennedy's words are clipped, and he speaks too fast. He has slept very little in the past week, filling his days and nights with political meetings, parties, and rendezvous with would-be girlfriends.* "I accept it with a full and grateful heart — without reservation — and with only one obligation — the obligation to devote every effort of body, mind and spirit to lead our Party back to victory and our Nation back to greatness."

Kennedy now launches into what will become known as the "New Frontier"

* Among them are Judith Campbell and the actress Marilyn Monroe. Campbell, who once dated Frank Sinatra, will go on to become the mistress of mobster Sam Giancana.

speech, telling Americans, "Today our concern must be with that future. For the world is changing. The old era is ending. The old ways will not do." As he outlines his vision for the future, Kennedy launches a series of personal attacks on his likely Republican opponent, current vice president of the United States Richard Milhous Nixon.

A continent away, Nixon himself cannot sleep. The CBS Television network is broadcasting Kennedy's speech live. Despite its being 11:00 p.m. in Washington, Nixon is riveted to the black-and-white TV in the family room of his Tudor-style home in the city's Wesley Heights neighborhood.* He endures every one of his opponent's assaults, taking each slight personally but also knowing that Kennedy does this all the time, as he is fond of hardball politics.

"Mr. Nixon may feel it is his turn now,"

* The official residence of the vice president is now the U.S. Naval Observatory in northwestern Washington, DC. However, Congress did not make this official until 1974. Until that time, vice presidents maintained their own private residence. Nixon purchased the five-thousand-square-foot house on Forest Lane in 1957.

Kennedy says somewhat sarcastically. Nixon, an acute observer, notes Kennedy's lean face is tense, despite the senator's attempts to appear at ease.

"After the New Deal and the Fair Deal — but before he deals, someone had better cut the cards."

The audience laughs.

Kennedy continues: "That 'someone' may be the millions of Americans who voted for President Eisenhower but balk at his would-be, self-appointed successor. For just as historians tell us that Richard I was not fit to fill the shoes of bold Henry II — and that Richard Cromwell was not fit to wear the mantle of his uncle — they might add in future years that Richard Nixon did not measure to the footsteps of Dwight D. Eisenhower."

Nixon is forty-seven years old, but his thick jowls and receding hairline make him look ten years older. He is a man of humble beginnings — unlike Kennedy, who was born into great wealth. In truth, JFK is closer to the commonly held image of a Republican — "fraternity presidents, tax-board assessors, community leaders, surgeons, Pullman porters, head nurses and the fat sons of rich fathers," as one writer described the party faithful.*

Nixon put himself through law school, served in the navy during World War II, then successfully ran for Congress in 1946. He believes strongly in the Republican virtues of fiscal conservatism, small government, and a powerful military. Nixon has a keen political mind. He has watched Kennedy's rise to power closely, recognizing for almost a year that JFK will be his likely opponent for the presidency. Now, mentally cataloguing each item in Kennedy's New Frontier agenda, knowing he must co-opt some of these themes and give them a Republican spin, Nixon concentrates heavily upon his rival.

Nixon's wife, Pat, and two young daughters, Tricia and Julie, are fast asleep, but he has no immediate plans to join them. He listens closely as Kennedy concludes his speech to thunderous applause.

"As we face the coming challenge, we too shall wait upon the Lord, and ask that he renew our strength. Then shall we be equal to the test. Then we shall not be weary. And

* The writer was Norman Mailer, in a piece for *Esquire* about the 1960 Democratic National Convention titled "Superman Comes to the Supermarket."

then we shall prevail."

Nixon is not impressed. Those eighty thousand Democrats might seem like a lot, but he well knows the Coliseum can hold many thousands more. Nixon also considers himself a better politician than his rival, and believes he can win the election if he can convince some Democrats to swing away from their party. Nixon needs crossover votes.

"In this campaign I make a prediction," he will tell the audience when he accepts the Republican nomination for the presidency thirteen days from now. "I say that just as in 1952 and 1956, millions of Democrats will join us — not because they are deserting their party, but because their party deserted them at Los Angeles two weeks ago."

Another man is also intensely watching John F. Kennedy.

Sitting in the living room of his lavish Pacific Palisades home, Ronald Reagan is disgusted by what he is hearing. At the conclusion of Kennedy's speech, Reagan gets up and wanders to the floor-to-ceiling windows overlooking the spectacular view of the distant lights of Los Angeles.

Reagan's mind is made up: he will cast his

vote for Richard Nixon.

This will come as no surprise to anyone in Hollywood. While still technically a Democrat, Reagan has been heavily influenced by the more conservative views espoused by his wife, Nancy, who grew up in an extremely Republican household and likes to brag that she has been reading the right-leaning *National Review* since its first issue.*

The motion picture industry is deeply divided between liberals and conservatives. A minority of actors such as Reagan and John Wayne openly espouse anticommunist, small-government views. But a much larger contingent, led by singer Frank Sinatra and his Rat Pack, have fallen under John F. Kennedy's spell. This group includes actors Paul Newman, Joanne Woodward, Elizabeth Taylor, Cary Grant, and Angie Dickinson. While some keep a distance between their personal and professional lives, Sinatra, in particular, has made it clear that he despises not only Ronald Reagan's views but also

* November 19, 1955. The *National Review* was founded by William F. Buckley Jr., a wealthy former CIA operative who believed that conservative commentary was all too often missing from American political debate.

Reagan himself. "Dumb and dangerous," Sinatra calls Reagan, "and so simpleminded." The singer takes his vitriol a step further by also attacking Nancy Reagan, calling her "a dope with fat ankles who could never make it as an actress."

Despite his career resurgence on television, and the wealth that has allowed him to build this spectacular four-bedroom, 4,700-square-foot home at the end of a long private road in the Pacific Palisades, Ronald Reagan and his wife have become social pariahs. They are rarely invited to the best parties, and even when a dinner offer comes their way, Reagan has a bad habit of lecturing all within earshot about politics. Nancy, for her part, does not help matters by appearing condescending. "We got stuck with them at a dinner party, and it was awful," the wife of screenwriter Philip Dunne once remembered. "Nancy is so assessing — she always looks you up and down before she deigns to speak."

Turning away from the window, Reagan walks past the large stone fireplace and into his small corner office. He sits down and takes pen and paper from a drawer. General Electric has taken great pride in turning his home into "The House of the Future" and has capitalized on that concept by having

Reagan film commercials for the *General Electric Theater* from his own kitchen, surrounded by a GE toaster, dishwasher, and electric garbage disposal. But no modern gadget will help Reagan perform the simple task of writing a letter.

Ronald Reagan is not afraid to mail his thoughts to anyone who will read them — as well as many who don't want to. Letter writing from his home office has become the nexus for Reagan's personal conservative movement, and with each letter he sends, his political ambition advances.

With Kennedy's words still echoing in his mind, Reagan picks up his pen and begins writing a letter to Richard Nixon.

"Dear Mr. Vice President," the letter begins. "I know this is presumptuous of me, but I'm passing on some thoughts after viewing the convention here in L.A. . . . I heard a frightening call to arms. Unfortunately, he is a powerful speaker with an appeal to the emotions. He leaves little doubt that his idea of the 'challenging new world' is one in which the Federal Government will grow bigger and do more, and of course spend more."

Ronald Reagan and Richard Nixon first became acquainted back in 1947, when Reagan appeared before Congress. They rekindled that relationship in 1950, when Reagan campaigned for Nixon's opponent in the race for a U.S. Senate seat from California. They've since become friends, and Nixon is actually the reason Reagan still maintains his Democratic Party membership. When Reagan told Nixon he was planning to switch parties in time for the 1960 election, the canny Nixon said he could do more for the Republican Party by remaining a Democrat and using his fame to convince other Democrats to cross party lines with him.

So Reagan remains a Democrat — at least for now. He has no idea that Nixon actually considers him "shallow" and of "limited mental capacity." But even if he did know that, it might not matter. Ronald Reagan simply wants to see John F. Kennedy and his liberal dogma defeated.

Reagan continues his letter: "I know there must be some short-sighted people within the Republican Party who will advise that the Republicans should try to 'out-liberal' him. In my opinion this would be fatal . . . I don't pose as an infallible pundit, but I have a strong feeling that the 20 million nonvoters in this country just might be conservatives."

But Nixon is not planning to take Reagan's advice. In one week's time, he will fly to New York and meet with Republican governor Nelson Rockefeller. After a dinner of lamb chops in Rocky's Fifth Avenue apartment, the two men will stay up all night drafting a more liberal Republican platform. The "Treaty of Fifth Avenue," as it will be dubbed, is designed to appeal to independent and Democratic voters.

Reagan concludes the letter, scalding John F. Kennedy: "Under the tousled boyish haircut is still old Karl Marx — first launched a century ago. There is nothing new in the idea of a government being Big Brother to us all. Hitler called his 'State Socialism.' "*

* Reagan's animosity toward John F. Kennedy will continue even after the young president is shot dead by an assassin's bullet. On November 22, 1963, just a few hours after JFK is assassinated, Ronald and Nancy Reagan will hold a dinner. "Why should we cancel our dinner party just because John F. Kennedy died? Don't be silly," Nancy Reagan told one guest who called to ask if the party was still on. The man, a film producer and former U.S. Army brigadier general named Frank McCarthy, arrived to find Ronald Reagan, John Wayne, and actor Robert Taylor socializing. As a film producer, McCarthy will go

Signing the letter "Ronnie Reagan," the actor fervently hopes his offer to campaign for Richard Nixon will be accepted. Though Nixon will lose the 1960 presidential election by less than one percentage point of all votes polled, Reagan will speak on his behalf whenever asked.

"Have you registered as a Republican yet?" shouts a voice from the audience. The year is 1962. As Ronald Reagan predicted, Richard Nixon's attempt to "out-liberal" John Kennedy is among the factors that cost him the presidency. Now Reagan is once again campaigning for Nixon, this time as the former vice president runs for governor of California.

Reagan stands before a small crowd of Republican supporters. The fund-raising event is being held in a house just down the street from his Pacific Palisades home. Reagan knows many of those in attendance but does not recognize this voice speaking to him in the middle of the living room.

"Have you registered as a Republican yet?" she asks a second time.

"Well, no. I haven't yet. But I intend to."

---

on to win the Academy Award for Best Picture in 1970 for *Patton.*

The truth is Ronald Reagan no longer has any reason to remain a Democrat. His conservative affiliations have become so notorious that General Electric recently fired him as a spokesman, under pressure from some powerful liberal concerns. So, once again, Ronald Reagan is an unemployed actor searching for his next paycheck. He has absolutely, positively nothing to lose by switching political parties.

"I'm a registrar," the woman says, standing up and walking toward Reagan with a slip of paper in her hand.

She hands the paper to Reagan. It is a registration form. The woman has already filled in all the blanks, meaning that with a simple swipe of his pen, Ronald Reagan will officially become a Republican.

The registrar hands Reagan a pen.

He signs the form without a moment's hesitation.

As the room erupts in applause, Reagan smiles. There will come a time when few will even remember his thirty years as a Democrat. "I did not leave the Democratic Party," he will tell people, borrowing a line from Richard Nixon. "The Democratic Party left me."

Now, in the first moments of his new life

as a Republican, Ronald Reagan gets back to the task at hand.

"Now, where was I?" he asks, before continuing the speech he has been perfecting for the last eight years.

A bitter Richard Nixon strides purposefully onto the stage at the Beverly Hilton Hotel in Los Angeles. The date is November 7, 1962. Despite Ronald Reagan's campaign efforts, Nixon has just lost the election for governor of California, an election he assumed he would win easily.* The governorship was meant to be a job that would keep Nixon in the public eye until 1968. He believed that John F. Kennedy would be president for two terms, so he would wait until then to tender another presidential bid.

Now an exhausted and angry Richard Nixon faces the harsh reality that he is finished. It will be a political near impossibility to recover from this loss.

* Polls showed that Richard Nixon would win the 1962 California gubernatorial election. However, Nixon failed to reach out to the more conservative elements of the Republican Party, a blunder that cost him dearly. The incumbent, Pat Brown, won in a landslide, garnering 52 percent of the popular vote to Nixon's 47 percent.

But before he goes, Nixon has a few words he would like to say.

His face lined with tension, Nixon forces a smile as he looks at the reporters assembled before him. There is no podium, just a cluster of microphones. He is nervous about the speech he is about to give but is attempting to appear jovial. The forty-nine-year-old Nixon considers the media to be his personal enemy and believes that after years of frustrated silence, the time has come to tell them off.

Nixon digs his right hand deep into the pocket of his suit pants. An elaborate chandelier hovers to one side of the room. Reporters sit at a long table in front of him, poised with pencil and paper to write down his words. To his right, television cameras and newspaper photographers prepare to capture this moment of defeat.

"For sixteen years," Nixon begins, "you've had an opportunity to attack me, and I think I've given as good as I've taken."

A hush fills the small ballroom. Nixon has just crossed a line. It is one thing to confront a journalist about his coverage in private, but to do so in public is taboo. And thanks to all those television cameras, this verbal assault is now being filmed for posterity.

Pencils scribble frantically as the reporters eagerly await Nixon's next words.

"I will leave you gentlemen now. And, uh . . . You will now write it. You will interpret it. That's your right. But as I leave you, I want you to know — just think how much you're going to be missing. You won't have Nixon to kick around anymore, because gentlemen, this is my last press conference."

Fifty-nine seconds. That's all it takes. Nixon does not field questions. He is whisked from the room and walks quickly out of the hotel, stopping only to shake the hand of a front-desk clerk before stepping into the front seat of a waiting car.

He is thrilled to have gotten the last word.

Yet fate will allow him many more press conferences. And if Richard Nixon thinks the media have gotten the best of him in the past, that is nothing compared to what they will do to him in the future.

Two years later, television cameras again capture a historic moment. The night is October 27, 1964. Ronald Reagan is eagerly anticipating watching himself on television. The occasion is a speech he taped one week earlier in support of Republican presidential nominee Barry Goldwater.* At first, Goldwater's people wanted Reagan to deliver the speech live. But Reagan is by now a canny politician, and although he would have liked the spontaneous applause and laughter that he knew each line would engender, he didn't want to take any chances on making a mistake — thus the live scenario was scrapped.

"Nancy and I went to the home of some friends to watch the broadcast," he will later write of the night that changed his life. Reagan's presentation for Goldwater was so successful that scribes simply dubbed Reagan's words "The Speech."

Reagan realizes his career is now in public life. After a seven-year break between films, he has made one last motion picture. He

---

* One young supporter of Goldwater, and an active member of the Young Republican movement, was a seventeen-year-old Chicago-area young lady named Hillary Rodham. She was fond of wearing a cowgirl outfit and a straw hat emblazoned with the Goldwater campaign's AuH_2O slogan (Au is the periodic symbol for gold; H_2O the symbol for water). Shortly afterward, she would switch her party allegiance to the Democrats, perhaps under pressure from her liberal friends at Wellesley College.

played a villain in *The Killers,* a movie that sank without a trace at the box office.*

Even though the speech is a sensation, Barry Goldwater's advisers did not want Reagan's talk to air. With the election just one week away, they were terrified that the conservative themes he was espousing would drive some voters into the Democratic camp.

As the Reagans sit side by side before the television set in the den of their friends' home, the black-and-white screen flickers, showing him standing behind a podium draped with patriotic bunting. The edited presentation then cuts to the back of the room, allowing the nation to see the audience awaiting his words. Some hold placards. Others wear cowboy hats. All are dressed informally and are meant to look like a homey cross-section of the American public.

This works perfectly with Reagan's homespun delivery, the gentle, parental voice that he perfected at those GE

* Reagan's previous film was 1957's *Hellcats of the Navy,* which costarred Nancy Reagan. Their final on-camera performance as a couple was the 1958 *GE Theater* episode with the prescient title "A Turkey for the President."

Reagan in The Killers, *his last movie role*

factories, after-dinner speeches, and count-less other conservative venues across the country. "Unlike most television programs, the performer hasn't been provided with a script," he assures the audience as he begins. "As a matter of fact, I have been permitted to choose my own words and discuss my own ideas regarding the choice that we face in the next few weeks."

Then Reagan begins a twenty-seven-minute soliloquy on the virtues of the America in which he truly believes. The

Republican presidential nominee, Barry Goldwater, is hardly mentioned. Reagan delivers a dazzling speech full of allusions to the American dream, fiscal conservatism, and small government. He speaks of freedom and the Founding Fathers as if they were brand-new concepts that Americans need to embrace immediately. He talks about poverty, farmers, the Vietnam War, Cuban immigrants, and American veterans. There is no hesitation in Reagan's voice, no fumbling with the words of his self-written script, for this is the summation of what he has believed for years.

"You and I have a rendezvous with destiny," he concludes, his voice at its most earnest and inspirational. "We'll preserve for our children this, the last best hope of man on earth, or we'll sentence them to take the last step into a thousand years of darkness."

Ronald and Nancy Reagan drive home in their Lincoln Continental after watching the filmed speech. The fifty-three-year-old Reagan is nervous, unsure if his talk has been a success. Others who watched the speech with them insist that Reagan did his job well, but he is still uncertain.

The October night is partly cloudy, with

temperatures in the low seventies. The Reagans park their car, then walk inside the house and go to bed, still not knowing if the speech has been a success or a flop.

It is midnight when the bedside phone rings. The Goldwater campaign is on the other end. Reagan's speech has been such a smash that people from all across the country have called in, pledging support and money for the candidate. "A Time for Choosing," as the speech will come to be known, will be described by reporters as "the most successful national political debut since William Jennings Bryan electrified the 1896 Democratic convention with the 'Cross of Gold' speech."*

* Delivered at the Democratic National Convention in Chicago on July 9, 1896. Bryan was a thirty-six-year-old former Nebraska congressman when he delivered the address. His oration was so powerful that the audience screamed in agreement, waving hats and canes. Some audience members threw their coats into the air. The speech, which advocated the use of silver coinage to increase American prosperity, was so effective that Bryan won the nomination. He ultimately lost the general election to Republican candidate William McKinley (who was shot by an assassin's bullet on September 6, 1901, died eight days later,

Nancy Reagan and Ronald Reagan after winning the Republican nomination for governor of California in 1966

and was succeeded in office by Theodore Roosevelt). William Jennings Bryan ran for the presidency twice more and later in life supplemented his income by delivering the "Cross of Gold" speech during lecture appearances. Bryan is also well known as being the foil for famed attorney Clarence Darrow during the

"That speech was one of the most important milestones of my life," Reagan will later remember. Until that day, he had been skeptical of any suggestion that he run for political office. Now that is about to change. "A Time for Choosing" will turn out to be, in his words, "another one of those unexpected turns that led me onto a path I never expected to take."

Scopes Monkey Trial, which argued the legality of teaching evolution in schools. Bryan, a devout Presbyterian, argued against the practice. He died in his sleep five days after winning the case.

8

Rotunda
State Capitol Building
Sacramento, California
January 2, 1967
12:11 A.M.

Despite making fifty-three films, Ronald Reagan has never known a moment of drama quite like the one he is experiencing right now. Dressed in a black suit with a thin dark tie, he stands, head held high and feet planted twelve inches apart, like a conquering hero from the Western movies he loves so much. His left hand rests on a Bible. A hulking bald man stands in front of him. A glance to his left shows Nancy Reagan prim and straight at his elbow, beaming after plastic surgery to repair her drooping eyelids. Thirty-two television cameras light Reagan's face. "America the Beautiful" echoes in his head, thanks to a choir from the University of Southern California, who serenaded him at the stroke of midnight.

This is Ronald Reagan's greatest moment, a time when at long last he gets to play the leading man. Just two years ago he was hosting yet another television show.* Now he is the newly elected governor of California. There's not a single writer in Hollywood who could have scripted this better.

Reagan raises his right hand, and the swearing-in begins. One hundred fifty guests are closely watching him, waiting for the trademark smile and nod of the head he has used to such populist effect while campaigning.

Yet there is one problem this early morning. The man facing him from two feet away is an annoyance. California Supreme Court justice Marshall McComb is reflecting light off his bald skull directly into Ronald Reagan's eyes. In this, his finest hour, Reagan is forced to squint, barely able to see the man to whom he is speaking.

"I, Ronald Reagan, do solemnly swear that I will faithfully defend the Constitution of the United States," he pledges, repeating

* *Death Valley Days,* a Western-themed production that ran for 452 episodes from 1952 to 1970. Reagan was the second of four men who hosted the show. He also acted in eight episodes.

the words that McComb has just recited to him. Reagan's voice fills the Rotunda, bouncing off the marble floors and the life-size statue of Spanish queen Isabella looking over him.

Reagan lets his gaze float out over the room. It is impossible not to be distracted. Men, women, and children surround him, watching the proceedings with hushed reverence. Many are standing on tiptoe to better witness the historic moment.

These are Reagan's people. They also represent something of an anachronism. America is descending into turmoil, torn apart by the Vietnam War, a deep racial divide, drug use, and a sexual revolution. But in this room, at this moment, Reagan sees none of that conflict.

Many filling this towering ceremonial space are as conservative as he is. The men wear crisp dark suits. Their hair is cut short, in sharp contrast to the shoulder-length locks so many men are beginning to wear these days. The knee-length dresses worn by the women are a throwback to the more formal styles of the 1950s, and nothing at all like the miniskirts that ride high up a woman's thigh and leave little to the imagination. Recently, when Ronald and Nancy Reagan visited their fourteen-year-

131

old daughter, Patti, at her boarding school and discovered her in one such short skirt, Nancy was so furious that she stormed out and sat in the car.

Reagan has nothing against the miniskirt. He is still fond of admiring the ladies. "He liked to look at women, no doubt about it," one of his aides will one day recall. "But if he did anything about it, he was very discreet." In truth, Reagan's days of womanizing are mostly behind him. The politically reinvented Reagan prefers to put forth a strong paternal public image.

Of course, no man is perfect. And Reagan still possesses idiosyncrasies that must be kept quiet, such as his trust in astrologers. Both he and Nancy use stargazers in order to divine the future. The conservative folks who admire the Reagans might be troubled if they knew.

Even the details of the swearing-in ceremony have been influenced by Reagan's astrologers. Normally, the gubernatorial inauguration takes place in broad daylight, but Ronald Reagan's stargazers have noted that Jupiter is visible in the nighttime sky at this precise midnight hour. The solar system's largest planet is thought to be a harbinger of fame, prosperity, and power. Rather than tempt fate by holding the inauguration in the morning, when Jupiter is absent, Ronald and Nancy Reagan insist that the ceremony be held at midnight, to reap the full benefit of Jupiter's largesse. This is why a state supreme court justice, chaplain, dozens of members of the press, and a select gathering of invited benefactors and dignitaries now stand in a broad circle around Ronald Wilson Reagan and his beloved wife at this witching hour.*

Reagan knows that in their hearts some in the crowd might doubt his ability to lead, thinking him just an actor. He is also well aware that his political views are at odds with current trends in American and California politics, thus making him a dinosaur in the eyes of many beyond the curved walls of the Rotunda. Reagan's victory notwithstanding, the landslide loss by Barry Goldwater in the 1964 presidential election makes it abundantly clear that conservative Republican values are falling out of fashion.

* When confronted many years later, Ronald Reagan will deny that astrologers played a role in his gubernatorial swearing-in, stating that the unusual midnight ceremony was due to the fact that then governor Pat Brown was making last-minute bureaucratic appointments.

As Justice McComb concludes the lengthy recitation of the oath, Ronald Reagan is keen to begin his new journey. He is absorbing a significant pay cut so that he might hold this position. The forty-four-thousand-dollar governor's salary is so low that the Reagans have had to sell the Malibu ranch.

That is a hardship Reagan will have to endure.*

For, on this cold January night, Ronald Reagan has a secret: The governorship will not be enough. One day Reagan hopes to be president of the United States.

His astrologers think it might be in the stars.

Four months after his inauguration, Ronald Reagan is facing a CBS Television camera in Los Angeles, about to participate in a

* Reagan's sadness about the sale of the ranch to Twentieth Century–Fox in 1966 was tempered by the $1.9 million selling price, which made him a millionaire for the first time. The property is now part of Malibu Creek State Park, but during the time that Twentieth Century–Fox owned it, the ranch was the location for many motion pictures, including *Butch Cassidy and the Sundance Kid*. It was also the location for the television show *M*A*S*H*.

debate entitled "The Image of America and the Youth of the World." It is 10:00 p.m. at the CBS headquarters in New York, 7:00 p.m. in Los Angeles, and 3:00 a.m. in London, England, where a panel of international college students sits ready to ask questions of Ronald Reagan and his fellow panelist, liberal senator Robert F. Kennedy.

The program will be broadcast live around the world.

Kennedy is in Paris and is the more seasoned political professional. Boyishly handsome at the age of forty-one, RFK is legendary, having served as attorney general under his late brother, the assassinated president John F. Kennedy. In 1964, Bobby, as he is known, was elected U.S. senator from New York. He is cocky and powerful, and tonight he is confident that he will get the best of Ronald Reagan. Kennedy's suit and tie are dark blue; his demeanor is nonchalant. He thinks so little of Reagan's mental prowess that he barely studied for the intellectual debate.

Reagan is far more cautious. He knows that fifteen million Americans will likely watch this broadcast, as will millions more around the world. So he has prepared for weeks, memorizing statistics about the Vietnam War and the history of Southeast Asia. He cannot afford to appear ill prepared or to let Kennedy make a fool of him, and that concern is etched deeply in Reagan's face. Though he is tanned and rested, his trademark smile is nowhere to be seen. In fact, gazing into the camera, his eyes are cold.

This debate is personal to Reagan. Unbeknownst to the vast audience, he believes it was Bobby Kennedy who pressured General Electric into firing him as host of *GE Theater* back in 1962. RFK allegedly told the giant corporation that no government contracts would come their way if they allowed the conservative Reagan to remain host.*

Ronald Reagan is not a vengeful man, but his memory is long, and now he desperately wants to win this contest and humiliate Kennedy.

"I'm Charles Collingwood," says the CBS

---

* Reagan might also have been fired from *GE Theater* because he was speaking out against the Tennessee Valley Authority, in which General Electric had a financial interest. And there was also a drop in the ratings, due to *Bonanza* being moved to a Sunday night slot opposite *GE Theater*. The popular Western won the top spot easily.

host, beginning the proceedings. "And this is *Town Meeting of the World,* the latest in an occasional series of trans-Atlantic confrontations that's been going on [*sic*] ever since communication satellites made them possible. With me here in the studio of the BBC in London are a group of young people, university students from — one from the United States, but the rest of them from Europe, Africa and Asia. They are all attending universities in Great Britain. They have ideas, all of them, sometimes provocative ones, about the United States, its role and its image."*

The dialogue begins, and the students in London immediately attack. "Senator Kennedy," asks a young man with short bangs,

* The lone American student on the panel is a former Princeton basketball player and Olympic gold medalist currently attending Oxford University on a Rhodes scholarship. Bill Bradley is twenty-three years old and will one day go on to play ten seasons in the National Basketball Association and serve three terms in the U.S. Senate. He was called upon to speak just once during the Kennedy-Reagan debate, and his comments were notable for his civil tone and a failed attempt to defuse the arrogant hostility of many of his fellow panelists.

"I'd like to ask you what you think of Dean Rusk's recent claim that the effect of anti–Vietnam War demonstrations in the States may actually be to prolong the war rather than to shorten it."

Kennedy responds timidly, his voice soft. He plans on running for president in one year and is courting the votes of college students who might be watching the broadcast. "I certainly don't think that's why the war is continuing," he says, giving tacit approval to the antiwar protests that some Americans see as unpatriotic. Kennedy glances away from the camera as he talks, looking at notes.

But when it is Reagan's turn to speak, he looks bold and confident: "I definitely think that the demonstrations are prolonging the war," he says emphatically, and then lists the reasons.

Just like that, Reagan is in charge. He dominates the rest of the debate, making Kennedy appear weak and passive. Kennedy does not help matters, allowing the panel to interrogate him as if he were some misguided professor. Sensing weakness, the students grow bolder.

"Answer my question," one demands, cutting RFK off in midsentence. When Kennedy gives him a lengthy response, the student once again interrupts, insisting that Kennedy has not answered the question.

Rather than appear indignant, however, Kennedy mildly accepts the rebuke, despite the fact that he is seething inside. "Who the fuck got me into this?" the deflated Kennedy will demand of an aide as soon as the show ends.

Ronald Reagan gently scolds the students when they interrupt or their statistics are incorrect. An increasingly bolder Reagan espouses freedom, democracy, and the American way. Kennedy apologizes for American foreign policy "mistakes," but Reagan refuses to do so. There is no fear in his eyes as he speaks, no hesitation or hint of backing down when the students harass and attack. A *Newsweek* reporter will write of this evening that "Reagan effortlessly reeled off more facts and quasi-facts about the Vietnam conflict than anyone suspected he ever knew."

As the broadcast enters its second half hour, Reagan veers away from Vietnam and waxes poetic about the greatness of the United States. His tone is evangelical. Most of the students on the panel have spent the hour painting America as the root of all global evil, and it is to them that he preaches most fervently.

Reagan's hatred of communism has not abated one bit since his days as president of the Screen Actors Guild. If anything, his convictions have become more intense: "I think it would be very admirable if the Berlin Wall, which was built in direct contravention to a treaty, should disappear. I think this would be a step toward peace and toward self-determination for all people, if it were."

As the broadcast winds down, it is Reagan who gets the last word. Among the students on the panel is a young man from the Soviet Union, who lives in a totalitarian state. Reagan's words are aimed directly at him. "I believe the highest aspiration of man should be individual freedom and the development of the individual. That there is a sacredness to individual rights!"

With Reagan's words ringing worldwide, Charles Collingwood ends the broadcast.

In Los Angeles, Ronald Reagan removes the earpiece that has allowed him to hear the students' questions from London. Unlike after the "Time for Choosing" speech of three years ago, there is no question in Reagan's mind that this night has been a triumph. "Political rookie Reagan," *Newsweek* will write, "left old campaigner Kennedy blinking when the session ended."

In Paris, Bobby Kennedy storms out of the studio into the predawn light. Furious at his embarrassing performance, he turns to an aide: "Never again put me on the stage with that son of a bitch."

One year later, it is Bobby Kennedy who is triumphant. Shortly after midnight, he briskly strides through the kitchen of the Ambassador Hotel in Los Angeles, on his way to meet the press. He has just won the highly coveted California Democratic presidential primary. Lyndon Johnson, the Democrat currently serving as president, announced two months ago that he would not seek another term in office. This leaves the door wide open for the popular and handsome Kennedy. At the age of forty-two, he appears to be just five months away from being elected president.

A crowd of enthusiastic supporters follows Kennedy through the kitchen. Among them are the famous writer George Plimpton and NFL player "Rosey" Grier. An ecstatic Kennedy stops to shake the hand of an immigrant busboy, unaware that an assassin stands just a few feet away.

Suddenly, shots ring out. Bobby Kennedy is hit and immediately slumps to the concrete floor. A single bullet has passed through his brain, entering just behind the right ear. Two other bullets have pierced his upper torso. He is an athletic man who has always taken care of his physical health. And for twenty-six long hours, Kennedy fights for his life. But at 1:44 a.m. on June 6, 1968, Robert Francis Kennedy loses that fight.

Ronald Reagan is on television the day after the RFK assassination, speaking to talk show host Joey Bishop on ABC. "The enemy sits in Moscow," Reagan says, because he believes that it was agents of the Soviet Union who killed Robert Kennedy, as well as his brother John F. Kennedy in 1963. "The actions of the enemy led to, and precipitated, the tragedy of last night."

Four months later, Ronald Reagan smells of Royal Briar cologne as he steps out into the night. A blast of unseasonably cold air chills him as he walks toward the swimming pool, a gin and orange juice cocktail in hand. As on most weekends, Reagan and Nancy have flown down from Sacramento to spend a few days at their Pacific Palisades home in Los Angeles.

But on this night, Nancy has not joined Reagan at this political event in Studio City, a few miles from his home.

Reagan sees a young girl sitting alone by the pool. She appears to be distraught. Slowly, he walks over to see if she is all right.

In truth, it is Ronald Reagan who needs a few kind words. Reagan's first year in office has been a challenge. His personal and political views are not popular. His first real battle came when members of a radical group of African Americans known as the Black Panther Party occupied the California State Capitol Building in Sacramento. In accordance with the Second Amendment to the U.S. Constitution, which allows citizens the right to bear arms, these twenty-four men and six women openly displayed the .357 Magnum pistols and 12-gauge shotguns they carried. California law states that carrying weapons openly in public is legal, and the Panthers were in Sacramento to argue against impending legislation that would revoke this right. The protest ended peacefully, but not before Republicans in the state legislature pushed through a bill that made gun control in California a reality. And it is the gun-loving Reagan himself who gladly signed the bill into law.

A few months later, in a controversy that trails him almost all the way through his first year in the governor's office, Reagan learned that two of his top aides are engaging in homosexual relations. He tries to defuse the situation by quietly letting the men resign. Homosexuality is still illegal in many areas of the country, and there is very little public support for gay rights in most parts of California. But Reagan's Hollywood background infused him with a tolerance for homosexuals. While he will go on record as condemning gay behavior, he is not personally bothered by it. In fact, Carroll Righter, an astrologer on whom he and Nancy depend, is openly gay.

The matter might have subsided if *Newsweek* magazine had not run an item on October 31, 1967, that made Reagan's problem into a national scandal. Making matters even worse, Reagan lied about it, telling the press that the homosexual aides were not fired for their private conduct. By the time the scandal died down, there were many who believed that Reagan's hopes of running for president in 1968 were long gone.

And they were right. In May 1967 it appeared that the battle for president of the United States might be a contest between Ronald Reagan and either Robert Kennedy or Lyndon Johnson. Now Johnson is done, Kennedy is dead, and Reagan's presidential hopes have vanished. In the ultimate irony, the Republican nomination goes to Richard Nixon. In just a few weeks' time, Americans will elect Nixon president over Hubert Humphrey.*

Now, on this October night in 1968, taking a break from the Studio City party to clear his head by the pool, Ronald Reagan is relaxed and loose. It helps that Nancy is not here. As much as Reagan adores his wife, she is extremely jealous. Nancy gets outraged if he so much as hugs a woman he knows. Reagan has to be very careful in Nancy's presence.

The young woman sitting before him is just eighteen years old. She looks at Reagan but does not recognize him as the governor. Perhaps feeling some sympathy, Reagan sits down.

The girl's name is Patricia Taylor. Years later she will try to capitalize on her relation-

---

* The 1968 election was one of the closest in American history. Nixon beat Democratic nominee Hubert Humphrey by winning thirty-two states and 301 electoral votes. The results were so close that Nixon was not assured of victory for more than fifteen hours after the polls closed on Election Day.

ship with Ronald Reagan by taping interviews suggesting that intimacy soon followed. Reagan's personal behavior as governor, however, is so exemplary that few question his clearly stated traditional values.

9

White House
Washington, DC
August 9, 1974
7:30 A.M.

A barefoot Richard Nixon wears blue pajamas as he eats his breakfast of grapefruit, wheat germ, and milk. He is alone in his bedroom, having just walked upstairs from the White House kitchen, where he ordered the morning meal. His forty-five-year-old Cuban-born butler Manolo Sanchez delivered the food, opened the drapes, laid out Nixon's clothes for the day, then left the president alone to eat.

Nixon does not sleep with his wife, Pat.*

---

* "Pat" Nixon was born Thelma Catherine Ryan in 1912. She earned the nickname Pat as a child because of her family's Irish heritage and because she was born the day before St. Patrick's Day. She is older than her husband by ten months.

He is prone to talking during the night and gets up at all hours because of insomnia. It's not unusual that Pat Nixon does not sleep with her husband in the White House. The Kennedys and Johnsons before him did not sleep in the same bed, either. Pat Nixon has an adjoining bedroom, separated from her husband's sleeping quarters by a door.

Nixon's high-ceilinged chamber has a fireplace in one corner and two large south-facing windows with views of the Washington Monument. Outside, the morning dawns muggy and overcast. This same bedroom once housed presidents Wilson, Harding, Roosevelt, Truman, Eisenhower, Kennedy, and Johnson.* World-changing decisions have been made within these walls. Yet none of those men has come to

---

* Nixon slept in the very bed used by Truman and Eisenhower. It was not until Gerald Ford's residence that a president and First Lady slept in the same bedroom. Pat Nixon's room was officially known as the master bedroom of the White House and was where Abraham Lincoln slept. The room we know as the Lincoln Bedroom was actually an office used by Lincoln and is often said to be the scene of ghost sightings. The White House was completely gutted during the 1948–52 renovation.

the shattering conclusion that Nixon reached just yesterday. In fact, none of the thirty-five men to hold the office of president has ever done what Richard Nixon is about to do.

Nixon strips off his pajamas, showers, and changes into the dark blue suit, white shirt, and maroon tie that Sanchez has laid out for him. He is just moments away from walking downstairs to the Oval Office and affixing his signature to a one-line document: "I hereby resign the Office of President of the United States."

The scandal that would bring down a president begins over two years earlier, on June 17, 1972. Richard Nixon is seeking reelection. His first four years in office have been a triumph, marked by significant efforts to end the war in Vietnam and the historic moment when American astronauts Neil Armstrong and Buzz Aldrin walked on the moon. Sixty-two percent of Americans approve of Nixon's job performance. No matter whom the Democrats select to run against him, he should win the election handily.

Yet the paranoid Nixon is not taking any chances. His reelection committee is undertaking a stealth campaign of political espionage to defeat the Democrats. This operation includes planting eavesdropping devices in the offices of the Democratic National Committee at the Watergate Hotel complex. On June 18, 1972, the *Washington Post* publishes a curious dispatch noting arrests made at the DNC's offices:

> Five men, one of whom said he is a former employee of the Central Intelligence Agency, were arrested at 2:30 a.m. yesterday in what authorities described as an elaborate plot to bug the offices of the Democratic National Committee here.
>
> Three of the men were native-born Cubans and another was said to have trained Cuban exiles for guerrilla activity after the 1961 Bay of Pigs invasion.
>
> They were surprised at gunpoint by three plain-clothes officers of the metropolitan police department in a sixth floor office at the plush Watergate, 2600 Virginia Ave., NW, where the Democratic National Committee occupies the entire floor.
>
> There was no immediate explanation as to why the five suspects would want to bug the Democratic National Committee offices or whether or not they were working for any other individuals or organizations.

But as the media would reveal over the course of the next 852 days, the Watergate burglars were ultimately working for one very specific individual: Richard Milhous Nixon.

More than three thousand miles away, California governor Ronald Reagan is well into his sixth year in office. Reagan has been extraordinarily successful, despite having survived a recall effort during his first term.* Reagan has achieved much as California's leader, cracking down on violent student protests against the Vietnam War, successfully raising taxes in order to balance the budget, and then issuing a tax rebate. In October 1971, Reagan traveled on one of his four trips to Asia as a special envoy of Richard Nixon to calm foreign heads of state who were nervous about the thawing of relations between the United States and China.

* An anti-Reagan group led by organized labor and the California teachers' unions failed to collect the signatures necessary to recall Governor Reagan. The only successful recall attempt in that state occurred in 2003, when Governor Gray Davis was removed from office and replaced by Hollywood actor Arnold Schwarzenegger.

Meantime, Nancy Reagan has also prospered as California's First Lady. She has come to enjoy the trappings of power, such as private jet travel, an aide to carry her purse, and the surprise friendship of singer Frank Sinatra. Once an enemy, Sinatra has become a big supporter of Governor Reagan and a close personal confidant to Nancy.*

Even though her husband has stated publicly that he will not seek a third term as governor, Nancy is not about to give up a life of perks and celebrity adulation. She is working behind the scenes to plan a presidential campaign. The time will come, Nancy believes, when her Ronnie will be ready for the big job.

Her astrologers agree.

But no seer can save Richard Nixon. Nine months after their arrest, the Watergate burglars and the men who helped them plan the break-in of the DNC headquarters are being sentenced. They have all pleaded

* Sinatra was furious when President John Kennedy refused to stay at his Palm Springs home because of the singer's alleged Mafia connections. Sinatra switched his allegiance to the Republican Party as a result.

guilty and have maintained a code of silence as to their motives. All insist they acted without help. At this point, there is absolutely no evidence connecting Richard Nixon or the White House to the break-in.

But John Sirica, the short-tempered, sixty-nine-year-old chief judge for the U.S. District Court for the District of Columbia, is convinced there is more to the story. He stuns the burglars with sentences ranging from thirty-five to forty-five years in federal prison for charges of burglary, conspiracy, and wiretapping. The sentences, however, are provisional: if the defendants break their silence, prison time will be reduced to months instead of years.

The man in charge of security for the Republican National Committee, James McCord, a former CIA officer, is the first to crack. "I would appreciate the opportunity to talk with you privately in chambers," he informs Judge Sirica.

Five weeks later, on April 30, 1973, President Richard Nixon inhabits an old leather chair in the White House's second-floor Lincoln Sitting Room. Although it is April, flames dance in the fireplace. Nixon enjoys the fire, and even orders it lit during the hot summer months so that he can sit alone and listen to records.

But tonight the Lincoln Sitting Room is silent. Nixon broods and sips from a glass of twenty-year-old Ballantine scotch. Ever since McCord's confession, Judge Sirica's new grand jury investigation into the Watergate scandal has unveiled damning evidence linking the White House to the burglaries. McCord is naming names. Nixon is frantically working to distance himself from those names, even if it means firing men who have long been loyal to him. Just today, he accepted the resignations of three key members of his administration for their role in the Watergate fiasco and fired another.*

The phone rings.

"Governor Reagan on the line," a White House operator tells Nixon.

"Hello," Nixon responds coldly. Nixon has a famously low tolerance for alcohol and

---

* Nixon accepted the resignations of advisers H. R. Haldeman and John Ehrlichman, as well as that of Attorney General Richard Kleindienst. He fired White House counsel John Dean for his role in a Watergate cover-up, despite the fact that Dean had been ordered by the White House to lie. This makes an enemy out of Dean, who will subsequently provide very damning testimony against Nixon.

gets drunk quickly. Tonight is no exception.

"Mr. President?" says Reagan.

"Hello, Ron. How are you?" Nixon replies in a booming voice.

Reagan's is a courtesy call, one Republican to another. But in truth, the two men are battling for control of their party. Nixon is threatened by Reagan's popularity and his brand of staunch conservatism. He is vehemently opposed to the idea of Reagan succeeding him as president and has hand-picked former Texas governor John Connally as the man he will back for the Republican presidential nomination in 1976. Knowing this, Connally is preparing to switch over from the Democratic Party.

"Just fine and how are you?" Reagan responds. His words ring hollow because both men know that Nixon is in trouble. Earlier this evening, Nixon went on national television and lied to the American public, telling the country that he had nothing to do with Watergate. Furthermore, Nixon insisted he would be relentless in finding who was responsible.

"Couldn't be better," Richard Nixon says bitterly, then he immediately changes the subject. "You must have — the time is so far different. You're about only seven o'clock, or eight o'clock there."

"Yes. Yes," Reagan says.

"How nice of you to call." Again Nixon's voice is tinged with sarcasm. In his drunken state, he has a hard time hiding his loathing for Reagan.

"Well, I want you to know we watched," Reagan tells Nixon. "And my heart was with you. I know what this must have been, and all these days and what you've been through, and I just wanted you to know that, uh, for whatever it's worth, I'm still behind you. You can count on us. We're still behind you out here, and I want you to know you're in our prayers."

"How nice of you to say that," Nixon answers. He is determined to change the subject again. "Well, let me tell you this. That we can be — each of us has a different religion, you know, but goddammit, Ron, we have got to build peace in the world and that's what I'm working on. I want you to know I so appreciate your calling and give my love to Nancy. How — how'd you ever marry such a pretty girl? My God!"

Nixon is being disingenuous. He has confided to his staff that "Nancy Reagan's a bitch. A demanding one. And he listens to her."

Ronald Reagan knows none of this. "Well, I'm just lucky," he says, chuckling.

"You're lucky. Well, I was lucky."

"Yes. Yes. You were."

"How nice of you to call. You, you thought it was the right speech though?"

"I did. Very much so. Yes."

"Had to say it. Had to say it."

"Yeah. I know how difficult it was. And I know what it must be with the fellas having to do what they did. And they —"

Nixon cuts him off. "That's right. They had to get out."

"And I can understand —"

Again, Nixon interrupts to change the subject. "Right? Where are you at now? Are you in Sacramento?"

"No. Los Angeles."

"Ha, ha. Good for you to get out of that miserable city."

"Yeah."

"Right. Rod," Nixon says, unintentionally mangling Reagan's name. "Damn nice of you to call."

"Well —"

"OK."

"This too shall pass," Reagan says, trying to console the president.

"Everything passes. Thank you."

"You bet. Give our best to Pat," Reagan concludes.

The line goes dead.

Throughout 1973, the evidence that Richard Nixon funded acts of political espionage and engaged in a cover-up continues to grow. A brand-new cloud of scandal settles over the White House when it is revealed that Vice President Spiro Agnew has been taking bribes while in office.* In order to escape prosecution for conspiracy, extortion, and bribery, Agnew resigns on October

* Spiro Agnew served as vice president from 1969 to 1973. He was very controversial, particularly because he attacked the press, once famously calling journalists "nattering nabobs of negativism." He was accused of taking bribes and kickbacks from contractors during his time as governor of Maryland, a practice that continued into his vice presidency. He was ultimately accused of tax evasion, conspiracy, bribery, and tax fraud. However, he plea-bargained those charges down to just one: income tax evasion, to which he pleaded no contest. The terms of this deal included three years' probation and resignation from the office of vice president of the United States. Agnew never spoke to Richard Nixon again once he left office, but he was in attendance at Nixon's funeral in 1994. Spiro Agnew died of leukemia in 1996 at seventy-seven.

10, 1973.

Richard Nixon is torn about a successor. He would like to nominate John Connally for vice president, but the lifelong Democrat switched political parties only five months ago. There is still animosity among Democrats about the defection, and Nixon feels that they will block Connally's congressional confirmation.

The second choice is Nelson Rockefeller, the liberal Republican governor of New York. Given their long-ago Treaty of Fifth Avenue, which led to a blending of their personal political views into a road map sending the Republican Party on a more moderate course, Nixon fears that this choice will alienate the conservative elements of the party.

The third name on Nixon's list is Ronald Reagan. He is extremely popular among Republicans, and, despite conservative philosophies that are far to the right of Nixon's, Reagan has few enemies in Washington and should have little problem getting confirmed.

Reagan has campaigned for Nixon during three elections. He has called to offer condolences at a time of hardship. Reagan and Nixon have exchanged correspondence for more than a decade. They should be friends.

But because of envy on Nixon's part, they are not.

Nixon's nomination for the vice presidency is an old friend: Congressman Gerald Rudolph Ford Jr. of Grand Rapids, Michigan, the minority leader in the House.

Ronald Reagan will not be coming to Washington anytime soon.

All through the 1973 Christmas season, and into 1974, Richard Nixon battles to stay in office. As prosecutors circle ever closer, he denies them access to tape-recorded discussions he had about the Watergate situation. The prosecutors are forced to take the case all the way to the Supreme Court, which rules unanimously on July 24, 1974, that Nixon must turn over the recordings of sixty-four conversations related to Watergate that occurred in the Oval Office.* It is a

* Voice-activated tape recorders were located in the Oval Office, the Executive Office Building office, the Cabinet Room, and in the Aspen Lodge at Camp David. In addition, microphones were placed inside telephones in those locations and in the Lincoln Sitting Room. Nixon was taping the conversations for posterity, knowing that one day

crushing defeat for the president, made all the worse three days later, when the House Judiciary Committee files three articles of impeachment against him. There is a chance that Richard Nixon will be not only forced out of office but also sent to prison.

Every night throughout the crisis, comedian Johnny Carson performs a six-minute monologue of topical one-liners on *The Tonight Show.* Carson is "the most powerful single performer in television," one critic says of the late-night talk show host, and it is true, as many in the media take their cues from him.

Carson and other entertainers batter Richard Nixon, causing more and more Americans to believe that their president is indeed a crook. Cries for Richard Nixon to resign are relentless, and so is Johnny Carson: "Tonight's monologue is dedicated to Richard Nixon. I've got a monologue that

---

historians would be interested in the 3,700 hours of conversations that he taped between the installation of the tape recording system in early 1971 and July 12, 1973, when he stopped recording due to the Watergate scandal. Franklin Roosevelt, John F. Kennedy, and Lyndon Johnson had also made it a habit to tape White House conversations.

just won't quit."

Richard Nixon is not a quitter. But by August 7, 1974, it is clear that he has no other choice. He calls Secretary of State Henry Kissinger to explain his decision. The two men, who bonded over ending the Vietnam War, meet in the Lincoln Sitting Room, Nixon's favorite room in the White House. Richard Nixon's mental health has become an issue as the Watergate crisis has dragged on for more than two years. He has hinted at suicide. He drinks too much and often takes sleeping pills to allow himself at least a few hours of peace. But the pills don't always work: Nixon has begun wandering the White House hallways late at night, engaging in loud verbal debates with the paintings of former presidents that hang on the walls.*

But on this evening, Nixon is not in an

---

* Edward Cox, who is married to Nixon's daughter Tricia, had been a staunch defender of Nixon throughout Watergate. But by August 6, 1974, he realized that Nixon was no longer capable of governing. When Michigan senator Robert Griffin told Cox that Nixon seemed completely rational, Cox informed him, "The President was up walking the halls last night, talk-

162

argumentative mood. Instead, he is defeated and drunk. Kissinger enters the White House to find Nixon slumped in his favorite leather chair. The room is nearly dark. Even though Nixon is still technically the president, his powers are deeply diminished. The military Joint Chiefs of Staff no longer recognize his authority and actually refuse to take orders from him. Secretary of Defense James Schlesinger has even gone to the extreme of planning for the army's Eighty-Second Airborne Division to remove Nixon from office forcibly, if it should become necessary.

Suddenly, Nixon begins to cry. "Pray with me," he says to Kissinger, pushing back his ottoman and sinking to his knees on the light gray carpet.

Kissinger is startled and initially confused. He is Jewish and does not share Nixon's Quaker faith. But above all, Henry Kissinger is an accommodating man and soon joins Nixon on the floor.

Nixon continues to cry as he prays, then falls forward and presses his face into the carpet. "What have I done?" he laments, pounding the floor with his fists. "What has

---

ing to pictures of former presidents — giving speeches and talking to the pictures on the wall."

happened?"

Thirty-six hours later, Nixon signs his letter of resignation with a flourish. There is no precedent for his act. Per the Presidential Succession Act of 1792, Nixon addresses the letter to Henry Kissinger, his secretary of state and most trusted adviser.*

Now there is nothing to do but leave the White House. Nixon stops first to say good-bye to his household staff in the West Hall. The cooks and maids form a single line, and Nixon stops to shake each hand. Then it is on to the East Room, where a large crowd of family and supporters waits to hear him deliver one last speech. The U.S. Marine Band plays the theme song from *Oklahoma!* as Nixon enters and steps to the podium, followed by "Hail to the Chief."

* The Presidential Succession Act of 1792 (amended in 1886, 1947, and 1967) stipulated which individual would be next in line for the presidency. It was always understood that a president would leave office before the completion of his term only through death, not resignation. However, in the unlikely event resignation should take place, Section 11 of the act requires the president to submit an instrument of resignation in writing to the secretary of state.

Nixon's wife, Pat, stands to his left as he pulls out a pair of black-framed glasses and steps to the three microphones. His daughters, Julie and Tricia, also stand on the podium, next to their husbands. The women have all been crying. Nixon speaks for twenty minutes, fighting back tears at times, and concludes his remarks by reminding his audience, "Always give your best, never get discouraged, never be petty; always remember, others may hate you, but those who hate you don't win unless you hate them, and then you destroy yourself."

George H. W. Bush, head of the Republican National Committee, stands in the audience, marveling at Nixon's words. Later he will write in his journal, "The speech was vintage Nixon — a kick or two at the press — enormous strains. One couldn't help but look at the family and the whole thing and think of his accomplishments and then think of the shame and wonder [what] kind of man is this really. No morality — kicking his friends in those tapes — all of them. Gratuitous abuse."

Across the country, Ronald Reagan watches Nixon's resignation unfold on television. All three major networks are carrying the proceedings live. "It is a tragedy for America that we have come to this, but it does mean that the agony of many months has come to an end," Reagan says in a statement to the press.

As Nixon leaves the White House and steps into the Marine Corps helicopter that will fly him away from the presidency forever,* Ronald Reagan is left to wonder if Gerald Ford will ask him to be the new vice president of the United States. Reagan tells reporters he would consider such a request "a call to duty."

But that call never comes.

---

* Nixon's helicopter takes him to Andrews Air Force Base, where he boards Air Force One with his family. The plane flies to El Toro Marine Corps Station in Orange County, California, where Nixon then travels by car to his home on the ocean in San Clemente. Air Force One is thirteen miles southwest of Jefferson City, Missouri, when Gerald Ford takes the oath of office as president of the United States. As Air Force One carries that designation only when the president is on board, pilot Ralph Albertazzie radios ground control to ask for a new call sign. Thus, Richard Nixon's presidency finally and officially comes to an end.

10

Dallas, Texas
August 9, 1974
5:00 P.M.

As Richard Nixon flies into self-imposed exile, his plane passes just a few hundred miles north of this sprawling Texas city. Below, in a furnished rental apartment, John Hinckley Jr. lies around, strumming his guitar. The spartan room is tidy, for Hinckley is a fanatic about cleanliness and personal hygiene, often washing his face with such vigor that his father fears "he'd take the skin off."

Hinckley is nineteen years old now, living in Dallas near his elder sister, Diane, while on summer break from college. He works in a local pizza joint called Gordo's, where he sweeps the floor and clears tables. Hinckley is already gaining the sixty pounds he will soon add to his five-foot-ten-inch build. His Paul McCartney–type haircut frames his face, bangs sweeping low across the tops of his eyebrows. When he smiles, Hinckley's dull blue eyes come alive. Yet Hinckley rarely smiles; nor does he have any inclination to shed some of his expanding girth. He has little interest in physical fitness or presidential politics — or in anything, for that matter. While his elder brother, Scott, is being groomed to run their father's oil company, and his sister is newly married and settling down, John has retreated into a world all his own. He speaks with a flat affect, and his gaze often lacks expression. His only solace comes through music.

The truth is John Hinckley is at a loss to explain what is happening in his brain. He has some form of schizophrenia, a mental disorder that causes the mind to distort reality. A combination of inherited traits and environmental factors has altered his genetic makeup, beginning with subtle changes in his teenage years. If left untreated, his condition can tailspin into delusions and violent behavior that will become dangerous to him and those around him.

His parents are currently building a new home in Evergreen, Colorado, a small mountain town populated largely by wealthy conservatives. They moved there from Dallas just a year ago, as John was beginning his freshman year at Texas Tech University. Having no friends in Evergreen, John Hinckley prefers to spend the summer in scorching-hot Dallas before heading back to school in the fall.

But Hinckley has no friends in Dallas, either. This is nothing new. Once, his high school classmates called him "as nice a guy as you'd ever want to meet." He was popular and well liked, a member of the Spanish Club, Rodeo Club, and an association known as Students in Government. But halfway through high school, he abruptly stopped playing sports or taking part in school functions. His mother, Jo Ann, was heartbroken by the sudden change — and confused as to why it happened.

John Hinckley is no longer one to experience happiness. It has been a long time since he has known that emotion. But here in his room, at least he is content. He listens to the Beatles and plays guitar, day after day after day. Today is a Friday. The president of the United States has just quit. The world is in shock. Outside, the sun is shining on yet another baking-hot Texas summer afternoon. But John Hinckley does not notice. Within these walls, each day is just like any other. Friday might as well be Monday. It does not matter.

Hinckley's parents think themselves lucky that their son does not drink, take drugs, or engage in sexual promiscuity. They are deeply religious evangelical Christians, and to know that their son is not violating biblical principles gives them some peace. So they leave him alone.

One day they will look back and realize that their son's withdrawal from society was not normal.

By then, it will be too late.

11

Old Shadow Cabinet Room
House of Commons
London, England
April 9, 1975
Noon

Ronald Reagan sits on a small cloth-upholstered sofa, his left knee just inches away from touching that of a woman sitting in an adjacent chair. Reagan is now a former governor, having left his office in Sacramento three months ago. The still-handsome sixty-four-year-old senses an immediate chemistry between himself and the forty-nine-year-old Margaret Thatcher, Great Britain's new House of Commons opposition leader.

Thatcher is a homely woman, but Reagan considers her "warm, feminine, gracious, and intelligent" — so much so that he will take the unprecedented step of gushing about the British leader to Nancy Reagan when this meeting ends in two hours. For Margaret Thatcher, the feeling is mutual. "When we met in person I was immediately won over by his charm, sense of humor, and directness," Thatcher will later recall.

Thatcher wears her graying hair swept up in a high wave. Her dress features wide lapels and a zipper down the front, a style not often seen in the staid world of British politics. She is a complex woman, fond of working through the night and unwinding with a glass of whisky. She owns an American-made Ruger handgun for protection, and there is a growing legend that she helped invent soft-serve ice cream back in the days when she was a chemist instead of a member of Parliament.

Thatcher is a new breed of politician, eager to break her nation out of the cradle-to-grave welfare philosophy that has thwarted the British economy since the end of World War II. Though she is dedicated to politics, ideology means more to Thatcher than appearance. In time, she will learn to balance the two, burnishing her image by switching to power suits and a simple strand of pearls. Her favorite color is turquoise, but she often prefers the more powerful appearance of black, white, gray, and navy. She will soon begin dying her hair reddish blond, and, at the suggestion of legendary actor Laurence Olivier, she will hire a voice coach from London's Royal National Theatre to bring her speaking voice down an octave.

In time, Thatcher will earn the nickname Iron Lady, for her habit of imposing her will on Parliament and her staunch opposition to the Soviet Union and socialism.

But all this is yet to come. For now, Margaret Thatcher is more focused on talking policy with the man she has just met but who is obviously her political "soul mate," to use Reagan's words.

Thatcher presents her guest with a pair of cuff links. Reagan opens the small box and tries them on as a photographer snaps the moment for posterity. He wears a dark suit, polka-dot tie, and white shirt. The former governor's successful economic policies have led to an invitation to speak with British businessmen about ways to reduce the size of government and grow the economy. This sort of political proselytizing has become Reagan's primary occupation since moving from the governor's mansion in Sacramento back down to Los Angeles. He will make almost two hundred thousand dollars this year traveling the world giving

Ronald Reagan presents Margaret Thatcher with a silver dollar medallion, April 9, 1975.

speeches.* In addition, two ghostwriters help him prepare his weekly syndicated newspaper column, which goes out to 226 papers in the United States. And he personally writes the Saturday afternoon radio broadcast he delivers to 286 conservative stations nationwide.

When Margaret Thatcher requested the

* Bureau of Labor Statistics adjust this figure to roughly $872,000 in today's currency.

meeting, she hoped Ronald Reagan might spend forty-five minutes with her. But the two get along so well that they spend more than double that time in this small chamber crowded with many tables and chairs.

Thus begins a beautiful friendship.

A few days after Ronald Reagan flies home from London to America, there is staggering news: the capital of South Vietnam, Saigon, falls to the North Vietnamese Army. American television cameras capture vivid images of American military and intelligence personnel being hastily evacuated by helicopter from the rooftop of an apartment building near the U.S. embassy. After two decades, the Vietnam War finally ends in defeat.*

* The Department of Defense once considered January 1, 1961, as the first official day of the Vietnam War. However, American military advisers were in the country long before that. This meant that the name of U.S. Air Force Technical Sergeant Richard Fitzgibbon Jr., who died in 1956, before the war officially began, could not be listed on the Vietnam Veterans Memorial in Washington, DC. The policy was changed in 1998, shifting the start of the war to November 1, 1955. Fitzgibbon and eight others are now listed on the

"I have chosen a dark day to write a belated thank you," Reagan says in a letter to Margaret Thatcher on April 30, 1975. "The news has just arrived of Saigon's surrender and somehow the shadows seem to have lengthened."

Reagan's grim mood infects the whole country. Secretary of State Kissinger has compared America to the former Greek city-state of Athens, which suffered a long slide into oblivion. Kissinger also equates the Soviet Union with Sparta, the militaristic Greek state that constantly prepared for war. The rotund Kissinger is pessimistic about America's standing in the world. And he is not alone. Many believe America's decline began with the assassination of John F. Kennedy in 1963, continued through the antiwar protests of the late 1960s, and then accelerated with the chaos of Watergate in the early '70s.

Eight months before the fall of Saigon, new president Gerald R. Ford tried to stanch the bleeding by pardoning Richard

---

wall. Fitzgibbon's son was killed in action in Vietnam on September 7, 1965. This makes them one of only three father-and-son service members to die in that conflict. The others were Leo Hester Sr. and Leo Hester Jr.; and Fred and Bert Jenkins.

Nixon for any and all crimes he may have committed while in office, believing that the nation would not benefit from the prolonged spectacle of a president on trial. "My fellow Americans," Ford had promised in his inaugural address, "our long national nightmare is over."

But it is far from over. And the outrage continues to grow. America, a nation built upon integrity, honesty, and trust, has seen those principles twisted in a way that signals not some future form of greatness but imminent decay.

And no one seems to know how to stop it.

"Ladies and gentlemen," intones a booming offstage voice, "the President of the United States."

A lectern bearing the presidential seal stands in the middle of the speaker's platform. The president steps onstage, only to get tangled in the American flag. He drops the typed speech he is carrying. Quickly scooping up the pages, he steps to the lectern and composes himself. "My fellow Americans," he begins, "ladies and gentlemen, members of the press, and my immediate family."

Then things get worse. The president stumbles over his words, repeating himself again and again, bumbling his way through the address. "I do have two announcements to make," he says, before falling to the ground again. "Whoa. Uh oh. No problem. No problem," he says, gripping the lectern with two hands to right himself.

The date is November 8, 1975. The "president" is actually comedian Chevy Chase, playing the part of Gerald R. Ford. Earlier in the year, while visiting Austria on official business, Ford tumbled down the steps of Air Force One. He was not hurt, and blamed the spill on a bad knee. However, the fallout has been immense. The former University of Michigan football star's perceived clumsiness has become a national joke. A vast national audience roars at Chase's lampooning of a sitting American president. An office that was once revered and respected out of patriotic fervor has become fodder for farce. Gerald Ford's most difficult task since replacing Richard Nixon is restoring dignity to the presidency. He is failing.

Chevy Chase finally stumbles away from the lectern, trips on a folding chair, and falls hard to the ground. "Live from New York, it's Saturday Night," he yells into the camera.*

* The amiable Ford is a good sport about the

178

Nancy Reagan is not one to laugh easily. She is now decidedly unamused that her twenty-two-year-old daughter, Patti, is living with a rock musician and openly smoking marijuana. Nancy is also incensed that her seventeen-year-old son, Ron, recently seduced the thirty-year-old wife of musician Ricky Nelson in Nancy's own bedroom.[*]

"The bad news is you came home early and caught him," older son Michael Reagan reminds his father when he hears the news. "The good news is you found out he wasn't gay."[†]

---

send-up. He and Chase will go on to become friends, and Ford will even host a special comedy symposium at his presidential library in 1986 — at which Chase will appear.

[*] Patti Reagan takes her mother's maiden name while in college because her liberal political views clash with those of her father. Beginning in 1974, she has a four-year relationship with Bernie Leadon, a founding member of the Eagles. Together, they write the song "I Wish You Peace," which appears on the Eagles' One of These Nights album.

[†] The marriage of Kristin and Rick Nelson is already strained at the time, thanks to the constant

"I hadn't thought of that," Reagan responds. "But you're absolutely right. I guess it's a blessing. Thanks, Mike. I must tell Nancy."

But what really gets to Nancy Reagan's inner core is the growing celebrity of First Lady Betty Ford. America may not be completely sold on her husband as president, but the country loves Betty. The fifty-seven-year-old represents a huge relief from the heaviness of the Nixon White House. Betty Ford talks openly about premarital sex, abortion, and equal rights for women. Adding to that, she had a mastectomy just one month after her husband took office, losing her right breast to cancer. She speaks candidly about the scar it produced, along with the fact that she likes to have sex with her husband "as often as possible."

Nancy Reagan craves that level of celebrity

---

travel required by his musical career — and to his womanizing. They will reconcile and split several times before finally divorcing in 1982. Rick Nelson left his entire estate to his four children, leaving Kristin Nelson with nothing after he died in a plane crash in De Kalb, Texas, on New Year's Eve 1985. Kristin Nelson is the older sister of television star Mark Harmon.

for herself. Betty Ford notices this after dining with the Reagans in Palm Springs during the 1975 Easter vacation. "She's a cold fish," Ford later recalled. "Nancy could not have been colder. Then the flashbulbs went off, and she smiled and kissed me. Suddenly, an old friend. I couldn't get over that. Off camera, ice. On camera, warmth."

The purpose of the dinner was to suggest that Ronald Reagan not challenge Gerald Ford for the 1976 Republican presidential nomination. It is an uncomfortable night. This is not the first time Reagan and Ford have met, but they circle each other as if they are strangers. Aides note that both men are "uptight, unnatural, pathetically polite, and acutely on guard" at the dinner. "Betty Ford and Nancy Reagan hit it off even worse."*

Ford, a lifelong Republican who served in the navy during World War II, considers Reagan little more than a lightweight actor and former Democrat. However, he knows that Reagan represents the conservative vote, and this concerns him. Rather than

* The quote comes from White House counselor to the president Robert T. Hartmann, who is best known for penning Ford's inaugural address in 1974.

marginalizing his potential opponent, Ford has chosen to court Reagan. He has twice offered him a spot in his Cabinet, telling the former governor that he can select almost any position he likes. He has also offered Reagan the job as U.S. ambassador to Great Britain, to which Reagan replied, "Hell, I can't afford to be an ambassador."

In addition, Ford asked Reagan to be part of a panel investigating alleged abuses by the CIA. All this is an effort to prevent Reagan from running for president and splitting the Republican Party in two. Suspicious, Reagan keeps his distance from Ford, accepting the spot on the CIA panel in an effort to gain national exposure, but turning down any scenarios that would make him subservient to Ford. Finally, in an effort to gain conservative support, Gerald Ford strongly suggests that Nelson Rockefeller step down as vice president when his term comes to an end.* Rockefeller cooperates, and the path is now open to Reagan run-

---

* On that same day, November 4, 1975, Ford also appoints Donald Rumsfeld as secretary of defense, Dick Cheney as White House chief of staff, and George H. W. Bush as director of the Central Intelligence Agency. All three men will play pivotal roles in American politics for the next thirty years.

ning as Ford's new vice president in 1976.

But it is not to be. Believing he has the resources to defeat Ford for the nomination, Reagan makes it clear that he has no interest in the secondary position. Still, he keeps Gerald Ford guessing as to whether or not he will challenge him. "I tried to get to know Reagan, but I failed," Ford will later write. "I never knew what he was really thinking behind that winning smile."

Gerald Ford quickly finds out what is on Reagan's mind. On November 19, 1975, Ford is working in the Oval Office at 4:28 in the afternoon, with Vice President Nelson Rockefeller and Chief of Staff Dick Cheney, when the phone rings. Governor Reagan is on the line.

Ford does not take the call.

Reagan tries again at 4:57 p.m. This time, Ford picks up. Reagan is calling from his suite at the Madison Hotel in Washington, where he and Nancy have just checked in. In the morning, Reagan tells Ford, he is going to announce his candidacy for president at the National Press Club.

"I trust we can have a good contest," Reagan tells Ford.

At first, Gerald Ford is not upset by the news, for he has anticipated Reagan's decision ever since that Easter dinner in Palm

Springs. He takes a thirty-minute stroll to gather his thoughts, stopping first at the White House barbershop for a quick trim. By the time he returns to the Oval Office, Ford is convinced that he will breeze to victory.

The *New York Times* echoes Ford's sentiments, writing that a Reagan presidential bid "makes a lot of news, but it doesn't make much sense."

However, a Gallup poll shortly after Reagan's announcement shatters Gerald Ford's illusion.

The poll finds Republican voters favoring Ronald Reagan over Gerald Ford by a margin of 40 to 32 percent.

Let the games begin.

"When you leave the platform, turn to your left," a Secret Service agent whispers to Ronald Reagan as he prepares to deliver the first speech of his presidential campaign. The new candidate is in Miami. He and Nancy now have a Secret Service detail, offering round-the-clock protection against would-be attackers.

The whirlwind life of a presidential candidate has already begun for the Reagans. They flew by chartered plane from Washington, DC, down to Florida this morning. After his speech in the main ballroom at the Ramada Inn on Twenty-Second Street, they will be whisked back to Miami International Airport, where they will then fly to Manchester, New Hampshire. Tomorrow it's on to Charlotte and then Chicago, and finally California. This will be life for the Reagans for the next nine months until the Republican National Convention in August. If they are lucky, they will get to continue the nonstop travel into November, when the presidential election is held. While the pace will be frantic, it will be well worth it. The ultimate goal for Ronald Reagan is being elected president of the United States and thus being recognized as the most powerful man on earth.

In Miami, Reagan speaks for twenty minutes. At 2:00 p.m. he steps down from the dais but chooses to ignore the Secret Service's demand that he turn left. Instead, Reagan goes right, hoping to say hello to an old friend he has spied from the stage.

"What the hell do you think you're doing?" campaign chairman Tommy Thomas says to Reagan as he plunges into the audience.

The crowd closes around Reagan. He is unafraid, eagerly shaking hands, working the room like the seasoned politician he has become. All around the governor, people smile and try to catch his eye. Suddenly, a twenty-year-old man with dark hair and dressed in a checkered shirt, who is standing just two feet in front of him, extends his right arm and points a .45-caliber pistol at Reagan's chest.

Before Reagan can react, his Secret Service detail surges past him and tackles Michael Lance Carvin. Reagan himself is thrown to the ground for his protection, the agents shielding his body with their own.

"I feel fine," Reagan later explains to the press.

"I hope it doesn't happen again," a startled Nancy Reagan tells the media. "I think you always have to keep it in the back of your mind."*

* Michael Lance Carvin is an admirer of convicted mass murderer Charles Manson's acolyte, Squeaky Fromme, who tried to assassinate Gerald Ford. The pistol turns out to be a toy replica of an actual pistol. Carvin, who phoned the Denver office of the Secret Service two weeks earlier to make death threats against Gerald Ford, Ronald Reagan, and Nelson Rockefeller, is arrested and later convicted of eight felony charges on April 19, 1976. Carvin is released on bail while awaiting sentencing and promptly flees. Federal agents

■ ■ ■ ■

Nine months later, Ronald and Nancy Reagan are running through the labyrinthine hallways and tunnels of Kansas City's Kemper Arena. The Republican National Convention is in its final moments, and the Reagans are on their way to the stage. The roar of the crowd echoes down the corridors, and delegates from all over America are in a state of near bedlam as they await the candidate and his wife. This is the first time Ronald Reagan has made an appearance at the four-day convention, and the moment he shows his face, a collective roar shakes the arena.

Reagan is unsteady. "What am I going to say?" he asks Nancy. He has not prepared a speech. The losing candidate is not sup-

---

finally capture him in Lake City, Florida, and Carvin is sent to prison. He is released on January 4, 1982, and resumes a normal life, including getting married and landing a steady job. However, in 1998 he is accused of making death threats against controversial disc jockey Howard Stern. He is sentenced to two years in federal prison, a period reduced to seven months. His current location is unknown.

posed to speak at the convention — and as of last night, Ronald Reagan has officially lost the Republican nomination for the presidency. Gerald Ford's slender margin of 1,187 votes to Reagan's 1,070 has ensured a Ford victory.* As he did so many months

* The enmity between Reagan and Ford only grew in the months leading up to the convention. Ford cleverly hired Stuart Spencer to run his campaign, well aware that Spencer managed both of Reagan's gubernatorial victories in California. This insider knowledge of Reagan's rhetoric helped Ford win the opening primary in New Hampshire by painting Reagan as keen to levy taxes. Should Ford have lost in New Hampshire, the election might have been over. Yet he continued his string of victories in Massachusetts, Florida, and Illinois. Then, just as Reagan's staffers were suggesting their candidate quit the race, Reagan won the North Carolina primary. He accused Ford of letting the United States fall behind the Soviet Union in the global arms race, which played into America's mourning over the loss in Vietnam. Ford countered with an attack ad suggesting Ronald Reagan would be quick to start a nuclear war. Ford also sowed seeds of discontent among Reagan backers by inviting influential delegates to the White House, campaigning for delegates seeking political office, and allowing key delegates to

ago, Reagan has made it clear that he will not accept the vice presidency if it is offered. So Ford has not offered.

The two candidates were neck and neck at the start of the convention. Ford won fifteen primaries, Reagan twelve. But Reagan committed a major blunder by announcing his running mate before the convention, selecting liberal Republican senator Richard Schweiker. This alienated Reagan's core conservative constituents. He tried to fix the error by suggesting that convention rules be changed to mandate that Ford also name his running mate early. The matter was taken before the Republican Party's Rules Committee, where it was voted down. Ford won the nomination on the first ballot. This is the first time Reagan has ever been beaten head-to-head in an election. He will remain bitter about the loss for years to come.

Gerald Ford's acceptance speech is masterful. He is interrupted by applause sixty-five times. Watching Ford on television, Jimmy Carter's campaign manager, Hamilton Jordan, parses no words in describing the strength of Ford's delivery: "It scares

---

be seen with him at important celebrations, such as the 1976 U.S. Bicentennial gala in New York.

the shit out of me."

Now Gerald Ford concludes his acceptance speech by calling Ronald and Nancy Reagan to the stage in a display of party unification. For Reagan, this will mean he must make a few brief remarks.

"Don't worry," Nancy tells him. "You'll think of something."

As the couple steps onto the stage, their appearance once again ignites a furor. "Viva!" Reagan's Texas supporters shout.

"Olé!" respond his California followers, trying to outdo them.

Over and over, they chant the words back and forth. The convention is no longer a political event but a massive party. Reagan lets go of Nancy's hand and moves to the lectern. The stage is a mob, with the Fords, the Rockefellers, and new vice presidential candidate Bob Dole and his wife, Elizabeth, all crowded onto the small space. Reagan still gropes for the words he will say, even as he steps up to the microphone. Nancy is at his side, pressing her white skirt against her thighs because she has chosen to stand atop a grate blowing air up under the garment.

Reagan begins by praising his party. "There are cynics who say that a party platform is something that no one bothers to read and it doesn't very often amount to much. Whether it is different this time than it has ever been before, I believe the Republican Party has a platform that is a banner of bold, unmistakable colors with no pale pastel shades. We have just heard a call to arms, based on that platform.

"And a call to us to really be successful in communicating and reveal to the American people the difference between this platform and the platform of the opposing party, which is nothing but a revamp and a reissue and a rerunning of a late, late show of the thing that we have been hearing from them for the last forty years."

Reagan's remarks provoke roaring applause, followed by hushed silence. Delegates hang on his every word.

There is no script to Reagan's speech, no notes. His impromptu address is dazzling. He veers away from generalities and into his own deeply held political beliefs, until it is as if Ford is not there at all. Reagan speaks of the Communist threat and the vast potential of America. "We live in a world in which the great powers have poised and aimed at each other horrible missiles of destruction — nuclear weapons — that can, in a matter of minutes, arrive at each other's country and destroy virtually the civilized world we live in."

Then Reagan articulates his thoughts on the peace and security of future Americans, and how everyone witnessing this speech can mold the country's future.

"Whether they have the freedoms we have known up until now will depend on what we do here. Will they look back in appreciation and say, 'Thank God for those people back in 1976 who headed off that loss of freedom'?"

His voice rises until Reagan is no longer a politician but a preacher. He stands not at a podium but at a pulpit. And Kemper Arena is his church. "This is our challenge, and this is why we're in this hall tonight."

"We must go forth from here, united," he concludes. " 'There is no substitute for victory.' "*

The speech is less than three minutes long, but the applause breaks stretch it to eight. That's all it takes for Republicans to see Reagan's vision, humanity, and charisma.

* Reagan is quoting Gen. Douglas MacArthur, in his final address to Congress on April 19, 1951, in which he concluded fifty-two years of military service with the same words. MacArthur also famously uttered the line "Old soldiers never die; they just fade away."

As Ronald Reagan waves good-bye to the crowd, it is quite clear to many across America that the Republican Party has nominated the wrong man for president.

12

Pacific Palisades, California
November 2, 1976
7:30 A.M.

Eleven weeks after former governor Reagan electrified America with his speech at the Republican National Convention, Election Day finally arrives. It is a cool Los Angeles morning, and Ronald and Nancy Reagan rise at seven thirty, taking their breakfast of fresh orange juice, toast, and decaffeinated coffee at the kitchen table.

As Ronald Reagan looks in the mirror to shave, he is pleased with himself. At age sixty-five, he is still an impressive physical specimen. His hair is thick. His teeth are white. Also, his body is toned from a daily regimen of calisthenics and from weekends chopping wood and clearing brush at the ranch. He will later joke that he should write an exercise book about his regimen entitled *Pumping Firewood.*

Nancy Reagan is also in good shape, though her physique comes more from diet than exercise. The Reagans are fastidious about watching how much they eat and drink, preferring a light breakfast and a lunch of soup so that they may indulge in favorite foods such as meat loaf or macaroni and cheese for dinner. The governor likes also to "hold a few calories back" at dinner so he can enjoy dessert.

After finishing their morning ablutions, the Reagans walk the half mile to the longtime residence of Robert and Sally Gulick. The former World War II navy pilot and his wife have allowed their house to be used as a polling place for more than two decades, and it is here that the Reagans will cast their ballots.

All across America, voters are deciding who will lead them. Either the incumbent president, Gerald R. Ford, or the Democratic candidate, James Earl "Jimmy" Carter, will be the next president of the United States. It is a choice between the man who pardoned the despised Richard Nixon but kept the nation from further chaos or a devoted Christian southern governor who some believe is far more secular than he pretends to be. Neither candidate inspires the nation. Watergate and

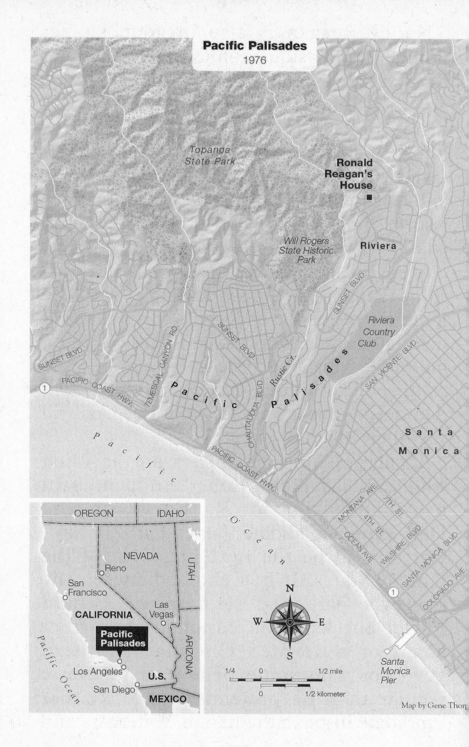

Pacific Palisades
1976

Topanga
State Park

Ronald
Reagan's
House

Will Rogers
State Historic
Park

Riviera

SUNSET BLVD.

Riviera
Country
Club

SUNSET BLVD.

SUNSET BLVD.

PACIFIC COAST HWY.

TEMESCAL CANYON RD.

CHAUTAUQUA BLVD.

Rustic Cr.

Pacific   Palisades

SAN VICENTE BLVD.

Santa
Monica

PACIFIC COAST HWY.

Pacific

Ocean

MONTANA AVE.

7TH ST.

4TH ST.

OCEAN AVE.

WILSHIRE BLVD.

SANTA MONICA BLVD.

COLORADO AVE.

Santa
Monica
Pier

OREGON   IDAHO

NEVADA

UTAH

Reno

San
Francisco

CALIFORNIA

Las
Vegas

Pacific
Palisades

ARIZONA

Pacific Ocean

Los Angeles

U.S.

San Diego

MEXICO

N

W   E

S

1/4   0   1/2 mile

0   1/2 kilometer

Map by Gene Thor

the Vietnam War have made many Americans cynical. Today will see the lowest voter turnout since 1948.*

The Gulick home, on a tree-lined suburban street, is where many other local celebrities, such as bandleader Lawrence Welk and Los Angeles Dodgers broadcaster Vin Scully, will cast ballots, but the Reagans are the reason the media stand waiting in the street. The former governor gives reporters a friendly hello and walks inside to vote.

Sally Gulick greets the Reagans warmly. The fifty-nine-year-old community doyenne is well known for three things: breeding German shepherds, her annual Army-Navy football game party, and having an avid

* Turnout for the Truman-Dewey race in 1948 was 51.1 percent. Carter-Ford in 1976 was 53.55 percent. The lowest turnout in modern history is 49 percent for the Clinton-Dole contest in 1996. Until 1900, voter turnout in the United States frequently exceeded 75 percent. The highest in recorded U.S. history was 81.8 percent in 1876, when Republican Rutherford B. Hayes of New York lost the popular vote but won the election over Democrat Samuel Tilden of New York by one vote cast by the congressionally appointed Electoral Commission.

interest in politics.

In anticipation of the Reagans' arrival, Sally has put out a jar of jellybeans, in case the governor wants to indulge his sweet tooth with his favorite candy. And while a polling place is required to be impartial, Sally Gulick is not above placing a papier-mâché Republican elephant in plain sight.

However, on this day, Ronald Reagan is not a loyal Republican. He has been bitter since the convention, avoiding showing any overt support for Gerald Ford. Later this afternoon he will write a letter to a supporter in Idaho, stating that he has campaigned for Ford in twenty-five states and sent a million letters to back the president's campaign.

But that will be disingenuous. Ronald Reagan did not take losing easily. He has refused to appear in public with Gerald Ford or even to be photographed with the president. Reagan's many campaign speeches were pro-Republican, but focused only on politicians who'd endorsed him during the primaries. Worst of all, in the final days of the campaign, at a time when Ford desperately needed Reagan to make a last-minute swing through the South to secure conservative votes, the governor flat-out refused.

Now, as Reagan pushes the lever casting his vote, he once again refuses Ford.

Stunningly, Ronald Reagan declines to vote for the office of the presidency. He cannot bring himself to cast a ballot for Gerald R. Ford. Neither can Nancy, whose disdain for Betty Ford was clear throughout the Republican convention.*

"I'm at peace with the world," Reagan tells the press as he and Nancy leave the polling place to begin their walk home.

"Will you run again in four years?" a reporter asks.

"I wouldn't rule it out," Reagan answers.

---

* Nancy Reagan and Betty Ford were a study in contrasts, with Betty's fun-loving persona a polar opposite to Nancy's steely self-control. The press called their appearance at the 1976 Republican National Convention the "battle of the queens" and wrote extensively on their choices of dress and hairstyle. At one point during the convention, an ovation for Nancy Reagan was cut short when the band launched into "Tie a Yellow Ribbon Round the Old Oak Tree," whereupon Betty Ford and singer Tony Orlando got up onstage and danced. Nancy Reagan seethed. The competition did not end at the convention, with Nancy making it a point to write critically of Betty Ford in her 1989 memoir, *My Turn.*

"And I wouldn't rule it in."

Several hours earlier, and two thousand miles east, Gerald Ford is eating pancakes. He cast his ballot at the Wealthy Elementary School polling place at 7:33 a.m. Michigan time. His hometown of Grand Rapids has just installed new voting machines, and Ford had to be given a tutorial on how to use them. Surrounded by watercolor drawings and a sign saying, "Welcome Mr. and Mrs. Ford" that schoolchildren prepared for this day, Gerald Ford punched out his ballot.

Now Ford sits in Granny's Kitchen Restaurant and indulges in his Election Day superstition. Granny's was where he ate blueberry pancakes the day he was first elected to Congress in 1948, and he keeps coming back.

Gerald Ford is nervous. That is understandable. His fate and future are now out of his hands. In just twenty-four hours, he will know whether he has been reelected or booted from office.

Gerald Ford is a man who has been through intense situations before and knows how to remain cool under pressure. While he was serving aboard the light aircraft carrier USS *Monterey* during World War II, the ship was struck by Typhoon Cobra near the Philippines. The storm was so severe that it sank several destroyers, killing nearly eight hundred U.S. sailors. On the morning of December 18, the pitching *Monterey* was buffeted by screaming winds and seventy-foot waves. Young lieutenant Gerald Ford ventured out onto the exposed flight deck in an attempt to climb a ladder to the ship's wheelhouse in order to secure his duty station. Suddenly, a wave taller than the *Monterey* itself broke over the side of the ship, knocking Ford from the ladder and sending him sliding toward the Pacific Ocean. Ford was powerless to stop his inevitable plummet into the churning sea. At the very last minute, the former University of Michigan football star reached out and grabbed hold of a small metal catwalk. Hanging on for dear life, he pulled himself to safety and worked his way up into the wheelhouse.

Heroic yet humble, Ford speaks infrequently about that terrifying moment. Few of his closest friends even know it occurred.

Now, thirty-two years and a political lifetime after Typhoon Cobra, Gerald and Betty Ford sit in a small corner booth sipping coffee and awaiting their food. A player piano in the corner puts forth "One Sweet Kiss." An antique sign hangs from the wall advertising "Genuine Ford Parts Used Here." Outside, a crowd of well-wishers peers through the windows, watching the president eat his breakfast.

Soon the Fords will board Air Force One to fly to Washington. There, Ford hopes to take a nap before having dinner with sports broadcaster Joe Garagiola and his wife.

The First Lady has already made peace with this election. In private statements to the press, she pretends to be fine with the outcome, whatever it might be. "Either the president wins," she says, "or if he loses we get to see more of him."

But Betty Ford is hiding her apprehension. Polls show her husband trailing Carter by a slim margin over the last few weeks. Betty, a realistic woman, understands there is a good chance that she and her husband will soon be evicted from the White House.

As President and Mrs. Ford fly back to Washington, Nancy Reagan is already planning for the next presidential election. Her husband spends the morning of Election Day in his office, composing handwritten letters to supporters. Then the two of them drive into Hollywood, where she listens as

Reagan records a whopping twenty radio commentaries.* In the waning moments of the Republican National Convention, Ronald Reagan made it clear that 1976 would not be his last bid for the presidency. "Nancy and I," he told his campaign staff, "we aren't going to sit back in our rocking chairs and say that's all for us."

Nancy Reagan cried publicly as he spoke on that day, refusing to stand at her husband's side when he said good-bye to his campaign staff because she was so emotional. She turned away from the crowd so no photographer could capture the tears in her eyes. Losing the nomination was hard on her husband but perhaps just as difficult for Nancy. Now she spends many nights alone here in Pacific Palisades as Reagan travels the country to give speeches. When not campaigning, her husband is usually ensconced in his study. Nancy knows Ron's focus is on building his political base. So she is forced to do everything else, taking charge of the family because her husband is too busy. Nancy deals with the drama of

* Reagan normally tapes just fifteen radio spots at a time. He does this with producer Harry O'Connor. Each address is three minutes long and most are written by Reagan himself.

her liberal daughter Patti's turbulent life, including her drug use and frequent changes of boyfriend.

Nancy is also concerned that her son, Ron Reagan Jr., is heading in the wrong direction. He wears his hair too long and is developing a passion for ballet dancing. This does not amuse his father, who prides himself on being rugged. Finally, Nancy Reagan watches as the children from Reagan's first marriage, to Jane Wyman, Maureen and Michael, grow more distant by the day, largely because they don't like her.

None of the blame for the family's troubles seems to fall on Ronald Reagan. It is Nancy who accepts the criticism. She knows that her controlling ways have alienated not just the children but also some of her husband's campaign staff.

But she could not care less.

To Nancy Reagan, a troublesome employee is just one more person who has to go. Nancy has terminated numerous staffers. The deed is almost always done by Michael Deaver, a longtime Reagan aide who has become very close to Mrs. Reagan.

Nancy is now fifty-five and still looks as if she is in the prime of her life. She is so devoted to her husband that Betty Ford tells *Time* magazine, "When Nancy met Ronnie, that was it as far as her own life was concerned."

But Nancy Reagan's single-mindedness toward her husband has paid off: Ronald Reagan has become a powerful man. Their income is assured, thanks to Reagan's radio contract and numerous paid speeches around the country. Nancy will never have to work again.

So it is that Ronald and Nancy Reagan end Election Day 1976 by themselves in their home on San Onofre Drive. Since Ron Jr. has left home to begin his studies at Yale, the Reagans are empty nesters. On most nights, they watch an old movie and unwind before going to bed at eleven. But with all three major television networks showing nothing but election returns, the Reagans cannot help but watch.

To them, neither presidential candidate offers the country the necessary ideology and passion. If only Reagan had defeated Ford in the primaries, this would have been their Election Day, and perhaps their night of triumph. Instead, they sit alone in the house, looking out over the lights of Los Angeles and wondering, "What if . . . ?"

But tomorrow is a new day.

As always, Ronald Reagan will spend a few hours in his study, writing his letters and speeches, laying the ideological groundwork to expand his conservative constituency.

But the story is different for Nancy Reagan. She has nothing at all to do. Shopping and socializing with her wealthy friends gets dull after a while.

So Nancy Reagan looks ahead to the day that her husband, Ronald Wilson Reagan, becomes the president of the United States in 1980.

She will see to it.

At 3:18 a.m. in Washington, DC, an exhausted Gerald Ford finally goes to bed. He has been watching the election returns for hours, and there is still no clear winner. Thirty-six invited guests have spent the last three hours in the White House watching with Ford. The family's gathering is private, as compared with the giddy scene on ABC, where broadcasters Howard K. Smith and Barbara Walters talk over images of a festive Jimmy Carter party, presided over by his aging mother, Lillian. The matriarch speaks as if she senses victory.

Still, Ford thinks he will win. Too tired to stay awake any longer, he plans to fall asleep and then arise to the news that he has been reelected. He steps out into the hallway with

Chief of Staff Dick Cheney, issues a few minor orders, and then walks to his bedroom. The president slips between the sheets, Betty Ford at his side. Good news or bad, in the morning it will all be over.

The fact that the election is this close is testament to Gerald Ford's tenacity. Back in the summer of 1976, as Ronald Reagan divided the Republican Party with his campaign attacks on Ford, Jimmy Carter held a thirty-three-point lead in the polls. America wanted to believe that the smiling small-town peanut farmer would heal the country's maladies.

But Carter almost self-destructed. Against the advice of his counselors, he gave an interview to *Playboy* magazine, hoping to attract voters who might have been put off by his conservative Christian religious views. In that interview, he admitted, "I've committed adultery in my heart many times."*

* Just as they did with Ford's pratfalls, *Saturday Night Live* was quick to spoof Carter's gaffe. In a skit that aired the night of October 16, 1976, Dan Aykroyd played the part of Carter in a mock interview with a female journalist, Liz Montgomery of the *New York Post,* played by Jane Curtin.

National headlines ensued, with Carter coming across as somewhat lurid.

The interview was a huge mistake. In attempting to be completely honest, the governor actually lost the support of some women voters and evangelical Christians who thought his admission unseemly.

The gap between Carter and Ford closed even further when the president won the first televised debate in late September. Looking physically robust and in command of the facts, Ford made it clear which candidate was the president and which was not.

MONTGOMERY: Governor Carter, you have said that the *Playboy* interview may have been a mistake. Do you think you are being too honest with the American people, and do you still lust after women?

GOVERNOR CARTER: Well, I don't think there's such a thing as being too honest, uh, Ms. Montgomery, and just to prove it I'm going to answer honestly how I feel right now . . . I want to say that you're a very attractive woman, and your hair looks kind of silky and kind of soft and, uh, at this moment, in my heart, I'm wearing a leather mask and breathing in your ear.

Now, as Gerald Ford turns out the light at 3:20 in the morning, he does so with the knowledge that he is on the verge of accomplishing something no other presidential candidate has ever done: closing a twenty-point gap in the polls in just eleven weeks' time.

The White House master bedroom goes dark.

Gerald Ford sleeps for five hours.

In the morning, he opens his eyes, hoping for good news.

He doesn't get it.*

* Carter narrowly beat Ford in the popular vote, 50 percent to 48 percent. However, he garnered 297 of the electoral votes to Ford's 240, thus sealing his victory.

13

Egyptian Theatre
Hollywood, California
Summer 1976
Afternoon

Just fifteen miles from the home of Ronald and Nancy Reagan, John Hinckley Jr. sits alone in this aging movie palace watching a new film called *Taxi Driver*. It's a motion picture Hinckley will eventually see more than fifteen times. The twenty-one-year-old drifter, who continues to put on weight, wears an army surplus jacket and combat boots, just like the film's main character, Travis Bickle. Hinckley's hair is now down to his shoulders, and his breath smells of peach brandy, another affectation he has picked up from Bickle, who is played with frightening intensity by actor Robert De Niro.

Screenwriter Paul Schrader based the character of Bickle on Arthur Bremer, the would-be assassin of presidential candidate George Wallace in 1972. Bremer shot Wallace to become famous and impress a girlfriend who had just broken up with him. He had originally intended to kill President Richard Nixon but botched several attempts.*

But it is not De Niro who stirs the most emotion in John Hinckley. Instead, it is the child prostitute Iris who brings him back to the Egyptian Theatre time after time. Portrayed by twelve-year-old Jodie Foster, Iris behaves like an innocent child by day while turning tricks with grown men at night. During the filming of *Taxi Driver,* Foster was so young that she had to undergo a psychological evaluation to make sure she could cope with the troubling subject matter. Her nineteen-year-old sister, Connie, was brought in to be a body double for her

* The twenty-one-year-old Bremer attacked Wallace at a campaign rally in Laurel, Maryland, firing four bullets into Wallace's body at close range. One bullet lodged in Wallace's spine, paralyzing him for life. Three other bullets wounded nearby police officers and campaign volunteers. Bremer was sentenced to fifty-three years in prison but was released after thirty-five. He is now a free man.

in explicit scenes.*

Hinckley does not know these things. Nor does he care. He is falling in love with Jodie Foster, no matter what her age.

Outside the Egyptian, the once-glamorous streets of Hollywood that Ronald Reagan knew when he was a movie star thirty years ago are no more. Hustlers, con artists, pimps, and drug addicts troll the sidewalks. There is an air of menace as solitary men enter cheap X-rated theaters. Street thugs and drug addicts mingle with tourists who buy tacky souvenirs and study the cement sidewalk handprints of the stars at Grauman's Chinese Theatre.

John Hinckley has come to Hollywood to be a star in his own right. He hopes to use his guitar skills to make his fortune, but that has not happened. His squalid accommodation at Howard's Weekly Apartments just

---

* Foster won the role over a reported 250 other actresses, including Kim Basinger, Mariel Hemingway, Carrie Fisher, Bo Derek, Jennifer Jason Leigh, Debra Winger, and Eve Plumb, best known for playing Jan Brady on the wholesome television show *The Brady Bunch.* Despite the extensive casting search, Scorcese told Brandy Foster, Jodie's mother, that he had never considered anyone else for Iris.

off Sunset Boulevard has become a prison. "I stayed by myself in my apartment," he would later write of his months in Southern California, "and dreamed of future glory in some undefined field, perhaps music or politics."

The lonely Hinckley keeps to himself, living on fast food and slowly becoming convinced that Jews and blacks are the enemies of white men like him. The more time he spends in Hollywood, the more Hinckley expands his circle of loathing. He now views the city of Los Angeles as "phony" and "impersonal."

Isolated, Hinckley does not even keep in contact with his parents unless he needs money. He has become a drifter, unwilling to finish his studies at Texas Tech or get a job, and would be homeless without their support. John and Jo Ann Hinckley are growing increasingly concerned about their son's behavior, but they support him financially, hoping that one day he will turn his life around and come back to Colorado. Hinckley gives them hope by writing that he is in a relationship with a woman named Lynn. But "Lynn Collins" is not real. She is a myth based on Betsy, Cybill Shepherd's character in *Taxi Driver* — a fact the Hinckleys will not learn for five more years.

Jodie Foster as Iris in Taxi Driver

There are more lies, such as the one about the rock music demo he fictitiously records. In reality, the only good thing in John Hinckley Jr.'s life right now is up there on the screen at the Egyptian. *Taxi Driver* gives him hope and a sense of purpose. The fog of depression hanging over him lifts. Adopting the same manner of dress and behavior as Robert De Niro's character is empowering for him. In *Taxi Driver,* Hinckley sees a series of clues that will lead him to a better life.

"You talking to me?" Travis Bickle says, alone in a ratty apartment not much different from Hinckley's. Bickle stares at his reflection in the mirror, taunting an imaginary antagonist. "You talking to *me*? Well, I'm the only one here. Who the fuck do you think you're talking to?"*

Hinckley is enthralled as the on-screen action shifts to an attempted political assassination. The scene shows Bickle intending to kill a presidential candidate in order to win the love of a woman. But the Secret Service foil Bickle's effort, and he slips away without firing a shot.

John Hinckley knows the next scene well. It is the final gun battle. Travis Bickle goes to rescue Jodie Foster's character from her pimp, who has sold her to an aging mobster. Jodie is beautiful up there on the screen, her blond hair rolled into tight curls, lips painted a vivid red. A one-man vigilante, Bickle blasts his way down the dingy hallway to where Iris's liaison is being consummated. Blood spatters the walls as the body count rises. The camera pulls in tight to the

* Robert De Niro reportedly stole the line from Bruce Springsteen, who said it onstage in response to fans shouting his name.

surprised look on Iris's face as she hears the approaching gunshots. It is her friend, Travis Bickle, who has come to save her. She is not afraid. Quite the opposite. She cries when it appears that Travis might die.

As the movie ends and the credits role, Travis Bickle is a hero in the eyes of Jodie Foster's character — and in the eyes of John Hinckley Jr.

And if Bickle can be a hero, then Hinckley can be a hero, too.

There are any number of reasons John Hinckley has fallen in love with that beautiful young girl up there on the screen. She is the one person the solitary Travis Bickle cares enough about to put his own life on the line for — and in real life, her name is Jodie, which is the nickname Hinckley's mother goes by. A delusion is beginning to take shape in Hinckley's disturbed brain: that Jodie Foster might just be capable of falling in love with him.*

The screen grows dark. John Hinckley steps out into the hot California sunlight. He walks the streets, just as Ronald Reagan

* This condition is known as erotomania, in which an individual believes someone he or she admires is harboring the same feelings toward him/her. It is often associated with mental illness.

once did. It was here on Hollywood Boulevard, near the corner of Cahuenga, that Reagan received his star on the Hollywood Walk of Fame in 1960. Hinckley strides over it without even noticing.

In addition to acquiring boots, a jacket, and a newfound thirst for peach brandy, John Hinckley now also keeps a journal, just like Travis Bickle. The only trait he has not borrowed from the taxi driver is a passion for owning guns.

That will soon change.

14

White House
April 25, 1980
5:43 A.M.

President Jimmy Carter is depressed. The White House switchboard wake-up call has not made his real-life nightmare disappear. In fact, it's getting worse. Having his press secretary leak the horrible news to the media in the dead of night was bad enough, but the weight of what he must do now feels like a heavy stone upon his chest.

Carter is a man who likes to micromanage. He dresses quickly, in a dark suit, light blue shirt, and yellow-and-blue tie. The president then picks up the bedroom phone to call his press secretary, Jody Powell. Throughout the last four years, Powell has been very busy, as Carter's presidency has seen one setback after another. Catastrophic inflation has weakened the dollar. Skyrocketing oil prices and long lines to purchase gasoline have shocked and angered the public.* And now there is humiliation overseas.

Jimmy Carter and Jody Powell talk intensely about what the president will say on television in just one hour. An anonymous scheduler keeps track of the president's calls, inserting a *P* next to this moment in the president's daily worksheet, indicating that it was Carter who placed the call to Powell. (An *R* is used when the president receives a call.)

The two men talk for five minutes. Neither has any interest in breakfast. They are used to working under pressure. But even though the day is still young, they are already drained. The speech on television should have been one of celebration, the president of the United States proclaiming jubilant news to the world: *A daring rescue attempt has freed the fifty-two American hostages.*

* The shortage of American gasoline was caused by the overthrow of the shah of Iran in January 1979. The Iranian ruler, Ayatollah Khomeini, cut Iran's oil production, drastically reducing the shipment of crude-oil shipments to the United States. The soaring price of gasoline plunged the American economy into a recession and sent interest rates soaring to as much as 20 percent.

The hostages have been held in Iran by Muslim militants for six harrowing months because of U.S. support for the shah of Iran, who was admitted to the United States for cancer treatment shortly after going into exile. The radicals holding the Americans hostage insisted that he be returned to Iran to be put on trial for crimes committed during his thirty-eight-year reign.

Instead of celebration, though, there is disaster: eight American soldiers and pilots lie dead in the hot sands of the Iranian desert following an aborted rescue attempt, their bodies burned beyond recognition. In a rush to flee without being captured, their fellow soldiers left the dead Americans behind. It is, perhaps, one of the greatest military humiliations in U.S. history.*

But Jimmy Carter's nightmare will not

---

* Operation Eagle Claw was aborted at the behest of its commanders shortly after the would-be rescuers arrived at Desert One, their preliminary staging area in the Iranian Dasht-e Kavir desert, due to mechanical problems with the mission's helicopters. Carter approved their request. However, as the Special Forces units began pulling out of Iran, a helicopter collided with a C-130 transport. The subsequent explosion resulted in the deaths of five air crewmen aboard the C-130

end with a public explanation of why he authorized the rescue attempt, why he suddenly ordered it aborted, and why eight American servicemen are now dead.

Iranian militants have long threatened to kill the hostages if any rescue attempt were launched. Carter finally called their bluff — only to fail miserably. Now he has to explain the tragedy to the American people.

Jimmy Carter walks downstairs from the second-floor residence. His wife, Rosalynn, a woman known for her frosty demeanor, is on her way home from Austin, Texas, where she was supposed to spend the day campaigning on her husband's behalf. It was shortly after midnight when Jimmy Carter asked his wife to come back to Washington. This would not be a day for campaigning.

Morose, the president steps into the Oval Office at 6:08 a.m. He sits at his desk in this great room and places phone calls to the First Lady and Secretary of Defense Harold Brown. A news camera and microphone are brought into the room. The president straightens his tie. His speech is laid before him on the famous

---

and three from the RH-53D helicopter. The press was informed of the debacle at 1:00 a.m.

Resolute desk.*

Finally, at 7:00 a.m., Carter looks into the camera. He wants to appear in command, but his eyes betray him, showing exhaustion. The president will speak for eight minutes. Afterward, he will receive condolences from former secretary of state Henry Kissinger, who will offer to explain the purpose behind the failed rescue mission to the major television networks on Carter's behalf.

Jimmy Carter never imagined such a moment when he was governor of Georgia. Then, he was a solitary man with huge ambitions, launching a long-shot campaign in 1974 eventually to become president of the United States. Carter has come a long way from his small hometown of Plains,

* A gift from Britain's Queen Victoria to the United States in 1880, the desk was made from timbers of the Arctic exploration vessel HMS *Resolute,* which was frozen in ice and later retrieved by American whaling vessels before being returned to Great Britain. It was used by Presidents Kennedy, Carter, Reagan, Clinton, Bush II, and Obama in the Oval Office. The first President Bush used the *Resolute* desk for the first five months of his presidency, then had it moved into his private study.

Georgia, but now it is all crashing down.

Carter speaks like a naval officer instead of a politician as he unemotionally explains his tactics to the nation, hoping his words will save his reelection campaign.

"I canceled a carefully planned operation which was under way in Iran to position our rescue team for later withdrawal of American hostages, who have been held captive there since November 4," he begins.

"Our rescue team knew, and I knew, that the operation was certain to be difficult and it was certain to be dangerous. We were all convinced that if and when the rescue operation had been commenced that it had an excellent chance of success. They were all volunteers; they were all highly trained. I met with their leaders before they went on this operation. They knew then what hopes of mine and of all Americans they carried with them," Carter explains.

"It was my decision to attempt the rescue operation. It was my decision to cancel it when problems developed in the placement of our rescue team for a future rescue operation.

"The responsibility is fully my own."

Carter exhales. It has been a brutal morning. And he fears the worst is yet to come.

Out of respect for the fifty-two captives,

Carter has done little campaigning for reelection. He believes this "Rose Garden strategy" of remaining in the White House to deal with the crisis makes him look more presidential — and that it will ultimately win him another term.

That strategy is doomed to fail. And so is Jimmy Carter's presidency.

After his nationwide address on the Iranian hostage-rescue disaster, Carter's job approval rating plunges to 28 percent.

Ronald Reagan takes notice.

Ten months before the failed rescue attempt, Jimmy Carter is responding to the news that Sen. Ted Kennedy plans to run against him for president. "I'll whip his ass," Jimmy Carter tells a group of Democratic members of Congress.

The two men are sworn enemies and will remain that way the rest of their lives. Kennedy, the blue-blooded youngest brother of the assassinated John and Robert Kennedy, is a forty-seven-year-old senator from Massachusetts. He's a man of many pleasures, drink and women being chief among them. Kennedy is the sentimental favorite among many Democrats who have bestowed sainthood upon his dead brothers.

But Teddy Kennedy is no saint, as the

events of a fateful summer night one decade ago clearly showed.

It was 11:15 p.m. on July 18, 1969. The senator was attending a party on Chappaquiddick Island, a short ferry ride from the main hamlet on Martha's Vineyard, Edgartown. Kennedy was restless and decided to leave the party with an attractive young campaign worker, twenty-eight-year-old Mary Jo Kopechne. The fresh-faced Mary Jo was infatuated with Kennedy, and he knew this as he led her to a 1967 Oldsmobile Delmont 88. Kennedy had been drinking but nevertheless got behind the wheel while Mary Jo, a former member of the Robert Kennedy 1968 presidential campaign, sat in the front passenger seat. Strangely, she'd left her purse and her hotel room key behind, as if expecting to return to the party later that night.

Kennedy and Mary Jo drove into the dark. Few people live on Chappaquiddick Island. First, the two made a stop on Cemetery Road, an out-of-the-way location. Suddenly, a police car approached, so Kennedy started up the Olds again.

Later, Ted Kennedy will tell investigators that he was driving Mary Jo Kopechne to the local ferry so she could make the last crossing to Edgartown. But that was a lie;

they were driving in the opposite direction from the ferry. Kennedy turned down a dirt road and onto a small wooden bridge that crossed a canal. There were no guardrails, and the car was traveling twenty miles per hour when it suddenly slid off the bridge and into the water. The Oldsmobile flipped upside down in the black current, disorienting Kennedy and Mary Jo. The senator quickly got free of the vehicle and then kicked hard for the surface. In the darkness, he did not see or hear Mary Jo Kopechne.

Kennedy panicked. Not only had he driven a car off a bridge in the dead of night, in the company of a woman who was not his wife, but that woman may also have drowned.

Soaking wet, Kennedy walked up the road until he came to the body of water separating Chappaquiddick from the main part of Martha's Vineyard. He dove into the water and swam five hundred feet to Edgartown. Incredibly, once on land, Kennedy returned to his hotel room, changed into dry clothes, and went to bed. He did not inform police about the accident for nine more hours. When he finally did talk to the authorities, he told them he'd called Mary Jo Kopechne's name many times and made an effort to swim down and find her in the submerged vehicle. Few believed his story.*

Soon, fishermen spotted the wreck, and rescue divers pulled Mary Jo Kopechne's body from the car. Quickly, investigators deduced that she'd initially survived the wreck, finding an air pocket inside the vehicle. Judging from the position of her body, police believed she'd remained alive for some time. Edgartown Rescue Squad diver John Farrar, who pulled Mary Jo's body from the vehicle, told friends that Mary Jo suffocated rather than drowned. The car's doors were all locked, but the windows were either open or shattered, leaving investigators to wonder how the six-foot-two Kennedy could successfully escape while the five-foot-two Mary Jo remained in the vehicle.

* Every effort was made to keep Ted Kennedy's name out of the media regarding the accident, but shortly after noon on July 19, 1969, radio station WBZ in Boston broke the story that Kennedy was the driver. The lurid headline in the *New York Daily News* the next day read, "Teddy Escapes, Blonde Drowns." The scandal was forced out of the headlines later that day, when Neil Armstrong and Buzz Aldrin became the first men to land on the moon. However, the story was quickly revived and followed Kennedy for the rest of his life.

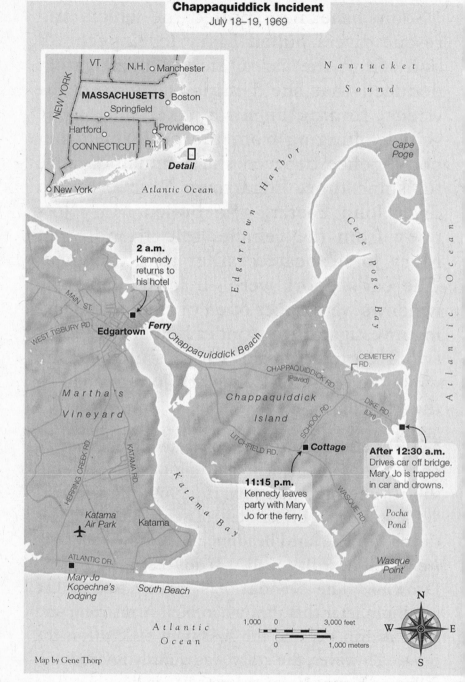

Chappaquiddick Incident
July 18–19, 1969

MASSACHUSETTS

VT.

N.H. ○ Manchester

NEW YORK

Boston ○
Springfield ○
Hartford ○ Providence ○
CONNECTICUT R.I.
○ New York

Detail

Atlantic Ocean

Nantucket Sound

Cape Poge

Edgartown Harbor

Cape Poge Bay

Atlantic Ocean

2 a.m.
Kennedy returns to his hotel

MAIN ST.

WEST TISBURY RD.

Edgartown **Ferry**

Chappaquiddick Beach

CEMETERY RD.

CHAPPAQUIDDICK RD. (Paved)

DIKE RD. (Dirt)

Martha's Vineyard

Chappaquiddick Island

SCHOOL RD.

HERRING CREEK RD.

KATAMA RD.

LITCHFIELD RD.

■ **Cottage**

After 12:30 a.m.
Drives car off bridge. Mary Jo is trapped in car and drowns.

Katama Bay

11:15 p.m.
Kennedy leaves party with Mary Jo for the ferry.

WASQUE RD.

Pocha Pond

Katama Air Park

Katama

ATLANTIC DR.

Mary Jo Kopechne's lodging

South Beach

Wasque Point

Atlantic Ocean

1,000   0   3,000 feet

0   1,000 meters

N
W   E
S

Map by Gene Thorp

In another incredible occurrence, there was no autopsy, in part because the Kopechne family opposed it. Almost immediately, the young woman, whose family lived outside Scranton, Pennsylvania, became the subject of rumor and innuendo.*

One week after Mary Jo Kopechne's death, Sen. Ted Kennedy learned that he would get off easy. An openly sympathetic judge, James Boyle, quickly wrapped up the case. Kennedy pled guilty to leaving the scene of an accident, and Boyle gave him a suspended sentence, saying, "You will continue to be punished far beyond anything this court can impose."

Now, more than ten years later, Boyle's words ring true. "Chappaquiddick," as the incident has become known, dogs Edward Kennedy as he challenges Jimmy Carter for the presidency. Two months after announcing his candidacy, CBS news interviewer Roger Mudd brings up that ill-fated night during a televised interview. Mudd also asks about the state of Kennedy's marriage.

* The body of Mary Jo was buried in Pennsylvania, where in December 1969 a local judge denied a request by the State of Massachusetts to exhume the body for a further inquiry into the cause of death.

Ill at ease, the senator fumbles for words. At one point, Mudd appears to accuse him of lying. Kennedy will later state that Mudd duped him into speaking about matters for which he was not prepared.

Making the situation even worse, the interview airs on November 4, 1979, the same day that fifty-two Americans are taken hostage in Iran. Immediately, the nation rallies around their president rather than the callow Kennedy. In primary after primary during the early months of 1980, Jimmy Carter is true to his word, whipping Kennedy's ass again and again, winning thirty-seven primaries to Kennedy's eleven.*

In the mind of Ted Kennedy, Jimmy Carter is a sanctimonious, weak man. "He loved to give the appearance of listening," Kennedy will one day write of visiting the Carter White House as a senator. "You'd arrive about 6 or 6:30, and the first thing you'd be reminded of, in case you needed reminding, was that he and Rosalynn had removed all liquor from the White House. No liquor was ever served during Jimmy Carter's term. He wanted no luxuries nor any sign

* Despite the lopsided total, Kennedy's victories in the crucial California and New York primaries kept him in the race.

230

of worldly living."

Kennedy also seethes about what he believes to be Carter's growing conservatism, thinking it an affront to the democratic ideals for which his brothers fought so hard. "Jimmy Carter," Kennedy will write, "held an inherently different view of America from mine."

So it is that, despite the lingering stain of Chappaquiddick and the many primary defeats, Ted Kennedy vows to continue his fight against Jimmy Carter all the way to the Democratic National Convention at New York's Madison Square Garden on August 11. In the same manner in which Ronald Reagan sought to unseat President Gerald Ford with a last-minute bid four years ago, Ted Kennedy and his staff now hatch a plan to take down Carter.

Polls support this plan. When asked, Democratic voters said they'd prefer Ronald Reagan over Jimmy Carter if those two candidates faced off for the presidency. Those same polls, however, show Ted Kennedy defeating Ronald Reagan.

On June 5, 1980, six weeks after Carter's televised national address about the failed hostage rescue, he and Ted Kennedy meet in the White House. Kennedy is giving Carter one last chance to avoid the sort of bruising convention that Ford endured — and that ultimately led to his defeat in the general election. All Kennedy wants is the chance to debate Jimmy Carter on national television, allowing voters to decide who should lead the country. The campaign has been a long one for Kennedy, taking him through forty states in nine months. He estimates that he has flown a hundred thousand miles in that time. He is not yet ready to concede the nomination, particularly against an opponent he despises.

"We were not victorious," Kennedy will write of his mind-set going into the meeting; "nor were we defeated."

Kennedy and Carter meet in the Oval Office, at 4:35 in the afternoon. The senator will remember the meeting as lasting fifteen minutes, when in fact they speak for forty. The president is secure in the knowledge that he has more than enough delegates to win the nomination. Kennedy knows this but is hatching an audacious scheme to steal those delegates and make them his own. Kennedy's plan is to force a shift in convention rules that will allow delegates the freedom to vote for anyone they want, rather than the candidate to which their state's primary results bind them.

By the time the meeting is done, Carter has made his intentions clear: there will be no debate.

Two months later, the end finally arrives for Ted Kennedy. His scheme hasn't worked. His campaign staff works the convention floor in a frenzy, determined to find some last-minute way to avoid defeat. But it is not to be. Kennedy has lost his bid for the presidency.

Unbowed, Kennedy gives a concession speech that sounds more like a call to arms. "The commitment I seek is not to outworn ideas, but to old values that will never wear out. Programs may sometimes become obsolete but the idea of fairness always endures," Kennedy tells the convention. "For all those whose cares have been our concern, the work goes on, the cause endures, the hope still lives, and the dream shall never die."

Kennedy is lucid and focused. Many will say it is the finest speech he has ever delivered.

Two nights later, as the convention closes, Ted Kennedy has scotch on his breath as Jimmy Carter invites him onto the dais in a display of party unity. Rosalynn Carter stands at her husband's side, looking every bit the "Steel Magnolia" who has had so much influence in the White House. Speaker of the House Tip O'Neill is on the crowded stage, as are a host of Democratic Party big shots.

But it is the body language between Ted Kennedy and Jimmy Carter that the crowd watches closely. Kennedy wears a pinstriped suit and has a look on his face that his staff calls "the smirk." The senator strides purposely to the lectern, making no attempt to heal any lingering wounds from the campaign. He shakes Carter's hand in the most perfunctory manner possible, then immediately walks to the side of the stage, where he can look out over the Massachusetts delegation. As they roar their approval, Kennedy thrusts a triumphant fist into the air.

Unbeknownst to Kennedy, Jimmy Carter follows him. He, too, puts up a victor's fist for the Massachusetts contingent, hoping for a side-by-side display of party unity with his opponent. But as Carter's fist goes up, Kennedy's goes down. There will be no partnership in this campaign.*

* Though often discussed as a candidate, Edward Moore "Ted" Kennedy never again sought the

In Ronald Reagan's mind, defeating Jimmy Carter for the presidency was just a matter of time.

After accommodating his closest Republican rival, George H. W. Bush, with the vice presidential nomination at the Republican National Convention in New York City, Reagan had a united party at his disposal. Nevertheless, he campaigned hard, crisscrossing the country and denigrating Carter's performance both at home and abroad. He had plenty of ammunition: high inflation, high unemployment, high gas

---

presidency after Carter defeated him in 1980. He went on to serve forty-seven years in the Senate, the fourth longest of any senator in U.S. history. Despite many legislative achievements, his career was tarnished by a propensity for drink and women. He divorced his wife, Joan, in 1982, and married for a second time, to Victoria Reggie, in 1992. After his nephew John F. Kennedy Jr. was killed in an airplane crash in 1999, Ted Kennedy appeared to settle down, adopting the role of family patriarch. He died of brain cancer on August 25, 2009. Ted Kennedy was seventy-seven years old.

prices, and voter outrage about the Iranian debacle.

On November 4, 1980, the landslide is so great that Jimmy Carter concedes the election before the polls even close in California. He phones his Republican opponent at home to give him the news.*

It is Nancy Reagan who answers the phone. Her astrologer has predicted that she and her husband are in for a long night of awaiting returns. But the stargazer is wrong. Therefore, the call at 5:35 p.m. is such a surprise that Ronald Reagan is in the shower. Nancy calls him to the phone. He steps out half-naked and reaches for the phone.

"Standing in my bathroom with a wrapped towel around me, my hair dripping with water," Reagan will later recall, "I had just learned I was going to be the fortieth President of the United States."

* Reagan won the popular vote 50.8 percent to 41.0 percent, with third-party candidate Illinois senator John Anderson getting 6.0 percent. The results were even more punishing in the Electoral College, where Reagan won 489–49. Despite these lopsided numbers, Carter later blamed his loss on the participation of John Anderson in the race.

15

Nashville, Tennessee
October 9, 1980
12:02 P.M.

Losing the election may have saved Jimmy Carter's life.

It is three weeks before the vote when John Hinckley finally makes up his addled mind. He will assassinate President Carter in order to impress actress Jodie Foster, with whom he has fallen deeply in love. Hinckley's plan comes right out of the movie *Taxi Driver.*

But today the frenzied Hinckley has reluctantly decided to delay the killing. He is now running through the Nashville airport, late for his plane. Over the last month, Hinckley has stalked Carter at appearances in Dayton and Columbus, Ohio; Washington, DC; and now Nashville. In Dayton, he got within six feet of Carter but did not shoot because he was not in "a frame of mind in which I could carry out

237

the act."*

That has not been the case in Nashville. President Carter arrived in the city less than an hour ago. He is now onstage at the Grand Ole Opry, speaking to 4,400 local residents. In two more hours, Carter will board Air Force One for the flight to his next campaign stop in Winston-Salem, North Carolina. Hinckley's frame of mind has nothing to do with his inability to murder Jimmy Carter today. The fact of the matter is Hinckley could not get close enough to squeeze off a shot. Security was too tight, so the would-be assassin decided to get out of town.

The handle of Hinckley's oversize gray suitcase is clutched in one fist as he bears down on the security checkpoint. He bought his first handgun just a year ago, and now owns several. Three of them — two .22-caliber pistols and one .38-caliber revolver — are inside his luggage. Hinckley is nervous. His heart races and he feels short of breath as he approaches the X-ray machine.†

* Hinckley made this comment to court psychiatrists when he went on trial for shooting the president.
† Hinckley usually checked his luggage, knowing

"I'm running late," he yells, doing his best to bluff his way through without having his suitcase scanned.

Laura Farmer and Evelyn Braun of the Wackenhut Security Corporation are unfazed. In fact, Sergeant Braun thinks that the pudgy young man looks extremely suspicious. Rather than passing him through, she instructs Mrs. Farmer to pay extra attention to the X-ray of Hinckley's bag.

John Hinckley reluctantly places the suitcase on the conveyor belt. The security officers notice that his hands are shaking.

Laura Farmer studies the video screen as it reveals the contents.

She signals to Nashville airport police offi-

---

his guns would not be x-rayed. The practice of x-raying carry-on luggage began in 1973, in an effort to curb the extremely high rate of airline hijackings (forty in 1969 alone). At the time, most airlines were opposed to individual passenger screening, and it was not even necessary to show identification when checking in for a flight. The Air Transportation Security Act of 1974 made x-raying carry-on luggage the law. Checked luggage was not x-rayed or searched until 1988, in response to the bombing that brought down Pan Am Flight 103 over Lockerbie, Scotland.

cer John A. Lynch, who walks over and opens Hinckley's suitcase. Not only does he find the three handguns, but Hinckley is also carrying fifty .22-caliber bullets and a set of handcuffs.

Hinckley begins to argue, claiming that he is selling the guns, and insists that he is late for his plane.

Airport police officer Lynch ignores him. "You have the right to remain silent," he informs Hinckley, officially placing him under arrest.

The four years since his first summer in Los Angeles have been largely a haze for John Hinckley. He continued to wander, shuttling from one state to another in an attempt to find himself, often returning to Texas Tech University, in Lubbock, to take a few courses. His grades were Bs and Cs, and Hinckley has been in no hurry to graduate. At school, he woke up each morning and ate a half-pound hamburger from Bill's Lot-A-Burger. Once fastidious about neatness, Hinckley has become a slob. He keeps no food in his simple apartment, where a fine layer of dust from the local sandstorms and a pile of white Lot-A-Burger bags cover the dining table.

In Lubbock, Hinckley often walked into

Acco Rentals to talk football with owner Don Barrett. Other days, he sat alone in silence by the pool at the Westernaire Apartments.

But recently, John Hinckley has developed a new passion. He's become enamored of Adolf Hitler and recently purchased a two-volume set of the German dictator's ideological opus, *Mein Kampf,* for thirty dollars at a Lubbock bookstore. Hinckley even joined the American Nazi Party for a year. He proudly wore the official brown uniform, with its swastika armband and storm-trooper jackboots. But Hinckley was asked to leave the fascist group because he consistently advocated violence.

"Rallies and demonstrations were not enough," neo-Nazi leader Michael Allen explained. "He said he believed violence and bloodshed was [*sic*] the answer. He advocated illegal acts, and we believe in acting within the law. We don't want his kind in our organization."

Another neo-Nazi official was blunter, saying that Hinckley was "violent, irrational and advocated terrorism."

But this is not the side of his persona John Hinckley wants Jodie Foster to see. Just one month ago, on September 17, Hinckley flew to New Haven, Connecticut, where the actress has begun attending Yale University. The image of her beautiful innocence in *Taxi Driver* continues to haunt Hinckley, who still watches the film on a regular basis. He is determined to win Jodie's love, but the journey to Yale proved to be a setback. He wrote her letters and poems, and even managed to speak with her on the phone. But rather than find the attention romantic, Foster was disturbed. She told Hinckley he was rude and dangerous, and ordered him never to call her again.

Initially, Hinckley was devastated. He attempted suicide by swallowing antidepressants but failed. Rather than try again, Hinckley vowed to renew his pursuit of Foster by imitating Travis Bickle's strategy for romancing women: political assassination.

So it is that John Hinckley spent what little money he had on handguns and airfare, following the president of the United States around the country, hoping to put a bullet in his head.

Within an hour of his arrest in Nashville, John Hinckley stands before Judge William E. Higgins. The location is not a courtroom but a small office in police headquarters. He is being charged with possession of a firearm.

A terrified Hinckley can only imagine what will happen next. He has never been in jail before. With President Carter just a few miles away at the Grand Ole Opry, it is logical that Judge Higgins or the FBI would question Hinckley about his guns and his intent. Even though it might appear to be a coincidence, the president's presence in Nashville demands that those questions be asked.

But on this day, John Hinckley is in luck. The FBI is so overwhelmed by Jimmy Carter's visit to Nashville that every last agent has been tasked with ensuring his safety. So there is effectively no interrogation of Hinckley.

Judge Higgins's verdict is swift: John Hinckley will be punished to the maximum letter of the law. He is immediately ordered to pay a $50 fine, along with $12.50 in court costs. He also loses his guns.*

John Hinckley walks out of Judge Higgins's courtroom a free man. He immediately returns to the airport, where he

* Hinckley was charged with possession of concealed weapons. Carrying a gun without a permit was not against the law in Tennessee at the time.

takes the next plane to Dallas.

In 1980 the Secret Service has a computer file listing the four hundred individuals most likely to attempt a presidential assassination. There is also a secondary list of the more than twenty-five thousand people who might be capable of carrying out such a killing.

Despite his troubles in Nashville, John Hinckley does not make either list.

Four days after his arrest, Hinckley enters Rocky's Pawn Shop at 2018 East Elm Street in Dallas. There, in a strip mall whose tenants include a bail bondsman and a dive bar, he purchases two snub-nosed pistols of the same model. Its official name is the RG-14 .22-caliber revolver. In police parlance, the gun is known as the Saturday Night Special.

The intensity of John Hinckley's quest for the love of Jodie Foster ratchets up. His compulsion has now overwhelmed him.

16

Smithsonian National Museum of Natural History
Washington, DC
January 20, 1981
11:47 P.M.

Ronald Reagan stares at the elephant in the room. It stands thirteen feet tall and measures twenty-seven feet from trunk to tail. It took thirteen four-inch bullets to kill him. The Fénykövi elephant, as the regal animal is known, is poised for battle in the center of this festive rotunda. Its flanks are draped in patriotic red, white, and blue bunting, making it the very symbol of the Republican Party.*

* At the time of its shooting by Hungarian big-game hunter Joseph Fénykövi on November 12, 1955, it was the largest-ever African elephant in recorded history. On March 6, 1959, Fénykövi donated the preserved hide of the elephant to the

The other symbol of the party stands at a lectern bearing the official seal of the president of the United States of America. Ronald Wilson Reagan gazes out over the hundreds of supporters dressed in formal wear who have come to celebrate his inauguration. He wears white tie and tails. Nancy Reagan, on his right, is draped in a white satin sheath that took a team of dressmakers four weeks to embroider. Her full-length Maximilian mink coat and alligator handbag are backstage, watched over by the Secret Service. Unbeknownst to the crowd, Nancy's outfit for the evening costs close to twenty-five thousand dollars.*

This is the Reagans' ninth inaugural ball of the evening. And with midnight just moments away, they still have one more to go. The festivities began the previous night, at the inaugural gala organized by Frank Sinatra. Johnny Carson was the emcee, introducing performances by Sinatra and comedian Bob Hope, who poked fun at Reagan's Hollywood days by joking that the new president "doesn't know how to lie, exag-

---

Smithsonian, where a team of taxidermists labored for sixteen months to prepare it for display.

* More than sixty-eight thousand dollars in today's money.

gerate or cheat — he's always had an agent for that!"

Tonight is even more glamorous. Priced at a steep five hundred dollars a ticket, seats are in such demand that the press will compare these formally dressed men and women to "drunken soccer fans" as they battle for their places at the table, where swordfish and chateaubriand are washed down with California wine and Kentucky bourbon. Hundreds of corporate titans have flown in from all over the country — so many, in fact, that their private jets have disrupted normal flight patterns at Washington's National Airport this morning. As limousines clog the city streets, California socialite and longtime Nancy Reagan confidante Betsy Bloomingdale actually gets out of her stretch limo to direct traffic at Dupont Circle. A mink stole draped around her shoulders, the fifty-eight-year-old Bloomingdale doesn't have time for gridlock.

Indeed, so many women have worn expensive furs to these inaugural balls that the press will report coatracks looking like "giant furry beasts." The Washington caterer Ridgewells will serve four hundred thousand hors d'oeuvres at the various parties tonight. Lavish consumption is on display, something Jimmy and Rosalynn Carter would never have allowed.

Throughout the night, Ronald Reagan remains unfazed. "I want to thank all of you," he tells the crowd at the Smithsonian. His voice is growing hoarse after hours of speeches, but though he is just weeks away from turning seventy years old, the new president shows no signs of fatigue. "Without you there wouldn't be this successful inaugural."

Four years ago, Jimmy Carter did not feel it appropriate to celebrate his inauguration with even one formal ball, let alone ten. No partying for the man from Plains. Instead, Carter's 1977 inaugural address was somber, pointing out America's limitations as a nation. The tone of pessimism and defeat that marked Carter's first day in office came to define his entire presidency.

If Ronald Reagan's first day in office is any indication of what is to come, the United States of America is in for a far more upbeat presidency. He and Nancy spent last night at Blair House, the official state residence where presidents-elect sleep the night before their inauguration.* The first

* Blair House is a 120-room, 60,600-square-foot mansion across the street from the White House.

couple is rested and ready to take full advantage of the celebration.

The Reagans have been in Washington for a week, adapting to the capital's routine after more than a year living out of suitcases on the campaign trail. With their new life comes intense public scrutiny. A litany of personal facts is finding their way into the media. Given his age, many wonder about Reagan's health. Despite a medical history that includes a shattered femur suffered in a celebrity baseball game thirty years ago, the worst of his maladies right now is minor arthritis in his right thumb and chronic hay fever. He continues to work out each night, using a small exercise wheel before taking an evening shower. To some doctors, for a man about to enter his eighth decade, Reagan is an amazing physical specimen.

In fact, the biggest physical problem Reagan has right now might be his hair color. It has become a national mystery. The

---

Built in 1824, it was originally the home of Surgeon General of the U.S. Army Joseph Lovell. Francis Preston Blair Sr., adviser to several presidents, including Abraham Lincoln, purchased the home in 1836. The United States bought the property in 1942 to avoid having guests of the president sleep in hotels.

president says he does not dye his dark hair, but many are skeptical.*

There is no question that Ronald Reagan is a vain man. He is almost deaf in his right ear, thanks to standing too close to gunfire while filming a series of movies about the Secret Service in the late 1940s. But Reagan refuses to wear a hearing aid. Also, he can get testy at times. Some of his campaign staff whisper about Irish rages. In one case, candidate Reagan became so annoyed with his speechwriters that he took off his glasses and threw them against the wall. Such outbursts are rare, but Reagan's closest confidants know that when they see his jaw tighten, it is time to back off.

The Reagans are often pedestrian in their tastes. Reagan's favorite Christmas carol is "Silent Night," and his favorite song is the "Battle Hymn of the Republic." He enjoys lasagna and hamburgers for dinner, followed by a dessert of brownies or carrot

---

* Gerald Ford once noted that Reagan's hair was "prematurely orange." This occasional side effect is often seen as evidence of the use of Clairol hair dye, and in 2009 a former Clairol executive stated to the *New York Times* that the Reagans brought their own personal hair colorist into the White House. However, it has never been confirmed.

cake. When watching television, the Reagans prefer *The Waltons* and *Little House on the Prairie,* shows built around wholesome values.

Ronald Reagan's political hero is no longer Franklin Delano Roosevelt; he's been replaced by former Republican president Calvin Coolidge. "He [Coolidge] wasn't a man with flamboyant looks or style, but he got things done in a quiet way," Reagan will write of the man whose picture he will hang in the White House Cabinet Room. "He came into office after World War I facing a mountain of war debt, but instead of raising taxes, he cut the tax rate and government revenues increased, permitting him to eliminate the wartime debt."

This kind of analysis surprises observers in Washington, many of whom don't think that Ronald Reagan has a first-rate intellect. He has long studied the nuances of domestic and foreign policy and possesses a stunning ability to recollect the most minute facts for the purposes of a speech or debate. But Reagan often hides his knowledge in order to present himself as a simple man of humble opinions, an image he believes makes him more appealing to regular voters.

Yet Reagan does not pander. While many

politicians use religion as a campaign theme, the Reagans rarely go to church, and the new president does not make an issue out of his belief in God. However, his spirituality does influence him. On October 11, 1979, Reagan sends a letter to a writer for a pro-life Catholic magazine, in response to an article about Reagan's views on abortion. "To answer your questions; I have a very deep belief that interrupting a pregnancy means the taking of a human life. In our Judeo-Christian tradition, this can only be justified as a matter of self-defense."

But expressions like that for Ronald Reagan are rare. His experience in the secular state of California imbued him with a practical political strategy, so he mostly avoids the emotional issue of religion.

Nancy Reagan, on the other hand, avoids very little. She is known to blurt out her personal thoughts. When her son, Ron, attacks Jimmy Carter as having "the morals of a snake," Nancy publicly defends her boy.* In December, just one month after the election, she stands up against gun control by admitting to owning a "tiny little

* Ron Reagan Jr. made these comments in an interview with *New York* magazine in December 1980.

gun." Coming shortly after the assassination of singer John Lennon, the comment strikes many as callous, and there is public outrage over the incident in liberal circles. Reacting to the heat, Nancy fires her newly appointed press secretary for not "protecting" her from the media backlash.

Sensing blood, the press descends on Nancy Reagan. Soon, she is being described as being cheap and self-absorbed. *Tonight Show* host Johnny Carson refers to her as the "Evita of Bel-Air," comparing her to the imperious wife of Argentinian dictator Juan Perón, Eva, who longed for her own unlimited power.

In truth, Nancy Reagan is much more interested in high fashion and copies the dress and look of two icons: Jackie Kennedy and England's Duchess of Windsor. To cover the cost of such extravagance, the incoming First Lady expects designers to give her clothing and handbags gratis — under the pretense that they are merely being "borrowed."

Nancy Reagan wears one of those outfits now, a three-thousand-dollar dress, coat, and hat by the Cuban-born designer Adolfo, as she and Ronald Reagan are driven from Blair House to the White House shortly before noon on Inauguration Day. There they are met by a somber Jimmy Carter and his wife. Per tradition, the two men ride together in a limousine for the short two-mile journey to the Capitol building for Reagan's swearing-in. They sit side by side in the backseat but do not speak. Instead, each man looks out the window, waving to the crowds on his side of the limo. "He was polite," Reagan will later write of that stony ride. "He hardly said a word to me as we moved slowly toward the Capitol, and I think he hesitated to look me in the face."

Nancy Reagan and Rosalynn Carter are driven in a separate limousine, directly behind their husbands. Rosalynn Carter wears a dull brown skirt and coat with a matching scarf knotted at her throat, making her look somewhat dowdy next to Nancy in her fire-engine red outfit. Today is the end of a dream for Rosalynn, who grew up poor, with a widowed mother who took in sewing to make ends meet. The differences between her and Nancy Reagan, with her debutante past and wealthy stepfather, are many. Rosalynn has attempted to be kind to Nancy throughout the transition, as her husband has been to Ronald Reagan, for the Carters well remember the courtesies extended to them by the Ford family as they were leaving office four years ago.

However, Nancy Reagan has managed to annoy Rosalynn. She has visited the White House several times, intent most of all on gauging the amount of closet space so that her enormous wardrobe will have a home. Mrs. Carter tolerated having Nancy snoop around, even though the White House was still very much the Carter home. But when Nancy requested that the Carter family move out a week before the inauguration, Rosalynn drew the line. Her answer was a firm no. The Carters remained the White House's official residents until just a few minutes before noon on Inauguration Day.

Nevertheless, the transition of presidential power is well under way. The recorders who tally every moment of a president's day stopped recording Carter's activities one week ago. The Carters' furniture is being removed from the White House, replaced by that of the Reagans. Leaving office is hard on Jimmy Carter, for he is exhausted from staying up all night in a last-minute attempt to free the hostages in Iran. It is an act for which he will receive little credit. The Iranian militants would not set the Americans free until Reagan was sworn in, due to Carter's support for the

Ronald and Nancy wave from the presidential limousine on Inauguration Day, 1981.

shah of Iran.*

The Reagans have brought California's weather with them. Tens of thousands of people stand in shirtsleeves and light jackets on this fifty-six-degree day. The crowds stretch from the Capitol Building all the way down to the National Mall to the Lin-

* On January 19, 1981, the Algiers Accord resulted in the freeing up of $7.9 billion in Iranian assets that had been frozen by the United States once the hostage crisis began. This paved the way for the hostages' freedom.

coln Memorial. American flags and red, white, and blue bunting seem to be everywhere, imbuing this day with a jubilant sense of patriotism. Later on, once word gets out about the newly freed American hostages, yellow ribbons will be tied around every available tree, only heightening the festive atmosphere.*

But not everyone is joyful. There are many in the media who despise Ronald Reagan. Terms such as *lightweight, B-movie actor,* and even *dangerous* are sometimes used to denigrate him, both privately and in print. Ever since the failed Nixon administration, it has become commonplace in the media to disrespect Republican politicians.

Despite many preconceived notions and his familiar television persona, the press and most of the American people do not really know Ronald Reagan. He reveals himself to very few people. He is wary of the media

* This American tradition of welcoming home prisoners of war and soldiers was revived by the 1973 song "Tie a Yellow Ribbon Round the Ole Oak Tree," by Tony Orlando and Dawn. The practice dates to the nineteenth century, when American women wore a yellow ribbon to show their faithfulness to a husband or sweetheart serving in the U.S. Cavalry.

and easily guided by the strong personality of Nancy, who has more influence than any of his advisers — though even she is often frustrated by his unwillingness to share his feelings. Ronald Reagan is passive in many ways. He can be stubborn when he chooses to put his foot down but often allows others to make decisions for him. He craves approval and applause, thanks to growing up the son of an alcoholic father who gave him little of either. He often appears disengaged, preferring the company of his own thoughts to time with family and friends. He is a loyal man but has put little effort into fatherhood, often ignoring his children when they need him most. Reagan's world revolves around his conservative ideals and Nancy, with whom he has been known to get annoyed but rarely angry.

This is the real Ronald Reagan. But the public man is a far different story. To millions of his supporters, the new president is a benign father figure, a man who makes them proud to be Americans. And Reagan himself is proud of that image.

Vice President George H. W. Bush is sworn in first. The choice of running mate was a savvy move on Reagan's part, as it was Bush who proved the toughest opponent during the 1980 Republican presidential primaries. A longtime party workhorse, the World War II bomber pilot has served as a congressman from Texas, envoy to China, director of Central Intelligence, and chairman of the Republican National Committee. At six foot two, he stands an inch taller than Reagan and shares a similar athletic background. His eyes are blue, and he adds styling mousse to his gray-brown hair to keep it in place. "Poppy," as he was nicknamed in his youth, is known for being a gentle yet tough man.

Bush now steps into the thankless role of vice president with the same aplomb he brought to each of his previous jobs. Reagan has plans to make great use of George Bush and his many skills, in a manner normally unseen between a president and a vice president. Unlike Reagan, who can be privately aloof, Bush makes friends easily. He still keeps in touch with schoolmates and navy buddies he met decades ago. The same holds true in Washington, where Bush is deeply connected inside the Beltway. Reagan's practical side will not allow him to let such qualities go to waste.

At the stroke of noon, the new vice president steps away from the lectern. It is now Ronald Wilson Reagan's turn to take the oath of office. He wears a gray vest and tie under his black suit as he places his hand on a Bible that once belonged to his mother. A poised Nancy Reagan is at his side, resplendent in her matching red dress, coat, and hat. In what is a political first for Reagan, all four of his grown children are in attendance, standing with the other invited guests just behind him. And in what is a harbinger of things to come, none of the children is smiling.

A burst of sunshine plays on Reagan's face as Chief Justice Warren Burger reads him the oath. "I, Ronald Wilson Reagan, do solemnly swear . . ."

The oath takes just forty seconds. Reagan relishes each phrase, repeating words for dramatic impact and adding a pause here and there for emphasis.

"May I congratulate you, sir," the chief justice says, reaching over to shake Reagan's hand. As a twenty-one-gun salute echoes throughout Washington, DC, Reagan kisses his wife on the cheek. They turn together and look out on the thousands of Americans who have traveled to Washington to be here with them in person to witness this historic moment. Tonight there will be fireworks in the nation's capital. In New York, the Statue of Liberty will be bathed in spotlights. For the next twelve hours, Ronald and Nancy Reagan will be celebrated with a dazzling succession of parades, parties, and speeches. Then, finally, will come the humbling moment when Ronald Reagan steps into the Oval Office for the first time.*

As the most powerful man in the world, Ronald Reagan is preparing himself for the job by bringing in many political veterans. His chief of staff will be James Baker III, a fellow former Democrat who ran the presidential campaigns of Gerald Ford and then George H. W. Bush four years later. Reagan is willing to overlook that indiscretion for the sake of an organized and efficient White House. He likes that Baker is a no-nonsense manager known for his crisp analysis.

Reagan's deputy chief of staff, and the second man in what will become known as the Troika, will be Michael Deaver, a member of his California gubernatorial staff and a man whom both Ronald and Nancy Reagan prize for his loyalty.

And the third man upon whom Reagan will rely for advice in times of doubt is Edwin Meese, an attorney who served as

* This occurred at precisely 5:08 p.m. on January 20, 1981.

chief of staff during the California governorship. His official title is counselor to the president, but the forty-nine-year-old Meese's actual job description goes much deeper than merely giving legal advice. He and Reagan know each other so well that Meese is often considered the president's alter ego. However, knowing that such a role can carry too much clout in the White House, Meese has made it a point to meet with Baker in order to sharply define their roles. It is a balance of power that will be tested much sooner than either man is anticipating.

Thanks to his capable team, Reagan is confident that he can run the country. He is so eager to begin changing America that this afternoon he will sign his first executive order. With the swipe of a pen, he will order a federal hiring freeze. Within a week he will also lift price controls on oil and gasoline, simultaneously setting in motion his personal idea of a free-market economy and making his many donors from the gas and oil industry billions of dollars richer.*

* It was Richard Nixon who introduced the price controls on gasoline, in an attempt to stimulate greater domestic oil production. Carter instituted a levy known as a "windfall tax" against the oil

"It is time for us to realize that we are too great a nation to limit ourselves to small dreams," he preaches in his inaugural address. "We're not, as some would have us believe, doomed to inevitable decline. I do not believe in a fate that will fall on us no matter what we do.

"I believe in a fate that will fall on us if we do nothing."

The last inaugural ball winds down well past midnight, but at nine o'clock the same morning, Ronald Reagan sits down at the *Resolute* desk in the Oval Office and scans his list of scheduled meetings. He wears a coat and tie, as he will each and every time he sets foot in this legendary work space.

Reagan is firmly in command. Or so it seems to those around him.

Little does he know the violence that lies ahead.

---

companies during his administration, which promptly led to a decrease in domestic output. He later signed an executive order that would phase out price controls by October 1981. Reagan's lifting of the controls before that scheduled date caused production to soar, leading to a 50 percent drop in the price of oil.

17

Stapleton Airport
Denver, Colorado
March 7, 1981
6:00 P.M.

John Hinckley shuffles off the United Airlines flight from New York, eyes glazed from fatigue and face unshaven. He has spent a week on the East Coast in yet another futile attempt to win Jodie Foster's love. "Dear Mom and Dad," the twenty-five-year-old wrote in a note just seven days ago. "Your prodigal son has left again to exorcise some demons. I'll let you know in a week where I am."

But Foster once again rejected Hinckley, and yesterday morning at four thirty, a broke and incoherent Hinckley phoned his parents, begging for a ticket to fly home. He is unaware that Jodie Foster has given his love letters to the Yale University campus police, who are currently launching an investigation into his whereabouts.

Hinckley is among the last passengers to disembark. His fifty-five-year-old father, Jack, is waiting. His mother has not made the drive into the city from Evergreen because she is so distraught about her son that she has spent the day sobbing. The entire Hinckley family has been devastated by John's behavior. His sister, Diane, and elder brother, Scott, both phoned yesterday to encourage their parents to place John in a mental hospital. "He just keeps going down," Scott Hinckley told his father. "John doesn't seem like he can cope anymore."

But coping is the least of it. If Jack and Jo Ann Hinckley were the sort of people to pry, they would find a handgun, bullets, and paper targets in the shape of a man's torso in a small green suitcase hidden in their son's bedroom closet. But they do not believe in snooping into their son's belongings or his personal business. They have no idea why John impulsively flew back to New York City, and certainly no knowledge of the grandiose scheme to court Jodie Foster.

This does not mean that Jack and Jo Ann are completely hands-off parents. It was through their urging that their troubled son has begun seeing a Colorado psychiatrist about his failing mental health. Dr. John

Hopper, however, does not see anything greatly wrong with John Hinckley. In their sporadic sessions together over the last five months, Hopper has seen no signs of delusion or other symptoms of mental illness. John Hinckley trusts Hopper enough to confess that he is "on the breaking point" mentally, but rather than be alarmed, the psychiatrist thinks him a typical socially awkward young man who exaggerates his obsessions. Hopper treats Hinckley by attaching biofeedback electrodes to his forehead and thermometers to his fingers in an effort to teach him relaxation techniques.

Relaxation, Hopper believes, is vital to curing Hinckley.

The psychiatrist also believes that Jack and Jo Ann Hinckley are mostly to blame. He believes they coddle their son, not holding him accountable for his behavior. They allow him to live at home and don't force him to find a job. So Hopper has encouraged them to draw up a contract to set in motion the wheels of John Hinckley's independence. By March 1, he is to have a job; by March 30, he is to have moved out of the house. "Give John one hundred dollars," Dr. Hopper told the Hinckleys, "and tell him good-bye."

Technically, John Hinckley has remained

true to the contract. He beat the deadline for finding employment, landing a menial position with the local Evergreen newspaper. But he walked away from that job when he flew to New York. Now, in the busy Denver airport, a heartbroken Jack Hinckley must perform a most gut-wrenching act of parenting: he must tell his son good-bye.

Jack Hinckley guides John to an unused boarding gate. "Have you eaten anything?" he asks.

"I bought a hamburger in New York, and ate again on the plane," John replies.

They sit down. Jack is direct, telling his son that he is no longer welcome in their home. "You've broken every promise you've made to your mother and me. Our part of the agreement was to provide you with a home and an allowance while you've worked at becoming independent. I don't know what you've been doing these past months, but it hasn't been that. And we've reached the end of our rope."

John Hinckley is shocked. Even at age twenty-five, he is so accustomed to having his parents solve his problems that his father's words stun him.

Jack presses two hundred dollars into John's hands. "The YMCA is an inexpensive place to live," he says softly.

"I don't want to live at the Y."

"Well, it's your decision, John. From here on you're on your own."

The two men walk to the airport garage, where John Hinckley Jr. parked his white Plymouth Volare seven days ago. Jack Hinckley has brought along antifreeze, knowing that the car has been sitting in the winter cold all week. He empties the jug into the engine and then stands back as his son turns the key in the ignition.

"I watched him drive slowly down the ramp," Jack Hinckley will later write of that moment.

"I did not see my son face-to-face again until we met in prison."

Three weeks later, John Hinckley parks the white Volare in his parents' driveway. He has been living at a dive called the Golden Palms Hotel, thirty minutes away in Lakewood.

Jack is at work, so it is Hinckley's mother who answers the door. John is flying to California to start his new life, and Jo Ann Hinckley has agreed to drive him to the airport. The date is Wednesday, March 25, 1981. At this same moment, Ronald Reagan is taking advantage of one of the great perks that come with being president, flying by helicopter to Marine Corps Base Quantico, where he will spend two hours on horseback.

Mother and son barely speak during the hour-long ride into Denver. She does not want him to leave but forces herself to stick with what she and her husband now call the Plan.

John parks in front of the Western Airlines terminal. Jo Ann violates the Plan by giving him one hundred dollars. "He looked so bad and so sad and in absolutely total despair," she will later recall. "I thought he would take his own life."

But John Hinckley's flirtation with suicide has passed. He has a very different form of killing on his mind. "Mom," he tells her, saying good-bye once and for all to his former life, "I want to thank you for everything you've ever done for me."

Jo Ann Hinckley knows something is wrong. Her son never speaks with such formality. But the Plan must be obeyed, so she overrules her intuition and does nothing to stop John from leaving. If not for the Plan, the course of history might have been changed.★

★ Dr. John Hopper will be sued by Hinckley's many victims, saying that Hopper should have

269

"You're very welcome," Jo Ann tells her son. Her voice is intentionally cold because she knows she will start sobbing if she lets down her guard. Then, without a kiss or hug or even a handshake, she gets in the Volare and drives away.

Little does she know, her son is carrying one of his RG-14 .22-caliber Saturday Night Specials in his luggage.

It has become a vital part of *his* plan.

---

known he was dangerous and placed him in a hospital. The case was dismissed.

18

White House
Washington, DC
March 3, 1981
1:22 P.M.

Seated inside the Diplomatic Reception Room, President Ronald Reagan makes small talk with CBS anchorman Walter Cronkite as a sound engineer adjusts their lapel microphones. The two men sit opposite each other on simple wooden chairs. Behind them, the iconic Frederic Remington bronze sculpture *Broncho Buster* perches on a credenza. Reagan's legs are crossed, and he rests his hands on his knees to keep them still as he speaks. Both men are dressed in dark suits, with Reagan's maroon tie in subtle contrast to the blue and yellow favored by the newsman.

Walter Cronkite has been a major figure in broadcasting for forty years, and Reagan has specifically chosen him to conduct his first interview since taking office six weeks ago. The anchorman has personally known each president since Herbert Hoover and has an opinion on each.* Cronkite finds Reagan to be "a lot of fun to be with, the kind of guy you really like to have as a friend."

Despite that admiration, Cronkite has a job to do. In this instance, he must ask Reagan tough questions in an attempt to reassure the world that the president does not plan on waging a nuclear war against the Soviet Union. So far Reagan has done little to dispel that notion, taking the same hardline stance against the Soviets that he took against Communists in Hollywood almost

---

* Cronkite considers Hoover's presidency to have been "damned" by the Great Depression and Franklin Roosevelt to be a man of great charisma and personal strength. He considers Harry Truman one of the great presidents and was surprised by Dwight Eisenhower's total recall about the World War II D-Day landings more than a decade later. He thought John F. Kennedy handsome and sometimes arrogant; Lyndon Johnson larger than life; Richard Nixon an oddball; Gerald Ford a nice, straightforward guy; and Jimmy Carter to have been the smartest president he ever met.

four decades ago.

The situation has grown worse in the past week. On February 24, Soviet leader Leonid Brezhnev gave a three-hour speech in front of a Communist Party gathering in Moscow. The seventy-four-year-old Brezhnev is a short, overweight man with enormous bushy eyebrows who has ruled his nation for almost seventeen years. During that time, he has pursued a ruthless path of aggression against the United States and the rest of the West, secretly building a nuclear arsenal and military that now dwarf those of America and NATO.* This is in violation of several treaties between the two nations designed to keep world peace. Since the Nixon administration, the United States has pursued a policy of détente, in which the

---

* The Soviet Union had no nuclear warheads at the end of World War II, when Gen. George Patton urged Gen. Dwight D. Eisenhower and Undersecretary of War Robert Patterson to prolong that conflict by pushing for a show of strength against the encroaching Russian influence. Patton believed the Soviet Union was just as dangerous as the Third Reich. By 1981, as Reagan takes office, the Soviets have 32,146 nuclear warheads aimed at America, and the United States has 9,000 fewer aimed at Russia.

Soviet Union has often played the part of the aggressor and America has usually acceded to its demands in an effort to keep the peace.

It is a policy that Ronald Reagan abhors, and he is determined that Brezhnev understand that. "It has been a long time since an American president stood up to the Soviet Union," he says to his son Michael in 1976. "Every time we get into negotiations, the Soviets are telling us what we are going to have to give up in order for us to get along with them, and we forget who we are."*

At the time of Brezhnev's speech at the

* Reagan made this comment from his hotel suite during the 1976 Republican National Convention. He was lamenting his loss to Ford and the missed opportunity to implement his own foreign policy. His words continued: "I wanted to become president of the United States so I could sit down with Brezhnev. And I was going to let him pick out the size of the table, and I was going to listen to him tell me, the American president, what we were going to have to give up. And I was going to listen to him for maybe twenty minutes, and then I was going to get up from my side of the table, walk around to the other side, and lean over and whisper in his ear, 'Nyet.' It's been a long time

Kremlin, many within the KGB fear that the Soviet Union can no longer keep up with the United States economically or militarily.* A nation can be militarily successful for only so long. At some point, the economy must also be powerful, and this is where the Soviets are failing. The Cold War, that decades-old ideological conflict between capitalism and communism, could soon come to an end — and communism could lose.

For this reason, Brezhnev's speech included an invitation that Ronald Reagan sit down at the negotiating table. Pretending to seek peace, Brezhnev was again bluffing. He wanted to bully the untested American president.

But Ronald Reagan is in no mood to be bullied — not by Leonid Brezhnev, nor by Walter Cronkite.

From the very first question, Cronkite attempts to put Reagan on the defensive. He asks about the "crisis" in American foreign policy, drawing comparisons between the

---

since they've heard 'nyet' from an American president."

* KGB, for Komitet gosudarstvennoy bezopasnosti, translates from the Russian as "Committee for State Security."

United States military advisers in El Salvador and the early days of America's involvement in Vietnam.

Reagan fires back in a cordial yet firm tone of voice. "No, Walter," referring to the newsman by his first name, "the difference is so profound."

The president continues for a full minute, rattling off the details of the growing Communist threat in Central America thanks to military groups controlled by the Russians and Cubans.

Cronkite replies with another pointed question about the "wisdom" of Reagan's foreign policy. Reagan responds instantly, his command of the facts absolute. Back and forth they go for twenty minutes, two master communicators making sure their message is heard. And while Cronkite is speaking to the American people, Ronald Reagan is talking directly to Leonid Brezhnev. Every word of this interview, right down to each comma, will be transcribed and scrutinized in Moscow. Reagan wants the Russians to know one thing above all else: he is not Jimmy Carter.

Soon enough, the subject turns to Brezhnev's demand for a summit meeting.

"You might have overdone the rhetoric a little bit by laying into the Soviet leadership, calling them liars and thieves," Cronkite states, referring to a comment Reagan made at his first press conference. "The world, I think, is looking forward to some negotiations to stop the arms race, to get off this danger point."

But Reagan does not budge.

"I do believe this," Reagan begins, distancing himself from a détente that he considers phony. "It is rather foolish to have unilaterally disarmed, you might say, as we did by letting our defensive [*sic*], our margin of safety, deteriorate, and then you sit with the fellow who's got all the arms. What do you have to negotiate with?"

Leonid Brezhnev is not pleased.

The Soviet leader sits in his Kremlin office on this cold winter day, craving the cigarettes that doctors are forcing him to quit. The last time he met with an American president was a year and a half ago, at the Hofburg Palace in Vienna, Austria. There, after signing an arms-control treaty that limited the Soviet Union and United States to the same number of missiles and long-range bombers, a jubilant Brezhnev embraced Jimmy Carter, kissing him on both cheeks. To the millions worldwide watching this display on television, Brezh-

Soviet leader and Reagan nemesis Leonid Brezhnev in his Kremlin office

nev seemed to want to appear both charming and lighthearted.

"He has the Slavic love of physical contact — back slapping, bear hugs, and kisses," Secretary of State Henry Kissinger wrote in a confidential memo to President Gerald Ford in 1974. "His anecdotes and imagery, to which he resorts frequently, avoid the language of the barnyard. His humor is heavy, sometimes cynical, and frequently earthy.

"Brezhnev is a nervous man, partly because of his personal insecurity, partly for physiological reasons traced to his consumption of alcohol and tobacco," Kissinger continued. "You will find his hands perpetually in motion, twirling his gold watch chain, flicking ashes from his ever-present cigarette, clanging his cigarette holder against an ashtray. From time to time, he may stand up behind his chair or walk about. He is likely to interrupt by offering food and drink. His colleagues obviously humor him in these nervous habits."

But Brezhnev has a notorious dark side. Until recently, he womanized constantly, despite being married for more than fifty years. Physical ailments, however, have left him bloated and unable to speak without slurring, making sexual liaisons only a memory. His condition is so bad that the television broadcast of his February 24 speech to the Communist Party Congress was suddenly terminated after just six minutes. At this point, Brezhnev often seems incoherent, so much so that many Russians now mock him.

But they do so secretly. Brezhnev may be in poor health, but he still wields the power to make men disappear into the gulags of snowy Siberia or to vanish altogether.* After

* *Gulag* is short for *Glavnoe Upravelenie Lagerei,*

279

Brezhnev overthrew former Soviet dictator Nikita Khrushchev in 1964, sending him into house arrest on a farm outside Moscow, he made it clear that his role model was the ruthless Joseph Stalin, the World War II leader who murdered tens of millions of Russians and foreigners over the course of his brutal thirty-one-year reign.

Brezhnev is on a less extreme course. He and his KGB chief, the equally barbaric sixty-six-year-old Yuri Andropov, are fond of imprisoning dissidents and either declaring them insane or sending them to forced-labor gulags. There, the prisoners live on thin soup and hard black bread, laboring to chop down trees in temperatures as cold as seventy below zero. Soviet guards are known to shoot them on sight if they attempt to

---

or "main camp administration." Though often thought to have existed only above the Arctic Circle, in Siberia, they were located throughout the Soviet Union. These were prison, labor, and psychiatric camps designed to break the will of dissidents through torture, hard labor, and exposure to extreme cold. Sentences were determined in advance by Brezhnev's hierarchy. Trials were conducted in secret, with no chance for an appeal.

flee the barbed wire ringing their forest prisons.

Brezhnev copied the gulags from Joseph Stalin. So far, he has murdered approximately two million people in the camps. He is dedicated to Stalin's belief that communism should rule the world and that all brutality is permissible in this quest.

Sensing weakness in the West, Leonid Brezhnev has sent Soviet troops into Vietnam, Egypt, and Afghanistan and to the Chinese border — and those are just the nations where these forces are in the open. Soviet troops can also be found hidden within Angola, Cuba, Central America, and a host of smaller nations in which Brezhnev plots to spread global domination. Wherever the Soviets go, atrocities follow. The body count extends far beyond military intrusions. In Afghanistan, children are routinely maimed, mutilated, and murdered by a nefarious device known as the "butterfly" mine. Dropped by Soviet helicopters, millions of these explosive devices flutter to earth like small insects. But when a child tries to capture one of these delicate figures, the liquid explosive inside detonates, instantly severing their hands.

Ronald Reagan knows all this and despises the Communist leadership. He also understands he has four, perhaps eight, years to implement his strategy to reduce the Soviet threat. Brezhnev is intent on maintaining power for as long as he lives. He has marginalized his political rivals, keeping them on the fringes of power. For example, a fifty-year-old up-and-comer named Mikhail Gorbachev has just been named a voting member of the Soviet Politburo but is limited to a role in the Secretariat for Agriculture.

Brezhnev "has given his regime such strength and stability that a move to oust him, short of his physical incapacitation, seems almost inconceivable," the *New York Times* reports.

But the Soviet boss knows he must stay strong to maintain power. Now deeply angered by Ronald Reagan's comments to Walter Cronkite, Brezhnev feels his lighthearted manner vanish. He furiously dictates a nine-page personal letter to Reagan. "The Soviet Union has not sought, and does not seek superiority," he seethes. "But neither will we permit such superiority to be established over us. Such attempts, as well as attempts to talk to us from a position of strength, are absolutely futile . . . to attempt to win in the arms race, to count on victory in an atomic war — would be dangerous madness."

Ronald Reagan receives Brezhnev's letter at the White House on March 6. It is a Friday, and he is looking forward to a weekend at the Camp David presidential retreat for a dose of the outdoors. He knows Brezhnev, having met him at Richard Nixon's home in San Clemente, California, years ago, when he was still governor of California. World peace is contingent upon Reagan finding some way to relate to his Soviet counterpart. It is a delicate thing, to know that the fate of the world hangs on your next action.

"I didn't have much faith in Communists or put much stock in their word," Reagan will later write. "Still, it was dangerous to continue the East-West nuclear standoff forever, and I decided that if the Russians wouldn't take the first step, I should."

As he so often does in moments like these, Reagan consults with his advisers. This time, he turns to Secretary of State Alexander Haig, who has been insisting since the inauguration that he be given a more vital role in foreign affairs. Speaking in the Oval Office, he suggests to Haig that it might be good for Reagan himself to write Brezhnev a personal letter in reply.

But Haig is appalled. He knows the Soviets well from his years in the military as NATO commander, during which he often squared off against the Soviet-led Warsaw Pact allies. In Haig's estimation, Brezhnev's letter is typical Soviet rhetoric. He suggests that Reagan allow *him* to draft the return letter.

Ronald Reagan defers to Haig. He considers his secretary of state his chief adviser on foreign affairs. Nineteen days later, on March 25, Haig sends his draft of the letter to the White House.

That date is notable because it is the same day that John Hinckley is dropped off at the airport in Denver by his mother. Also on that Wednesday, Ronald Reagan flies by helicopter to Quantico for an afternoon of horseback riding.

"It felt great," Reagan writes in his journal that evening. "We should do this often."*

As he has done so frequently over the years, Reagan uses the time astride the small brown mare to sort out his thoughts. Haig

---

* Reagan begins keeping a journal on the very first day of his presidency. He will not miss a single entry over the course of his administration. Several days after the incident, he even took the time to write about the day he was shot.

has been a nettlesome presence in the White House, constantly wheedling power where he can find it, often at the expense of Vice President George Bush. The letter that Haig has drafted reflects that temerity. Reagan considers Haig's words inflammatory and not at all diplomatic.

The president sends the letter back to the State Department, asking for a new draft. Five days later his request is fulfilled.

But once again, it is not the letter Reagan has in mind. The date is March 30, 1981. Ronald Reagan has been in office sixty-nine days. But no letter will be written that day.

Instead, an act of pure evil intervenes.

19

Park Central Hotel
Washington, DC
March 30, 1981
9:00 A.M.

John Hinckley is hungry. He turns off *The Today Show* in his AAA-approved budget hotel room and steps out onto the corner of Eighteenth and G Street. The sky is overcast. A light rain settles on Hinckley's well-worn beige jacket as he strolls three blocks to the K Street McDonald's. He did not sleep well last night, troubled by how to play out his Jodie Foster obsession once and for all. Money is also on his mind. Once again, Hinckley is almost broke. After spending $47 on his room last night, and then spending a dollar for breakfast, he has less than $130 to his name. This is barely enough for a ticket back home to Denver, but John Hinckley does not care. He will never return to that home again.

On his way to breakfast, Hinckley turns into the local Crown Books. He browses, looking for literature about his two favorite topics: the Beatles and political assassination.

But little interests Hinckley this morning. He leaves the bookstore, crosses the street to McDonald's, orders an Egg McMuffin, and sits down in a booth to plan his day. Unlike most Washington tourists, Hinckley does not envisage hours of sightseeing. Instead, he will either take the train to New Haven and shoot himself dead in front of Jodie Foster, or he will murder Ted Kennedy, if only to add his name to the notorious list of assassins who have stalked and killed a member of that political dynasty.

If that target is not available, he might enter the U.S. Senate chamber and try to kill as many lawmakers as possible. And there is one other scenario in Hinckley's mind: assassinating President Ronald Reagan.

No matter which of the four schemes he chooses, Hinckley has the means to pull it off. Nestled within his large suitcase back at the Park Central Hotel are his snub-nosed pistol and forty-three lethal bullets.

Hinckley sits alone in the McDonald's for an hour. He cannot make up his mind.

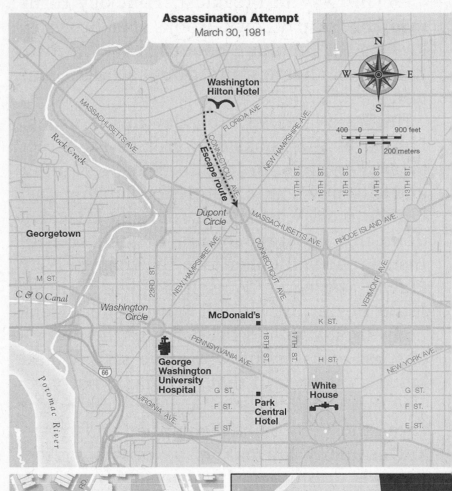

Assassination Attempt
March 30, 1981

Washington
Hilton Hotel

Escape route

N
W E
S

400 0 900 feet
0 200 meters

FLORIDA AVE.
CONNECTICUT AVE.
NEW HAMPSHIRE AVE.
17TH ST.
16TH ST.
15TH ST.
14TH ST.
13TH ST.

MASSACHUSETTS AVE.

Dupont
Circle

MASSACHUSETTS AVE.

RHODE ISLAND AVE.

Georgetown

Rock Creek

NEW HAMPSHIRE AVE.

CONNECTICUT AVE.

VERMONT AVE.

M ST.
23RD ST.

C & O Canal

Washington
Circle

McDonald's

K ST.

18TH ST.
17TH ST.

PENNSYLVANIA AVE.

George
Washington
University
Hospital

66

Potomac River

G ST.

Park
Central
Hotel

White
House

G ST.

F ST.

F ST.

VIRGINIA AVE.

NEW YORK AVE.

H ST.

E ST.

E ST.

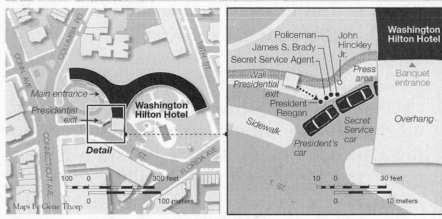

CONN. AVE.
COLUMBIA RD.
18TH ST.

Main entrance →

Presidential
exit →

Washington
Hilton Hotel

CONNECTICUT AVE.

Detail

T ST.

FLORIDA AVE.

100 0 300 feet
0 100 meters

Maps by Gene Thorp

Policeman
James S. Brady
Secret Service Agent

John
Hinckley
Jr.

Press
area

Wall
Presidential
exit
President
Reagan

President's
car

Sidewalk

Secret
Service
car

Washington
Hilton Hotel

Banquet
entrance

Overhang

T ST.

10 0 30 feet
0 10 meters

Shortly before eleven he walks back to the Park Central, stopping along the way to buy a copy of the *Washington Star.*

At the same moment, two blocks away in the White House, President Ronald Reagan is just concluding a ceremonial fourteen-minute meeting in the Cabinet Room with a group of Hispanic leaders. It has been a long morning, beginning with a breakfast for his political appointees in the Blue Room at 8:34, then a fifteen-minute session with his top advisers. Four more meetings round out the morning, each with a cast of dignitaries and administration officials. Among them is a relatively new face: James Brady. As Reagan's recently hired press secretary, Brady has the job of dealing with the media, using wit and intelligence to get the president's message to the public.

The husky Brady, a political veteran from Illinois, is forty years old. Nancy Reagan initially opposed him for the high-profile position, thinking him too old and too heavy. But Brady's sense of humor and his candor impressed the president and have made him popular with the Washington press corps.

Brady is hoping to tighten his bond with Ronald Reagan in the coming months by spending time with him. This afternoon, Reagan is due to give a short speech at the Washington Hilton, but Brady is unsure if he will attend. The president will not be taking questions from the press, and Brady's time might be better spent at the White House.

As James Brady deliberates, Ronald Reagan spends thirty minutes alone in the Oval Office, tinkering with his upcoming speech. The audience will be liberal union members who oppose his politics, but Reagan is confident he can win them over with his Irish charm.

Finally, at 11:24 a.m., Ronald Reagan slips out of the Oval Office and walks along the Colonnade, next to the Rose Garden, then takes the elevator upstairs to his private residence. There, he changes into a new blue suit before sitting down to a lunch of soup and fruit. Nancy Reagan is attending a luncheon in Georgetown, so the president dines with an old friend from California, the openly gay interior decorator Ted Graber.

As the president eats lunch, John Hinckley is taking a shower. He is deep in thought as the water beats down on him. An item on page A-4 in the *Washington Star* has caught his eye. Under the heading "President's Schedule," the piece mentions that Ronald Reagan will be giving a speech at the Washington Hilton this afternoon. This presents Hinckley with a dilemma: should he murder the president or kill himself in front of Jodie Foster? He has already decided against murdering Ted Kennedy or shooting up the Senate Chamber. Now, with his options down to just two, Hinckley soaks under the shower spray, trying to make up his mind.

"It was in the shower," he will later explain, "that I debated whether to detour to the Hilton or go up to New Haven. I was thinking, should I go over to the Hilton with my little pistol and see how close I could . . . well, see what the scene was like."

Hinckley rinses off the soap and turns off the water.

His mind is made up. He is going to the Hilton.

He towels off and gets dressed in a pair of simple trousers, a shirt, and ankle-high boots. His wallet contains $129 in cash along with two library cards, a Texas driver's license, a chess club membership, and folded magazine photos of Jodie Foster. There is no guarantee he will fire his gun this afternoon, but if he does get close enough to squeeze off a round, John Hinckley wants Jodie Foster to know he is doing it for her. He sits down at a small wooden desk and composes a letter to his beloved: "Dear Jodie," he writes. "There is a definite possibility I will be killed in my attempt to get Reagan. This is why I am writing you this letter now.

As you well know by now I love you very much. Over the past seven months I've left you dozens of poems, letters and love messages in the faint hope that you could develop an interest in me. Although we talked on the phone a couple of times, I never had the nerve to simply approach you and introduce myself. Besides my shyness, I honestly did not wish to bother you with my constant presence. I know the many messages left at your door and in your mailbox were a nuisance, but I felt that it was the most painless way for me to express my love for you.

I feel very good about the fact that you at least know my name and how I feel about you. And by hanging around your dormitory, I've come to realize that I'm the topic of more than a little conversation, however full of ridicule it may be. At least you know that I'll always love you.

Jodie, I would abandon the idea of getting Reagan in a second if I could only win your heart and live out the rest of my life with you, whether it be in total obscurity or whatever. I will admit to you that the reason I'm going ahead with this attempt now is because I cannot wait any longer to impress you. I've got to do something now to make you understand, in no uncertain terms, that I'm doing all of this for your sake!

By sacrificing my freedom and possibly my life, I hope to change your mind about me. This letter is being written only an hour before I leave for the Hilton Hotel. Jodie, I'm asking you to please look into your heart and at least give me the chance, with this historical deed, to gain your respect and love.

I love you forever — John Hinckley.

He adds the time, 12:45 p.m., to his signature and then places the letter in an envelope. This will be left behind in his suitcase for investigators should he succeed in murdering the president.

John Hinckley stands and removes the Saturday Night Special from his suitcase, along with boxes of ammunition. Several types of bullets soon litter his bedspread.

Hinckley has the choice of normal, round-nosed bullets or six rounds of an especially brutal bullet designed to blow a hole in the target by exploding on impact, spewing hot shrapnel.

Appropriately, these bullets are known as "Devastators."

He chooses them.

Armed and dangerous, Hinckley then takes a cab for the short ride to the Washington Hilton. He is nervous and has to urinate, so he asks the driver to stop at the Holiday Inn across the street. Hinckley uses the restroom and then hurries back to the entrance of the Hilton. A small crowd of seven journalists and a dozen eager spectators await Ronald Reagan's arrival. A padded black rope has been hung across the sidewalk by hotel security to keep the crowd a safe distance from the president.

Pistol snug in his jacket pocket, John Hinckley joins the crowd.

The time is 1:46 p.m.

At almost the exact same time, Ronald Reagan and his fifteen-vehicle motorcade depart the White House for the Hilton. Reagan's 1972 Lincoln Continental, with its backward-opening "suicide doors," is nicknamed Stagecoach. The president, whose Secret Service code name is Rawhide, a reference to the Westerns he loves, rides in the backseat with Secretary of Labor Raymond Donovan.

Trailing behind are several limousines carrying members of the White House staff; the president's personal physician, Dr. Daniel Ruge; and a bevy of Secret Service agents. It is a 1.3-mile drive to the Hilton.

Press secretary James Brady is also in the caravan. At the last moment he decided to make the trip in order to hear what Reagan will say.

At 1:51 p.m., the presidential motorcade arrives at the Hilton.

John Hinckley stands in the crowd of spectators behind the security rope, watching the motorcade approach. The main entrance of the Hilton is behind him. The president will not enter through this door. Instead, he will use the canopy-covered VIP entrance just forty feet away.

The assassin feels an unlikely burst of excitement at the prospect of seeing Reagan in person. Hinckley pats the pistol in his right pocket.* Ample time at the rifle range

* A button featuring the image of his hero John Lennon is in his left pocket. Lennon was shot dead

295

has prepared him for what is to come. He knows the .22-caliber Rohm must be fired at close range for peak accuracy, and the spot where he now stands is well within the pistol's optimal range of ninety feet.

Hinckley surveys the scene, seeing ABC newsman Sam Donaldson, among others. More than two dozen Secret Service agents stand ready to protect the president. Hotel security and Washington police also crowd around the Hilton, including two police officers facing the crowd on the other side of the security rope. Hinckley notices that there are some Secret Service agents on

---

by an assassin just four months previously. Hinckley attended a vigil for Lennon shortly afterward. His father, Jack Hinckley, was actively involved in a Christian relief organization known as World Vision during the mid-1970s. Some believe the global missionary group was engaged in espionage on behalf of the U.S. government. The Catholic human rights group Pax Christi accused World Vision of being "a Trojan horse for U.S. foreign policy." The fact that Lennon's assassin, Mark David Chapman, also worked for World Vision has led some to suggest a link between the two shootings. However, a link between the two assassination attempts and World Vision has never been proven.

nearby rooftops.

Suddenly, President Reagan's limousine glides past the security rope and comes to a halt just outside the VIP entrance. An agent steps out the front passenger door and hustles to open Reagan's door on the right rear side of the vehicle. Quickly, the president emerges into the afternoon drizzle, taking a moment to wave to the crowd.

DC police officers Herbert Granger and Thomas Delahanty are working the security rope and should be facing toward the crowd, looking for signs of trouble. Instead, they crane their necks to the left to see the president.

This is the perfect time for John Hinckley to shoot.

But he does not. Hesitating, he responds to the president's wave with a wave of his own. It is not an assassin's kiss but rather the goofball motion of a confused man.

"He was looking right at me and I waved back," Hinckley will recall. "I was kind of startled."

In the blink of an eye, Reagan is inside the building.

The time is 2:02 p.m. The president is introduced by Robert A. Georgine, the forty-eight-year-old head of the AFL-CIO's Building and Construction Trades Department. Reagan bounds onto the stage to the strains of "Hail to the Chief" and then launches into his speech. As always, the nearsighted Reagan has removed one contact lens, which will allow him to read the printed text with one eye while scanning the crowd with the other.

Ronald Reagan enjoys public speaking. It comes easily to him. He begins his speech, as usual, with a joke.

John Hinckley hears laughter coming from the ballroom. He has left the security rope to step inside the Hilton and wander around the lobby. "Should I? Should I?" he asks himself repeatedly, feeling the heft of the Saturday Night Special in his pocket. He is having second thoughts about killing Ronald Reagan. If he were to leave right now and go back to his hotel room, nobody would be the wiser. He could burn his letter to Jodie Foster and slide the .22-caliber back into his luggage. Rather than die in a hail of Secret Service bullets or spend the rest of his life in prison, John Hinckley could simply walk away. "I just wasn't that desperate. I just wasn't that desperate to act," he will later state. "Also, it was raining. And I wasn't going to stand around in the rain."

Hinckley makes up his mind: he will go back to the spectator area and wait. If Reagan does not appear in ten minutes, Hinckley tells himself, he will leave.

The time is 2:19 p.m. Ronald Reagan has five minutes left in his speech.

Meanwhile, less than two miles away, Nancy Reagan is lunching at the Georgetown home of Michael Ainslie. The president of the National Trust for Historic Preservation is hosting the First Lady and the wives of several Cabinet members after a brief morning tour of the Phillips Collection museum of art.

But at 2:20 p.m., Nancy Reagan suddenly tells Secret Service agent George Opfer she is not feeling well. It's nothing specific, just a general feeling of anxiety. The worried First Lady says her good-byes and is driven back to the White House.

John Hinckley is back in the spectator area outside the Hilton. He works his way to the very front of the crowd, so that the black rope presses against his belly and his right shoulder is against the hotel's façade. Three Washington police officers stand on the other side of the rope, facing him. Hinckley later remembers that they, as well as Secret Service agents, turned away from the crowd when President Reagan appeared.

The would-be assassin notices immediately that the Secret Service has moved Ronald Reagan's limousine to facilitate an easier departure from the hotel. Rather than being parked just outside the VIP entrance, it is now standing so close to the security rope that the right rear bumper almost touches the spectator area. Ronald Reagan will enter the Lincoln not forty feet but just ten feet away from where John Hinckley now stands.

All at once, Hinckley is jostled. Newsmen are pushing to get a better position in order to ask Reagan questions. Hinckley is outraged, shouting to the other spectators that the media should not be allowed to push their way to the front of the crowd. But then it becomes clear to him that the press is providing a vital distraction.

Everyone is paying attention to the media. No one is paying attention to John Hinckley.

Ronald Reagan finishes his speech at 2:24 p.m. The applause is polite, which disappoints him, for it is not the robust ovation he was hoping to hear. "Speech not riotously received," he will later write in his diary. "Still it was successful."

As part of his daily routine, Reagan places a checkmark next to each item on his agenda once it is concluded. The speech to the Building and Construction Trades Department having just earned its checkmark, the president leaves the stage and immediately follows his Secret Service escort to the car. Press secretary James Brady stands just inside the VIP door with Michael Deaver as Reagan approaches. A wave of Secret Service agents rushes past Brady, taking up their positions near the limousine. Agent Tim McCarthy is tasked with opening the right rear door for Reagan.

James Brady steps out of the VIP entrance before his boss, walking next to Deputy Chief of Staff Deaver. The president has chosen not to take questions, so Brady will now speak with the reporters himself. "Deal with them," Deaver says tersely as he heads toward the car that will ferry him back to the White House.

James Brady steps closer to the crowd, as Ronald Reagan walks out the hotel door. Secret Service agent Jerry Parr follows one step behind. It is his job to protect the president, so he now moves slightly to Reagan's left, placing his body between him and the crowd of spectators. If something were to happen within the first few steps outside the VIP door, Parr would immediately force Reagan back inside the safety of the hotel.

The first fifteen feet to the presidential limousine pass without incident. Parr is no longer thinking about pulling Reagan back. Now he is focused on moving the president forward into the car.

Agent McCarthy opens the right rear door of the limo. Like Press Secretary James Brady, McCarthy attended the University of Illinois at Urbana–Champaign. In a light blue suit, the former college football player is just shy of thirty-two. Brady stands ten feet from him, walking quickly to the security rope to meet with the press. McCarthy stands ready to close the door behind Reagan, unsure if the president will linger to wave to the crowd before getting inside the car.

The time is 2:27 p.m.

John Hinckley sees Ronald Reagan clearly. He also sees the small crowd of agents — "body men," in Secret Service parlance — accompanying the president. Hinckley notices James Brady moving toward the rope line. Things are happening very quickly.

The president raises his right arm and waves to the crowd. A woman calls out from the spectator area as if she knows him. A friendly Reagan motions in her direction. Normally the president wears a bulletproof vest when appearing in public, but the walk from the door to the car is so short that the Secret Service did not think he needed it today.

John Hinckley braces his right arm against the rough stone wall, dropping his hand into his pocket. Quickly, he pulls the gun out.

Later Hinckley testifies that his head tells him, "Put the gun away."

But he does not.

Tomorrow, the worldwide media will take one look at this loner and describe him as a deranged gunman, as if he has no idea what he is doing. But John Warnock Hinckley is a cold-blooded killer, a man who has trained himself in the art of murder.

Just as he has done so many times at the firing range, Hinckley grasps the butt of the pistol with two hands for maximum stability. He bends his knees and drops into a shooter's crouch, then extends both arms and pulls the trigger.

The first bullet hits James Brady square in the head, just above the left eye. He falls face-first to the sidewalk, his blood dripping through a sidewalk grate.

The second shot strikes Washington Metro police officer Thomas K. Delahanty in the neck, ricocheting off his spine and lodging against the spinal column. He falls to the ground in agony, screaming.

The third shot goes wild, hitting no one.

The fourth shot strikes Secret Service agent Tim McCarthy in the torso. He, too, falls to the sidewalk, seriously wounded, a bullet lodged in his liver.

The fifth shot bounces off the limousine.

The sixth also hits the Lincoln, but ricochets — piercing Ronald Reagan's body under his left arm. The bullet enters his lung, coming to rest just one inch from his heart.

The president of the United States staggers.

It takes just 1.7 seconds for Hinckley to fire all six Devastators.

The assassin is immediately punched in the head by a nearby spectator, then gang-tackled by the crowd. Hinckley is buried beneath several hundred pounds of angry citizens as Secret Service agents try to take him alive. Ironically, their job is to now protect Hinckley with the same vigor they devote to protecting the president.

John Hinckley Jr. being tackled by Secret Service agents and other onlookers after his attempt to assassinate Ronald Reagan, March 30, 1981

As Hinckley is subdued, three men are fighting for their lives.

One of them is Ronald Wilson Reagan.

At the sound of the first bullet, agent Jerry Parr grabs Reagan by the waist, shoving him hard into the back of the limo. The two men land in a heap, with Parr on top. As Reagan's face hits the armrest dividing the backseat, an intense wave of pain shoots through his body.

"Jerry," he cries. "Get off. I think you broke one of my ribs." The president is angry, believing Parr was unnecessarily rough.

Parr is not interested in delicacy. He needs to get the president to safety immediately. Long ago, as a boy, it was the 1939 Ronald Reagan movie *Code of the Secret Service* that inspired Parr to become an agent. Now, through a brutal coincidence, Jerry Parr has become the most important person in Reagan's life. "White House," he barks at Agent Drew Unrue, who sits at the wheel. "Let's get out of here! Haul ass!"

Parr climbs off the president. Neither man knows that Ronald Reagan has been shot. But as Reagan tries to sit up, he is "almost paralyzed by pain." He coughs hard, sending a stream of bright red blood onto his hand.

"You not only broke a rib," he tells Parr as the presidential limousine races to the safety of the White House, "I think the rib punctured my lung."

"Were you hit?" asks a concerned Parr.

"No, I don't think so."

Parr runs his hands over the president's shoulders, chest, and head. He sees no sign of blood. Reagan can barely sit up, his face ashen. He begins pressing his left arm against his chest as if having a heart attack. Reagan tastes blood and tells Parr that he might have also cut his mouth. The agent looks closely, seeing that the bright red blood on Reagan's lips contains numerous air bubbles, which is the sign of a lung injury.

"I think we should go to the hospital," Parr tells Reagan.

"Okay," Reagan answers, still believing that Parr broke his rib.

At the same time, in the third-floor White House solarium, Secret Service agent Opfer calmly enters the room and interrupts Nancy Reagan's conversation with the White House's chief usher. "There was a shooting," Opfer informs the First Lady. "The president is going to the hospital."

Immediately distraught, Nancy Reagan is led out of the White House. Her Secret Service code name is Rainbow, in reference to the many colors of her fiery personality. But there is no evidence of that on display right now. She is quiet and terrified. A car is brought around, and Nancy's frustration intensifies as the two-limousine motorcade gets caught in Washington gridlock on its ten-block journey. "I'm going to get out and walk," she yells. "I need to walk. I have to get there."

Traffic begins to flow, and fifteen minutes after leaving the White House, Nancy Reagan's limousine pulls up to the George

Washington University Hospital. As soon as the vehicle stops at the emergency entrance of the gray cinder-block building, she sprints toward the emergency room. Waiting at the door is Deputy Chief of Staff Mike Deaver.

"He's been hit," Deaver tells her.

"But they told me he wasn't hit," replies a shocked Nancy Reagan. "I want to see my husband," she pleads.

It takes Ronald Reagan's limousine four minutes to get to the hospital. He walks through the front door under his own power, then passes out and collapses hard to the floor. He is immediately transported to the emergency room. "I feel so bad," Ronald Reagan tells the paramedic, who quickly begins cutting the clothes off the president's body. "I feel really awful. I can't breathe."

This is the first indication that something is very wrong with Ronald Reagan. At first, doctors believe Reagan may die. Now an attempt to take his blood pressure has not yielded a systolic reading, meaning that his heart is barely pumping.

All around Reagan, the emergency room is a frantic scene of doctors, nurses, and well-armed Secret Service agents. Dr. Joseph Giordano, a surgeon who heads the hospital's trauma team, is inserting a clear plastic chest tube into Reagan, hoping to drain the blood from his chest cavity. "This better go well," Giordano tells himself as he slices open the president's skin.

"He was seriously injured," Giordano will later remember. "He was close to dying."

Ronald Reagan is a seventy-year-old man who has just suffered a devastating trauma. Not only was he shot, but he was thrown bodily into a car, and his head slammed hard into an armrest. His body may not have the ability to endure much more.

Reagan is conscious throughout the trauma procedure. Once he is stabilized, the next step will be surgery to remove the bullet. Spotting Jerry Parr just before being wheeled to the operating room, Reagan shows the first signs that he might make it: "I hope they're all Republicans," he tells the Secret Service agent who saved his life less than thirty minutes ago.

"Mr. President," Dr. Giordano, a lifelong Democrat, tells Reagan, "today we are all Republicans."

A pained but lucid Ronald Reagan is being prepped for surgery. Lying on the gurney, he looks up to find Nancy Reagan gazing down at him. She is unsteady. Blood loss has made her husband's skin the palest white she has ever seen. A nurse removes the president's oxygen mask from his mouth. "Honey," he tells her, hoping that a joke will erase the fear from her face, "I forgot to duck."

Nancy fights tears as she bends down to kiss him. "Please don't try to talk," she whispers.

Later, Nancy will remember this moment with sadness and fear. "I saw him lying naked, with strangers looking down at his naked body and watching the life ebb from him, and as a doctor's daughter I knew that he was dying," she will recount to her friends.

But Ronald Reagan is experiencing another reaction. He will later write of the joy this moment gives him. "Seeing Nancy in the hospital gave me an enormous lift. As long as I live, I will never forget the thought that rushed into my head as I looked up into her face. Later, I wrote it down in my diary: 'I pray I'll never face a day when she isn't there . . . [O]f all the ways God had blessed me, giving her to me was the great-est — beyond anything I can ever hope to deserve."

Reagan is wheeled into surgery. Nancy

clings to the bed's handrail the whole while, walking with the team of doctors and the now surgically gowned Secret Service agents who will accompany her husband into Operating Room Two.

"Who's minding the store?" Reagan asks Ed Meese as the gurney passes the White House counselor.

At the double doors leading into the surgery center, Nancy is told she cannot accompany her husband any farther.

The time is 3:24 p.m.

All she can do is wait.*

At 4:00 p.m., Ronald Reagan lies unconscious on the operating table. A rib spreader pulls his fifth and sixth ribs apart, allowing Dr. Ben Aaron to see clearly inside Reagan's chest. The seventh rib is indeed

* Eighteen years before, First Lady Jacqueline Kennedy suffered through the same ordeal, entering a hospital emergency room to await the outcome of surgery on her husband after JFK was shot. Jackie Kennedy first handed doctors pieces of his skull she'd retrieved from the presidential limousine, then stood patiently in a corner of the trauma room as doctors tried to revive him. Her pink suit was still drenched in the blood of her husband.

fractured, thanks to the bullet glancing off it. More troublesome is the blood filling the chest cavity. The president has lost half his total blood supply. Tubes running into Reagan's body fill him with new blood, antibiotics, and hydration fluid.

Dr. Aaron's goal is to remove the bullet from Reagan's body, but there is a big problem. While he can trace its path through the half-inch-wide hole it has left in the tissue and lung, he cannot find the location of the .22-caliber round.

Using his fingers, Aaron reaches inside the president's body and feels for the bullet, delicately working around Reagan's slowly beating heart as he does so. "I might call it quits," the surgeon says, frustrated he can find no sign of the bullet.

Frustration also reigns one mile away, at the White House.

"Who is running the government in the absence of President Reagan?" a journalist asks Deputy Press Secretary Larry Speakes on live television.

All across America, millions are glued to their TV sets as regular programming has been interrupted. A somber America awaits news about the severely wounded Ronald Reagan.

But if viewers are looking for reassurance, Speakes's words do not provide it.

"I cannot answer that question at this time," he responds.

One floor below where the press conference is taking place, members of Ronald Reagan's Cabinet huddle in the White House Situation Room, horrified at Speakes's response. Even worse, they know something that the press secretary does not: the Soviets are taking advantage of Reagan's condition by moving their submarines alarmingly close to America's East Coast. A nuclear missile could strike Washington in just eleven minutes. Secretary of Defense Caspar Weinberger has ordered America's bomber crews to go on high standby alert. Yet with the president now unconscious and Vice President George H. W. Bush in the air somewhere over Texas, no one at the White House has the direct authority to respond to the Soviet threat.★

Fearing the worst, National Security Adviser Richard Allen has ordered that the special briefcase known as "the football,"

★ Vice President George H. W. Bush was slated to give a speech in Austin, Texas. When news came that Reagan had been shot, he returned to Washington.

which contains the nuclear launch codes that could begin World War III, be brought to him. It now sits on a conference table here in the Situation Room, safely concealed beneath a small pile of papers.

Suddenly, Gen. Alexander Haig takes charge. The secretary of state, who has long sought to expand his power, appoints himself temporary president.

"The helm is right here," he declares to the startled Cabinet members. "And that means in this chair, right now, constitutionally until the vice president gets here."

Haig, an intimidating man, looks around, daring anyone to dispute him. Constitutionally, the general is incorrect. Speaker of the House Tip O'Neill should be next in line. But no one in the Situation Room cares to defy the former four-star army general who fought in Vietnam and Korea.

"How do you get to the press room?" he asks, rising from his chair.

The room goes silent. Before anyone can stop him, Haig races upstairs and barges into the press center. Knees buckling, voice cracking, and hands grasping the lectern so hard his knuckles turn white, Alexander Haig proclaims his authority to the nation on live TV.

"As of now, I am in control here in the

White House."

Nancy Reagan is not in control. She is desperately praying. She sits in the hospital chapel along with the wives of Press Secretary James Brady and Secret Service agent Tim McCarthy. All three of their husbands are currently in surgery. The women are unaware that the media will soon report that James Brady is dead.

The women are not alone in this small second-floor sanctuary. White House chief of staff James Baker kneels in prayer, while Mike Deaver and Ed Meese join the vigil. They are as close to the president as any group of advisers could be, and the wait is torturous.

Finally, at 5:25 p.m., thanks to a set of X-rays that show the bullet's location, Dr. Aaron feels the dime-size chunk of metal. The surgeon plucks the bullet from Reagan's lung with his fingertips.

"I've got it," he tells the surgical team, which includes a member of the Secret Service, who now steps forward to retrieve the bullet as evidence.

Dr. Aaron now turns his attention to the nonstop internal bleeding that still might kill Ronald Reagan.

Finally, at 6:46 p.m., an unconscious Reagan is closed up and wheeled from the operating room. The greatest crisis has passed, but danger remains.

Within an hour, Reagan is awake, though groggy. A breathing tube in his throat makes it impossible for him to talk, so he scribbles a note to his nurse. "If I'd had this much attention in Hollywood, I'd have stayed there."

Twenty miles away, at Andrews Air Force Base, the plane carrying Vice President George H. W. Bush has finally touched down on the runway. His return marks the end of Alexander Haig's self-declared three-hour reign as leader of the free world. And while Haig was legally wrong to declare himself in charge, his blunt behavior has had one positive effect: Soviet forces are backing down.

In the White House Situation Room, National Security Adviser Richard Allen breathes a sigh of relief that there will be no need to open the special briefcase containing the nuclear launch codes.

Not today, at least.*

* Haig never recovered from the public perception that he had become unglued in this time of crisis. He was fired as secretary of state fifteen

Alexander Haig briefs the press in the aftermath of the attempted assassination of Ronald Reagan.

■ ■ ■ ■

Meanwhile, John Hinckley sits in a Washington, DC, interrogation room. He complains that his wrist might be broken; there are also cuts and bruises on his face from being shoved to the concrete sidewalk. But for the most part, Hinckley is calm as Detective Eddie Myers of the Washington Metro Police Department's Homicide Divi-

months later and ran unsuccessfully for president in 1988.

sion interrogates him.

"How do you spell 'assassinate'?" Myers absentmindedly asks a fellow officer during the questioning.

"A-s-s-a-s-s-i-n-a-t-e," Hinckley answers, grinning.

The FBI has requested Hinckley be given a physical, including retrieving a sample of his pubic hair.

"Pubic hair?" the grizzled Myers asks in disbelief. "For Chrissakes. He didn't fuck Reagan, he shot him."*

It is not until morning that Ronald and Nancy Reagan are allowed to see each other again. She has spent a long night alone in the White House, sleeping at the side of his bed, hugging one of her husband's T-shirts to feel his presence. At 10:00 a.m., Nancy enters the intensive care unit with Patti and Ron Reagan, who have made the flight to Washington upon hearing of the shooting. Although Michael and Maureen Reagan have traveled to the hospital, they are not ushered in until Nancy's children have had

* The FBI asked for the physical examination as a precautionary technicality. The exam was performed by Dr. William J. Brownlee.

their moment.*

Ronald Reagan is oblivious to any sibling rivalry. He sees his family and is deeply moved. His breathing tube has been taken out, allowing him to joke and visit with Nancy and his children. He knows the shooting has changed his life forever.

"Whatever happens now I owe my life to God," he will write in his diary, "and I will try to serve him in every way I can."

* Maureen Reagan has just announced her candidacy for the U.S. Senate from California, against her father's wishes. Several weeks before the shooting, Michael Reagan was accused by California investigators of felony stock fraud. He will be cleared of the fraud charges in November. Without her father's backing, Maureen's Senate bid is ill-fated, ending when she finishes fifth in a field of thirteen candidates during the primary election. The protective Nancy Reagan sees both actions as a betrayal on the part of Reagan's children from his first marriage.

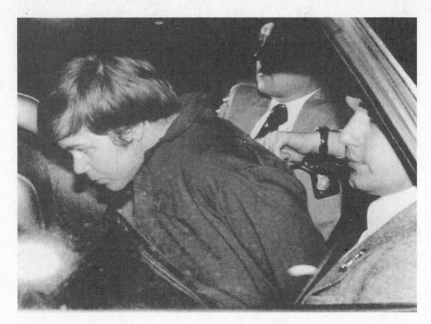

John Hinckley Jr. in police custody following the shooting of Ronald Reagan and three others, March 30, 1981

20

House of Representatives
Washington, DC
April 28, 1981
7:00 P.M.

The president who was nearly killed is bathed in applause. Members of Congress leap to their feet in bipartisan support of the man who was hit by an assassin's bullet a little more than four weeks ago. Ronald Reagan is visibly thinner and frail but is walking easily under his own power.

The roar continues as Reagan strolls to the podium and shakes hands with Vice President George Bush, who also serves as president of the Senate. Reagan greets the rotund white-haired Speaker of the House, Massachusetts congressman Tip O'Neill. The president then turns to address the Congress.

But the ovation will not end.

Reagan grins. He is genuinely thrilled by

the outpouring of warmth. His cheeks and forehead are red, thanks to hours spent enjoying the sun in the White House Solarium during his recovery. He wears a well-tailored dark blue suit with a gray-and-blue-striped tie.

Referring to the shooting, Reagan launches an unexpected joke: "You wouldn't want to talk me into an encore." Laughter erupts.

After three full minutes, the applause finally dies down, and Reagan begins his remarks. The purpose of the speech is to gain congressional approval for his economic recovery program. However, almost immediately, he detours from the details of that plan to speak from the heart.

"Mr. Speaker," Reagan begins, "distinguished Members of the Congress, honored guests, and fellow citizens: I have no words to express my appreciation for that greeting.

"I'd like to say a few words directly to all of you and to those who are watching and listening tonight, because this is the only way I know to express to all of you on behalf of Nancy and myself our appreciation for your messages and flowers and, most of all, your prayers, not only for me but for those others who fell beside me."

At the mention of her name, all eyes shift to Nancy Reagan. She sits in the front row of the congressional balcony, wearing a bright red dress. The murder attempt has rattled her so deeply that she has stricken the word *assassination* from her vocabulary. Her public approval rating is one of the worst a First Lady has ever experienced, for many consider her a controlling ice queen. But what the public does not know is that Nancy Reagan sobbed at the hospital after her husband was shot. Even now, there are moments when she completely breaks down emotionally.

Nancy knows the little things about her husband that every wife knows: that Ronald Reagan likes his eggs soft-boiled for precisely four minutes; that his favorite soup is a hardy combination of beef broth and lean ground hamburger served with a slice of French bread; and that the bumps on his left hand are caused by a hereditary disease that forces his pinky finger to curl permanently into his palm.*

Nancy Reagan is one of the few who saw

* Known as Dupuytren's contracture, this disorder is found most often in older males of northern

how pale and feeble her husband was in the hours after the shooting. For the first time, with those great dark circles under his eyes and haggard wrinkles, he looked like an old man. She saw the same frailty when he returned to the White House, walking in small, hesitant steps, his arms punctured by intravenous injections. In those days, he slept on a hospital bed in the Lincoln Bedroom, reliant on pain pills to get through the day and night. Nancy has even given up her own nightly sleeping pill to make sure that she will hear her husband should he cry out.

The First Lady's obsession with her husband's well-being extends to the public arena. Nancy Reagan now works with Deputy Chief of Staff Michael Deaver to regulate the president's schedule. Fearing that he will be overscheduled, Nancy decides whom Reagan will and will not see. This practice will continue throughout Reagan's presidency. Nancy's behavior is so hands-on that Deaver will one day state, "I always imagined that when I died there would be a phone in my coffin and at the other end of it would be Nancy Reagan."

European descent, which is why it is also known as Viking disease.

Ronald and Nancy Reagan at George Washington University Hospital during his recovery

She also watched with trepidation on April 16 as Ronald Reagan made his first public appearance since the shooting — taking a stroll around the Rose Garden before photographers. The nation marveled at his vigor and quick recovery, but Nancy knows it was all a carefully orchestrated façade, designed to reassure Americans that their seventy-year-old president was still very capable of leading the country.

On this evening, Nancy supervises her husband's meticulous pre-speech preparation. It begins with Ronald Reagan styling his hair immediately after stepping out of the shower. Reagan combs his still-wet locks forward until they hang over his eyes in long bangs. Then he applies a dab of Brylcreem in order to hold his hair in place and maintain the "wet look." Only then does the president sweep his hair back, deftly combing it into the trademark pompadour that takes years off his appearance.

"I never realized how much your face is changed when you comb your hair up in that pompadour," Michael Deaver once said to Reagan, after witnessing the hairstyling ritual. At first, with the hair hanging down on Reagan's face, Deaver was concerned that "Reagan looked eighty years old."

But with each stroke of the comb, youth magically reappears.

"Oh, yes," the president told Deaver. "It takes all the lines right out of my face."

Nancy has seen the combing ritual many times, just as she has seen countless makeup artists try to coax her husband into their chair before a big television appearance or a speech under bright lights. But harkening back to his old Hollywood days, Ronald

326

Reagan refuses to wear makeup. That red-rouged appearance he now displays on the congressional podium is all natural.

These are the peculiarities of a man who has long charted his own course, and after his near-death experience Nancy is thankful for the gift of being able to witness them at all. Not that the shooting is entirely behind the first couple. Nancy alone knows that even now, basking in the relieved applause of his political friends and rivals, Ronald Reagan is summoning all his strength and concealing a great deal of pain in order to give this address.

Nancy needs strength as well. She knows America does not like her. The press has been ruthless, disapproving of what they perceive to be her power over the president. The criticism nettles her, but Nancy endures it. She can be a vain, selfish, and even deluded woman, far too reliant on fortune-tellers. But she is also very clever. And her loyalty and love for Ronald Reagan are absolute.

The president feels Nancy's approval as his speech transitions from the personal to the patriotic. "The warmth of your words, the expression of friendship and, yes, love, meant more to us than you can ever know,"

Reagan tells America and the Congress. "You have given us a memory that we'll treasure forever. And you've provided an answer to those few voices that were raised saying that what happened was evidence that ours is a sick society."*

Reagan pauses for dramatic emphasis.

"Well, sick societies don't produce men like the two who recently returned from outer space."

The president is referring to astronauts John Young and Robert Crippen, who successfully piloted a new craft known as the Space Shuttle on its inaugural voyage into the heavens during Reagan's convalescence. *Columbia*'s journey forever changes manned space flight. What Crippen and Young accomplished is, indeed, revolutionary.[†] It

* After the shooting, it was Senator Bill Bradley (D-NJ) who proclaimed from the Senate floor that America was a "sick society."

† *Columbia* was launched April 12, 1981, twenty years to the day after Soviet cosmonaut Yuri Gagarin became the first man in space. Designed as a reusable platform, the Space Shuttle rocketed into space and landed back on Earth with wheels down, like a traditional airplane. Its versatility allowed its crew to actually live in space. The astronauts could float free of the spacecraft to

seems that the entire world has undergone a major transition in the twenty-nine days since John Hinckley opened fire.

The days of Reagan's recovery also marked the end of an era, when the last top American World War II general, Omar N. Bradley, died at the age of eighty-eight. Just one day later, on April 9, a frightening new epoch begins when the first confirmed diagnosis of a disease that will come to be known as AIDS takes place in San Francisco. And just four days previously, Reagan penned his long-delayed letter to Soviet premier Leonid Brezhnev, opening a new epoch of relations between the two nuclear superpowers.*

But the greatest changes to Reagan since

---

explore and to deliver supplies to the International Space Station. They could even make repairs of existing satellites. In the words of the National Aeronautics and Space Administration (NASA), the Space Shuttle "fundamentally changed our understanding of the universe."

* Reagan expressed a willingness to sit down at the negotiating table with Brezhnev, as the Soviet premier had demanded. However, Reagan also made it clear that "a great deal of tension in the world today is due to Soviet actions." He took Brezhnev to task for the Soviet nuclear and

the assassination attempt are more personal. In addition to allowing Nancy to assume control of his schedule, he surprised her one recent Sunday morning by suggesting they go to church. In the past, religion has been mostly politically expedient to the president. After the shooting, however, Ronald Reagan has become a man who understands his own mortality and is determined to draw closer to God.

"Sick societies," Reagan continues, "don't produce young men like Secret Service agent Tim McCarthy, who placed his body between mine and the man with the gun simply because he felt that's what his duty called for him to do."

Agent McCarthy, the recipient of John Hinckley's fourth bullet, checked out of George Washington University Hospital on April 7. He will spend the rest of his life joking that the Devastator round ruined his new woolen suit. More important, the Secret Service will soon begin showing new agents videotape of the Reagan assassina-

---

military buildup and for its ongoing attempts to use force directly and indirectly to increase its sphere of influence.

tion attempt, pointing to the way McCarthy shifted his body into a linebacker crouch, with arms up and legs slightly wider than shoulder width, to protect the president. In doing so, Tim McCarthy exposed himself to the bullet. The round spun McCarthy as it entered the right side of his abdomen, knocking him to the ground. In a split second, the .22-caliber slug hit a rib, punctured a lung, passed through his diaphragm, and came to rest in his liver. The surgery at George Washington to remove the bullet lasted a little more than an hour.

As Ronald Reagan speaks to Congress, Tim McCarthy has no regrets about what transpired. The devout Catholic father of two young children is a product of his rigorous training and is already making plans to get back on the job.

In this way, McCarthy and Ronald Reagan are two very similar Irishmen.

Ronald Reagan continues his speech: "Sick societies don't produce dedicated police officers like Tom Delahanty."

Officer Delahanty is also of Irish descent. He is considered an "exemplary officer" by his superiors, having received more than thirty commendations during his seventeen years on the force. But the Washington Metropolitan cop earned instant retirement when John Hinckley's second bullet struck him in the neck. His injuries make it impossible for him to stay on the job.

Delahanty wasn't supposed to be at the Hilton on March 30. When the forty-five-year-old Pittsburgh native reported for work that fateful morning, he assumed that he would be doing his usual job with a canine division in Washington's Third District.

But Delahanty's dog was suffering from heartworms. Kirk, as the mixed-breed canine is known, lives with Delahanty and his wife, Jane, in suburban Maryland. Delahanty chose to leave him home for the day and then accepted an assignment from the department's Special Services Division specifically to work the Hilton detail.

Secret Service protocol stipulates that an agent never turn his back on a crowd when a president is present. But Tom Delahanty and the other Metro police working the Hilton never received that training. This may have saved his life. The bullet that went into his neck as he turned to gawk at President Reagan would have hit him in the throat had he been facing the shooter.

That is small solace for Delahanty. The

bullet lodged in the lower left neck, dangerously close to his spinal column. Doctors at Washington Hospital Center initially decided against removing it, and only upon learning that the unexploded Devastator might detonate at any minute did the surgeons reverse that decision. As a safety precaution, they performed the operation wearing bulletproof vests.

However, by the time Delahanty was released from the hospital on April 10, the Devastator had left its mark. Irreversible nerve damage to his left arm means he must retire from the force. The department is also retiring Kirk, who will live out his days with Tom and Jean Delahanty.

Even in retirement, though, the incident haunts Officer Delahanty. He clearly proved himself to be far better in the protection of President Reagan than John F. Parker, the Washington Metro policeman who went drinking before President Abraham Lincoln was shot in Ford's Theater in 1865. Yet the Secret Service is now saying that Hinckley could have been stopped. All it would have taken was for Delahanty and the other Metro Police officers on the rope line to continue facing the crowd as Ronald Reagan departed the Hilton.

It is a question that will dog Thomas Delahanty the rest of his life.

Ronald Reagan pauses for emphasis. His eye contact with Congress is intense. He is firmly in control of the speech. "Sick societies don't produce . . . able and devoted public servants like Jim Brady."

As Ronald Reagan speaks his name, Press Secretary James Brady lies in a bed at George Washington University Hospital, his head resting at a twenty-degree angle to ease the pressure on his damaged brain.

Brady was pronounced dead by the media after John Hinckley shot him in the left side of the forehead. But those early reports were erroneous. Even as President Reagan speaks, Jim Brady is beginning a recovery process that will last a lifetime. The bullet that struck him was the only Devastator to explode on impact, sending shards of metal into his brain.

"The bear," as Brady calls himself, was comatose when the Secret Service brought him into George Washington University Hospital. Parts of his skull were missing, and his brain was visible. His eyes were swollen shut, and his breathing was rapid and shallow. Nerves were severed by the passage of the bullet, and a blood clot was forming on his brain.

The trauma team cut off Brady's blue business suit and stashed it in a plastic bag beneath the gurney. A catheter was installed, as were intravenous lines to replenish fluid and blood. But it appeared to be all for naught. James Brady's brain was swelling dramatically, squeezing the brain stem out through the bottom of the skull.

But Brady was in luck. He is right-handed, and while the bullet destroyed those portions of the brain that govern left-handed function, it spared those areas specific to right-handed behavior. He was also shot at a time of day when the hospital was at full staff, including a brain surgeon, allowing him to receive immediate assistance.

Within ten minutes, the trauma team stabilized Brady's condition.

But at 5:13 p.m., as word of Brady's grave condition leaked, Dan Rather of CBS News told America, "It is now confirmed that Jim Brady has died."

This was news to Sarah Brady, who was sitting with a social worker outside the emergency room.

It was also news to Dr. Arthur Kobrine, who was leading the surgical team then removing pieces of Brady's skull to relieve pressure on the brain.

Remarkably, the operation was a success. And though James Brady was still suffering in the hospital, he was alive. Amazingly, he will eventually recover a great portion of his brain function.

James Brady, the fourth Irish American shot by Hinckley, is also now forcibly retired. For the rest of the Reagan administration, the person taking his place will always be known as "acting" press secretary, out of respect for Brady.

Ronald Reagan is almost finished. "Sick societies don't make people like us so proud to be Americans and so very proud of our fellow citizens."

With those words, Reagan publicly puts the assassination behind him.

"Now, let's talk about getting spending and inflation under control and cutting your tax rates."

Three months later, standing in the Rose Garden at 10:55 on a sultry Washington summer morning, Ronald Reagan shows that he has rebounded from the shooting — and is not a man to be taken lightly.

"This morning at 7 a.m.," the president tells reporters, "the union representing those who man America's air traffic control facilities called a strike. This was the culmination of seven months of negotiations between the Federal Aviation Administration and the union. At one point in these negotiations agreement was reached and signed by both sides, granting a $40 million increase in salaries and benefits. This is twice what other government employees can expect. It was granted in recognition of the difficulties inherent in the work these people perform. Now, however, the union demands are 17 times what had been agreed to — $681 million. This would impose a tax burden on their fellow citizens which is unacceptable."

In Moscow, the Soviet leadership is watching this speech very carefully, even though it is a domestic matter. They are still unconvinced of Ronald Reagan's toughness. They do not know what sort of man he truly is. He may have survived an assassination attempt, but until now his leadership has not been tested by political crisis.

Shortly after Reagan won the election, the leadership of the Professional Air Traffic Controllers Organization demanded a 100 percent pay increase. These federal employees are not just responsible for the safety of America's skies but are also vital to national security, thanks to the military jets that rely on their guidance. PATCO was the rare union, along with the Teamsters, that supported Reagan during the election, and he sympathizes with their pay request. But it is too much. Such an enormous raise at a time when he is committed to cutting taxes is impossible.

So Reagan delivers an ultimatum: "If they do not report for work within 48 hours, they have forfeited their jobs and will be terminated."

A total of thirteen thousand air traffic controllers are now on strike. Their goal is to bring America to its knees, forcing Reagan to surrender. The threat of a major air disaster looms, an event that could destroy public faith in the president.

This is what the Soviets are watching so closely. If Reagan backs down, they will know how to negotiate with him in the future.

Understanding he is being personally challenged, Reagan is furious at the union. It has crossed the line. He may appear affable and easygoing, but he has a long history of holding tight to his convictions. In his mind, there can be no backing down. As he tells Secretary of Transportation Drew Lewis, quoting the words of his presidential idol, Calvin Coolidge, "There is no right to strike against the public safety, by anybody, anywhere, at any time."

In defiance of Reagan, more than eleven thousand air traffic controllers ignore his warning and continue to walk the picket lines. Forty-four hours later, Reagan makes good on his promise.

They are fired.

All of them.

"I'm sorry," Reagan tells the press. "I'm sorry for them. I certainly take no joy out of this."

Later, Reagan will reflect on this day with a sense of justification: "I think it convinced people who thought otherwise that I meant what I said."

Especially the Soviets.

George Shultz, who will one day serve as Reagan's secretary of state, will call this "the most important foreign policy decision Reagan has ever made."

The brutal firings send a signal worldwide: Ronald Reagan is back, and he is just getting started.

21

House of Commons
London, England
April 3, 1982
11:19 A.M.

Margaret Thatcher is terrified. Heart racing, but appearing calm on the outside, the British prime minister rises to speak. She is dressed immaculately, in a dark-blue suit accompanied by her trademark pearl necklace and earrings. Thatcher's reddish-brown hair, held in place by copious amounts of hair spray, rises several inches off her forehead and rings her face like a lion's mane. French president François Mitterrand likes to say that Thatcher has "the eyes of Caligula and the mouth of Marilyn Monroe," in reference to her cunning and her offbeat look. Those traits are very much in evidence today.

Mrs. Thatcher leans forward, her weak chin and blue eyes on full display. For the first times in fifteen years, Parliament is meeting on Saturday. Both sides of the chamber are filled, the elected members sitting comfortably on benches padded in green leather. They have come to debate whether Britain will go to war. But there is another issue at stake today, one that few in this room will say out loud: Margaret Thatcher's political career could be all but over.

"We are here," Thatcher begins, "because for the first time in many years, British sovereign territory has been invaded by a foreign power."

And it is all her fault.

Just yesterday, the Falklands, a collection of mountainous, windswept islands in the South Atlantic that Britain has controlled for nearly 150 years, were invaded by hundreds of Argentine commandos, infantry, and armored vehicles. Margaret Thatcher knew the Argentine military government had been rattling its sabers over the Falklands to deflect the public's attention from the country's wretched economy. But she did not take the threat seriously, believing the islands insignificant and of no military value.

"I thought that they would be so absurd and ridiculous to invade the Falklands that

I did not think it would happen," she will later tell a board of inquiry, adding that when she realized the invasion was imminent, "it was the worst, I think, moment of my life."*

Eight thousand miles away from London, the British Union Jack no longer snaps in the South Atlantic wind. It has now been replaced by the blue-and-white Argentine triband. In response, patriotic outrage seethes on the streets of Britain, almost all of it directed at Thatcher. In desperation, the Iron Lady has reached out to Ronald Reagan, asking the United States to help Britain retake the Falklands. But her fellow world leader and ideological soul mate is refusing. In fact, Reagan even suggests that Great Britain relinquish its claims to the Falklands, seeing the islands as a vestige of Britain's colonial past.

But Reagan is being shortsighted. This is about more than the Falkland Islands. This is about salvaging national pride at a time when Britain's global status is sinking and when its "special relationship" with the

* The Argentines call the islands the Malvinas and have laid claim to them since the nineteenth century, protesting British occupation multiple times since.

United States is overwhelmingly lopsided in America's favor. To allow a nation such as Argentina, and its arrogant military ruler, General Leopoldo Galtieri, to dictate terms is unthinkable to the British population.

No, this is a time for war, even if Margaret Thatcher and Great Britain must go it alone.

Thatcher has been prime minister for almost three years, and her conservative policies are fast losing popularity. The daughter of a grocer seems to have forgotten her humble beginnings.* Her greatest success has been in cutting taxes for the rich

* Thatcher was born Margaret Roberts, in the eastern England town of Grantham. Her father, Alfred Roberts, served as town alderman, a lay minister, and mayor of Grantham, in addition to owning two grocery stores. He was accused on several occasions of groping, fondling, and taking other sexual liberties with his young female employees, which was one plot thread of a thinly veiled 1937 satirical novel of Grantham, *Rotten Borough.* Some believe these accusations were false, spread by political opponents of his daughter. Neither of Margaret Thatcher's parents lived to see her rise to prime minister. Alfred Roberts died in 1970; Thatcher's mother, Beatrice, died in 1960.

while trimming services for the poor. Up until now she has shown little interest in foreign affairs and has been a lackluster leader on both the domestic and international stages. Her nation's mood matches her dour performance. With unemployment hovering in double digits, the people of Britain are defeatist and cynical, a far cry from the plucky can-do spirit that buoyed Great Britain in World War II. Opinion polls show that if an election were held today, Margaret Thatcher would lose to her liberal opponents in a rout.

Yet Thatcher has no intention of altering her policies. "This lady's not for turning," she has publicly announced. "People are prepared to put up with sacrifices if they know those sacrifices are the foundation of future prosperity."

British press secretary Bernard Ingham would later describe Thatcher as "macho in a man's world, determined to work men under the table; fierce in argument, asking no quarter and giving none; in the back row when tact was handed out; impetuous; secretive; inspirational, and utterly dedicated, with a constitution as tough as old boots."

Now that constitution will be sorely tested. On the surface, Margaret Thatcher appears ill suited to lead Great Britain into battle. But lead she must.

With little political opposition, the Iron Lady launches a most audacious scheme to get the Falklands back. She orders the head of the navy, Admiral of the Fleet Sir Henry Leach, to prepare an attack.* Within a day, an armada of British warships will set sail for the Falklands.

Four days after Margaret Thatcher's combat force sets sail from southern England, Ronald Reagan tiptoes into the Caribbean Sea. American warships are anchored offshore. The aquamarine ocean in Barbados is churning, with waves crashing onto the beach. Reagan begins to swim, though cautiously, knowing that he is not at full strength. It has been almost a year to the day since his release from the hospital after the assassination attempt. Part of Reagan's fitness regime now includes weight-

* Shortly after the crisis began, Leach insisted that Thatcher back a swift counterattack. "If we do not," Leach explained to the prime minister, "or if we pussyfoot in our actions and do not achieve complete success, in another few months we shall be living in a different country whose words count for little." Thatcher agreed.

lifting and stretching, and as he emerges from the surf after the brief swim, he is proud of the five pounds of muscle he has added to his upper body.

There are indications, however, that Ronald Reagan's health is not what it used to be. Reporters noted earlier in the week that he was completely exhausted by just two days of meetings with Caribbean leaders. And while Reagan made a point of venturing into the water for his swim, aware that photographers down the beach were capturing the moment, his vigorous session of backstroke and freestyle alongside his Secret Service bodyguard was brief.

Ronald Reagan walks up the white sand to where Nancy sits with their hostess, former Hollywood actress Claudette Colbert.* Nancy wears a strapless green-and-

---

* The French-born Colbert was born Emilie Chauchoin. She is best known for her role opposite Clark Gable in the 1934 comedy, *It Happened One Night,* for which she won the Best Actress Oscar. A staunch conservative Republican, Colbert died at Bellerive on Barbados on July 30, 1996. She had lived there alone ever since her husband of thirty-two years, a California surgeon named Joel Pressman, passed away in 1968 at the age of sixty-seven.

black bathing suit with a straw hat, while Colbert is clad in a white beach outfit. The actress did her own swim this morning, preferring thirty minutes of backstroke in the pool at the estate she has named Bellerive. *National Review* editor William F. Buckley Jr. and his wife, Pat, have joined Colbert and the Reagans for lunch.

Despite the state of world affairs, the president considers this a day off. He and Nancy flew to Barbados on official business, but the weekend is to be a time of sun and relaxation. Their get-together with Colbert and the Buckleys will stretch from just past noon until almost midnight. First, a cocktail hour, and then a dinner of curried chicken in Colbert's turquoise-colored dining room. Later, the Reagans will return to a private residence six miles away to sleep.

Yet world matters do not simply vanish because Reagan is in the mood to relax. Those warships anchored within view of Colbert's two-story villa are American navy communications ships, along with a hospital vessel standing by to treat Reagan should something once again go horribly wrong. Secretary of State Alexander Haig is currently in London, meeting with Margaret Thatcher about the Falklands, and Reagan is waiting on a report. While pretending to be neutral, the president is a firm backer of the British and has little sympathy for the Argentine dictator Galtieri, whom he considers a drunk. However, Reagan does believe the Argentine leader to be an ally in the war against communism. Evidence of this can be found in Argentina's military and financial support for a group known as the Contras, who are currently fighting the Marxist regime in Nicaragua. Since 1979 the United States has also backed the Contras. It is a policy that will soon lead to the greatest scandal of Reagan's presidency.

But there is another reason Reagan is adopting a tone of neutrality in the Falklands situation. The Soviet Union is courting Galtieri by threatening to join Argentina in the conflict against the British. Reagan does not want this to happen, so he is cautious in his public statements.

Secretary of State Haig's report from London is flashed to the White House Situation Room shortly after the Reagans finish lunch in Barbados. "The Prime Minister has the bit in her teeth, owing to the politics of a unified nation and an angry parliament," Haig reports. "She is clearly prepared to use force."

Reagan spends part of the afternoon thinking of his response. He finally writes back to Haig just before dusk. The larger problem facing the president is not the Falklands crisis but that he is still in the process of formulating his own foreign policy. In his one year in office there have been stirrings of unrest in Poland, delicate communiqués with the Soviet leadership, and an escalating crisis between Israel and Lebanon that now threatens to blossom into full-scale war.

"The report of your discussions in London makes clear how difficult it will be to foster a compromise that gives Maggie enough to carry on, and at the same time meets the test of 'equity' with our Latin neighbors," Reagan responds to Haig. "There isn't much room for maneuver in the British position."

Then, knowing his words mean war, Ronald Reagan gets dressed for happy hour.

On April 25, less than three weeks after sailing from England, British Special Forces and Royal Marines retake South Georgia Island.* The weather is terrible, a combina-

* First explored in 1775 by British sea captain James Cook, South Georgia was named for King George III and has been a British protectorate ever since. The remote island earned lasting fame

tion of force-ten gales and driving snow. Two British helicopters crash while attempting to rescue a group of commandos stranded on a glacier in the severe weather, and initial reports back to London indicate the loss of seventeen British soldiers. Thatcher weeps at the news, only to be told hours later that all the men survived. South Georgia Island is taken without a single casualty. "Rejoice!" she urges the citizens of Great Britain as the news breaks. "Just rejoice!"

But the Argentines are resolute. They still hold the islands' main city, Stanley, even as a full-scale British invasion looms. Argentine president Galtieri's nation, like Great Britain, is engulfed in patriotic fervor. Galtieri, the silver-haired former combat engineer, refuses to back down. He's been in office just four months, and this test of

---

in 1916, when Antarctic explorer Ernest Shackleton's ship *Endurance* was crushed by ice and he saved the lives of his crew by piloting a small boat across the Southern Ocean to the safety of a South Georgia Island whaling port. After his death in 1922, Shackleton was buried on South Georgia Island. Somewhat poignantly, one of the British vessels involved in retaking the island in 1982 is a modern vessel also christened *Endurance*.

his administration will be either his greatest triumph or his political undoing.

On April 30 the British declare a "total exclusion zone" around the Falklands. Any vessel found within a two-hundred-nautical-mile radius around the islands will be considered a ship of war and will be subject to immediate attack. Three days later, with Margaret Thatcher's complete approval, the Argentine cruiser *General Belgrano* is sunk by a British torpedo. Its two escort vessels refuse to stay and rescue the survivors, cowardly fleeing back to the mainland. Three hundred twenty-three sailors are sent to their graves in the icy South Atlantic waters.

Two days after the *Belgrano* is sunk, Argentina gets its revenge. The HMS *Sheffield* is part of a British task force patrolling seventy miles off the Falklands. "Shiny Sheff," as it is known for its highly polished stainless-steel fittings, is a state-of-the-art Type 42 destroyer.

At 7:50 a.m. on May 4, an Argentine patrol aircraft picks up the *Sheffield* on its radar. Two hours later, a pair of Super Etendard Argentine fighter jets take off from an air force base at the tip of South America. With French-made Exocet antiship missiles affixed to the bottom of their fuselages, the

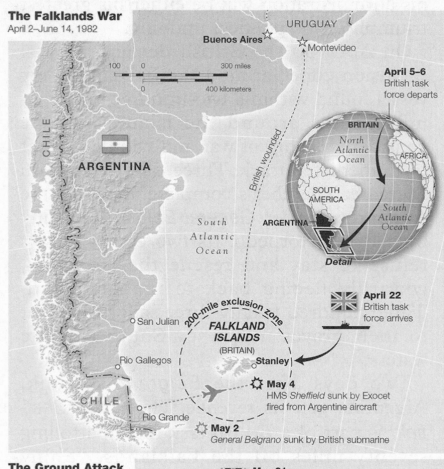

The Falklands War
April 2–June 14, 1982

100 0 300 miles

0 400 kilometers

URUGUAY

Buenos Aires ☆

☆ Montevideo

CHILE

🏳 ARGENTINA

South
Atlantic
Ocean

British wounded

April 5–6
British task
force departs

BRITAIN

North
Atlantic
Ocean

AFRICA

SOUTH
AMERICA

ARGENTINA

South
Atlantic
Ocean

Detail

200-mile exclusion zone

*FALKLAND
ISLANDS*
(BRITAIN)

○ San Julian

Rio Gallegos ○

Stanley

April 22
British task
force arrives

CHILE

Rio Grande ○

☆ **May 4**
HMS *Sheffield* sunk by Exocet
fired from Argentine aircraft

☆ **May 2**
General Belgrano sunk by British submarine

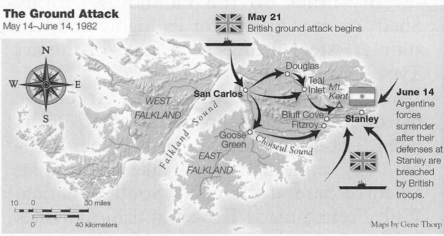

The Ground Attack
May 14–June 14, 1982

May 21
British ground attack begins

N
W E
S

Douglas

Teal
Inlet

*Mt.
Kent*

San Carlos

*WEST
FALKLAND*

Falkland Sound

Bluff Cove
Fitzroy

Stanley

June 14
Argentine
forces
surrender
after their
defenses at
Stanley are
breached
by British
troops.

Goose
Green

Choiseul Sound

*EAST
FALKLAND*

10 0 30 miles

0 40 kilometers

Maps by Gene Thorp

jets home in on the unsuspecting *Sheffield.*

Argentine pilots Lt. Armando Mayora and Lt. Cmdr. Augusto Bedacarratz use caution when approaching the ship, flying just a few feet above the ocean to avoid being detected.

Despite their stealth, radar operators on board the aircraft carrier HMS *Invincible* pick up the Etendards when the planes are 180 miles away. But the British fleet has undergone a number of false alarms in the past few days, thinking they see planes where none exists. The officer in charge of *Invincible*'s electronics ignores the sighting, telling his radar operators that they are "chasing rabbits." No warning is sent to *Sheffield* or any other British vessel in the vicinity.

On board the *Sheffield,* the mood is calm. The crew is not at battle stations, and the ship's officers are chatting with their superiors in London via satellite phone. The electromagnetic effects of the phone interfere with the ship's Type 965 radar, making it all but useless.

So it is that both Argentine planes fly within twelve miles of the *Sheffield* before launching their Exocets. Pilots Mayora and Bedacarratz fire their missiles and then split up to avoid detection. The Exocets' rocket propellant ignites both missiles one second after launch. The missiles drop to just six feet above the Atlantic and race toward the unsuspecting ship at seven hundred miles per hour.

"The sea was very calm," British sublieutenant Steve Iacovou will later remember. "We were looking out to sea and I thought it looked like a torpedo was on its way because the sea was shimmering and shaking."

With no time to undertake defensive measures, the crew takes cover. "Missile attack. Hit the deck!" is quickly broadcast throughout the ship.

One Exocet lands harmlessly in the sea.

The other does not.

The missile pierces the *Sheffield*'s hull on the starboard side. Quickly, a fifteen-foot hole opens up and the seawater pours in. Luckily for the men of the *Sheffield,* the missile is a dud, and the 165-kilogram warhead does not explode. However, flames from the rocket propellant ignite everything in the Exocet's path. Diesel fuel stored in the Forward Auxiliary Machine Room detonates, sending thick clouds of acrid black smoke throughout the vessel. The heat is so intense that all efforts to fight the fire are in vain. The blaze rages unabated, asphyxiating and burning all those trapped belowdecks. Amazingly, the *Sheffield* remains afloat, and the crew struggles to guide her into port. The order to abandon ship is given six days later, and the empty ship is towed into port. The *Sheffield* becomes the first British vessel sunk in combat since World War II.

"Twenty officers and ratings [enlisted men] died," the official report will read. "Some personnel, in the Galley area, were killed on impact."

This is the message that is read aloud to the House of Commons at 10:56 p.m. on May 4. Margaret Thatcher sits with her head bowed as British defense secretary John Nott tells the members of Parliament the sad news. The one thing she has feared more than any other was the loss of a ship. Now that has come to pass.

The prime minister does not reveal her emotions until she returns to 10 Downing Street, whereupon she breaks down. Margaret Thatcher weeps. Going to war was easy. But knowing that her decisions cost young men their lives, and that mothers throughout Great Britain are now learning the news that they have lost a son, is devastating. Her own boy, twenty-two-year-old Mark, and her husband, Denis, comfort

Thatcher in the sitting room at 10 Downing Street as she sobs.*

"What are you making all this fuss for?" Denis asks bluntly as the prime minister's crying continues. He is not always fond of being a politician's spouse, having suffered a nervous breakdown and abandoned his wife for two months early in her career. Fond of a large drink and a laugh, Denis was unsure of whether to divorce Margaret Thatcher or remain married to this workaholic woman with the buckteeth and frizzy hair who talks politics nonstop. In the end, he came back home, but Denis Thatcher is not one to mince words. "When there's a war on you've got to expect things to not go right all the time."

* Great Britain's version of the White House, 10 Downing Street is the official residence and workplace of the prime minister. While appearing relatively modest from the outside, it contains more than one hundred rooms and offices, along with the third-floor living quarters. Originally a collection of three houses built by Sir George Downing in 1682, it was first used for official state business in 1732 by Sir Robert Walpole and is within walking distance of the Parliament, Buckingham Palace, and Trafalgar Square.

■ ■ ■ ■

The next morning, the Iron Lady is stunned to get a message from Ronald Reagan, who once again suggests that the British consider leaving the Falklands to the Argentines. Reagan believes the conflict is not worth the price.★

Margaret Thatcher's mourning is replaced by rage. British soldiers and sailors are dying due to her decisions. Hundreds more are being wounded. In a scathing response, she makes one thing very clear: Great Britain is not backing down.

The men of the *Sheffield* will not have died in vain.

It is Memorial Day in Washington, DC. Ronald Reagan started his day at Arlington National Cemetery, in a moment of remembrance for the many Americans who lost their lives in war. Now he places a phone call to Margaret Thatcher.

"Margaret?"

"Yes, Ron?"

"Could you hear me all right?

★ Among the few countries that backed Great Britain were Ireland, New Zealand, and Argentina's antagonist neighbor, Chile.

357

"We could hear you very well. Can you hear me?"

"Yes, seems a little echo, but I guess that goes with the line we're on."

Ronald Reagan and Margaret Thatcher are speaking via the transatlantic hotline linking the White House with 10 Downing Street. It is 6:03 p.m. in Washington, close to midnight in London. Four more British ships have been sunk since the *Sheffield* went down, including her sister ship, the HMS *Coventry*. More than two hundred British servicemen have lost their lives on land and sea, but British troops have successfully retaken many parts of the Falklands. The war will not be over, however, until the British capture the capital city of Stanley.

"Could I impose and be presumptuous and give you some thoughts right now on the Falklands situation?" asks President Reagan.

"Yes, of course," Thatcher replies with a curt tone.

"I want to congratulate you on what you and your young men are doing down there. You've taken major risks and you've shown that unprovoked aggression does not pay."

Thatcher thanks the president and then listens in stony silence as Reagan puts forth a plan for a cease-fire to avoid "complete Argentinian humiliation." He hopes for a withdrawal of British troops and for peace to be maintained by a United Nations peacekeeping force. Thatcher is having none of it.

"Just supposing Alaska was invaded," she asks furiously.

"I have to say that I don't think Alaska is a similar situation."

"More or less so," Thatcher replies, not backing down an inch.

"It was always my understanding or feeling that you had in the past been prepared to offer independence to the islands."

With that, Reagan completes the last full sentence he will utter in this conversation. Despite the tone of civility, and the awareness that Great Britain is the weaker partner in their special relationship, Margaret Thatcher is uncowed by Ronald Reagan. Even as she speaks, British wounded are beginning the long journey back to Britain. Some maimed, some severely burned, they will bear the marks of the Falklands War the rest of their lives. Margaret Thatcher feels the emotional burden of their sacrifice and that of those who have fallen. She has slept little since the war began. The prime minister's official study is a short, seventeen-step walk up a staircase from her private apartment. She ascends those steps each night to listen to the BBC World News with her personal assistant, Cynthia Crawford. For the workaholic Thatcher, this is the closest she comes to an actual friendship. Crawford will remember: "We used to sit on the bedroom floor — the heating would have gone off and there was a two-bar electric fire in the bedroom — kick off our shoes and relax. . . . She had practically no sleep for three months. Just catnapping. She was so incredibly strong and determined. Not once did she flag."

After so many of these anxious nights, Margaret Thatcher has absolutely no intention of buckling under the suggestions of Ronald Reagan or any international peacekeeping body. She is not a woman fond of small talk, and her sense of humor is so dry that most people miss it. In a word, Margaret Thatcher is a serious woman.

So she lets the U.S. president know what's on her mind.

"Ron, I'm not handing over the island," Thatcher tells him. "I can't lose the lives and blood of our soldiers to hand over the islands to a contact. It's not possible." She continues: "You are surely not asking me, Ron, after we've lost some of our finest young men, you are surely not saying, that after the Argentine withdrawal, that our forces, and our administration, become immediately idle? I had to go to immense distances and mobilize half my country. I just had to go."

"Yes," says Reagan before Thatcher can cut him off.

She then launches into a long rant about Britain's territorial rights. Theirs is a friendship strong enough to endure this disagreement, so she plunges forward with abandon.*

"Margaret —" Reagan says, trying to get in a word during her tirade.

"Well —" He tries again.

"Yes —"

"Yes, well —"

"The point is this, Ron," Thatcher concludes. She has never been one to bully, unlike many politicians. However, she is relentless in making her point. "We have borne the brunt of this alone . . . we have some of our best ships lost because for seven weeks the Argentines refused to negotiate reasonable terms."

* "They disagreed over the Falklands, but that didn't hurt their friendship at all," Nancy Reagan will later comment.

"Well, Margaret, I'm sorry I intruded," Reagan says before hanging up.

"You haven't intruded at all. And I'm glad you telephoned."

Margaret Thatcher hangs up the hotline. Two weeks later, Stanley falls and Argentina surrenders. "She required guts to do it — her single greatest quality — and she deserved some cross-party support," liberal British leader David Owen will comment of the war. "Thatcher's personal resolve made all the difference between victory or defeat." Owen continued: "Thatcher would not have remained prime minister if General Galtieri's forces had not been thrown off the Falklands."

In the process, the British prime minister has emerged as a global force.

Her nation, as she has suggested, rejoices.

22

White House Oval Office
Washington, DC
April 15, 1983
9:57 A.M.

Ronald Reagan is struggling. As he presides over a mid-morning meeting of his speechwriters, the president strains to hear the words they are saying. Age is taking its toll. Weakened physically since the assassination attempt, he continues to go deaf in his right ear. His left ear is only marginally better. Reagan tries to keep this a secret, but everyone in the room is well aware that the president's hearing is impaired.

Seated in a cream-colored chair with his back to the fireplace, Reagan crosses his legs and pretends to listen as his six-person team sits on two couches in the center of the room. They are there to discuss the president's upcoming speaking engagements, but the Oval Office's poor acoustics are making it difficult for Reagan to decipher what is being said. To make matters even worse, the three men and three women often talk over one another.

Looking on silently, Reagan tries to follow the conversation by reading lips and watching body language to see if a direct question is aimed his way. The meeting is brisk and efficient, just fifteen minutes long. But during longer policy sessions with his senior advisers, Reagan has been known to grow so bored that he gives up all attempts to follow the proceedings, spending his time doodling on a yellow legal pad. This may not be normal behavior for most presidents, but the seventy-two-year-old Reagan knows he must husband his energy carefully in order to make it through the busy days.

Today, for example, began with breakfast. He dined with Nancy in the second-floor residence, eating his usual bran cereal, toast, and decaffeinated coffee. He said good-bye to Nancy with his usual gusto, pulling her to him as if they would be separated for months instead of mere hours. The president then took an elevator down to the first floor, where he was met by Secret Service agents. He then walked to the armored door of the Oval Office, via the West Wing Colonnade, where he began his workday.

After a series of morning meetings, Ronald Reagan will have a formal lunch with West German chancellor Helmut Kohl to discuss the growing Soviet threat.

By two thirty in the afternoon, his work will be done. This being a Friday, the Reagans will fly to Camp David for the weekend. But the time of their departure is always subject to change. As with all the president's travel arrangements, an astrologer living in San Francisco must first approve. Nancy Reagan keeps the Vassar-educated socialite Joan Quigley, fifty-six years old, on a three-thousand-dollar-per-month retainer secretly to provide astrological guidance. Nancy remains deeply superstitious, making sure to sleep with her head facing north, and constantly knocks on wood. But her dependence on Quigley runs much deeper. Very few members of the White House staff know that Nancy's astrologer controls much of the president's calendar.

To make sure that White House operators do not eavesdrop on their conversations, Nancy has a private phone line in the White House, and another at Camp David, connecting her directly to the stargazer. "Without her approval," Deputy Chief of

Staff Michael Deaver will one day write of Quigley, "Air Force One does not take off."

But there is one item on today's agenda so minor that Quigley has not been consulted, and Ronald Reagan's personal assistant Kathy Osborne has not typed it into the schedule. Sometime during the day, Reagan will take a moment to affix his signature to a proclamation naming April 10–16 as National Mental Health Week. The purpose is "to seek and encourage better understanding of mental disorders" and to bring "welcome hope to the mentally ill."

Eight miles away, in southeast Washington, DC, John Hinckley is finding that it pays to be mentally ill. Rather than suffer a heinous punishment for his attempted assassination of the president and near murder of three other men, Hinckley has been found not guilty of all crimes by reason of insanity. Thus, he spends his days in St. Elizabeth's Hospital, a century-old brick psychiatric facility. There, Hinckley has a soft life. He resides in a fourth-floor room, eats in the cafeteria, attends therapy sessions, shoots pool, plays his guitar, and watches TV. He can listen to any music he likes, and his hair remains long and shaggy. There are no shackles on his wrists or ankles. The only significant difference between this new life and his previous one is that Hinckley can no longer travel impulsively. His monetary woes are a thing of the past.

Shockingly, Hinckley still pines for Jodie Foster, telling the *New York Times* in a bizarre letter, "My actions of March 30, 1981 have given special meaning to my life and no amount of imprisonment or hospitalization can tarnish my historical deed. The shooting outside the Washington Hilton hotel was the greatest love offering in the history of the world. I sacrificed myself and committed the ultimate crime in hopes of winning the heart of a girl. It was an unprecedented demonstration of love. But does the American public appreciate what I've done? Does Jodie Foster appreciate what I've done?"

Hinckley continues: "I am Napoleon and she is Josephine. I am Romeo and she is Juliet. I am John Hinckley Jr. and she is Jodie Foster. The world can't touch us."

Ironically, one of the first things Ronald Reagan did when he came into office was slash federal funding for the treatment of mental illness, trimming the budget for the National Institute of Mental Health and repealing the Mental Health Systems Act of

1980. Yet, as the definition of mental impairment grows over time to include not just the insane or psychotic like John Hinckley but also those whose faculties are diminished by age, there are signs that the president himself may be sliding into this spectrum. The *New York Times* reported as early as 1980 that his "penchant for contradictory statements, forgetting names and general absent-mindedness" were considered by some to be a sign of Alzheimer's disease. This very specific form of dementia displays itself as confusion, impaired thought, and impaired speech.

In truth, Ronald Reagan can be sharp at times. Often, he spins entertaining yarns, adding dialects and jokes to his presentations. But on other occasions, the president gets lost mid-story. Sometimes he will tell a tale about some event in his life, when in fact he is confusing it with a movie role he once played. His staff is fond of saying that Reagan "has his good days and his bad days," and they know that the president tends to think more slowly in the evening than in the afternoon. In addition, Reagan has developed an "essential tremor," a slight shaking of the hands and nodding of the head. Though not a sign of brain impairment, it will grow worse with age.

Ronald Reagan has admitted to journalists that his mother died of "senility" and said that should such a condition ever affect him, he will resign the office of president of the United States.

But today, as his speechwriters rise promptly from their seats at 10:10 and file out of the Oval Office, nobody is realistically suggesting that Ronald Reagan is senile.

Or that he should resign.

Not yet.

23

White House Situation Room
Washington, DC
October 26, 1983
1:28 P.M.

Relief has arrived. Ronald Reagan wears a brand-new hearing aid, allowing him to make out the voice on the other end of the transatlantic hotline quite clearly.*

"Margaret Thatcher here."

The prime minister has excused herself from a parliamentary debate to take Reagan's call. The Iron Lady, just as Reagan's mother, will eventually live out the last dozen years of her life in a state of dementia.

But that confusion is seventeen years away.

Right now, Margaret Thatcher is completely furious.

* Reagan began using a hearing aid in his right ear in September 1983. He began wearing one in his left ear in 1985.

Yesterday, on Reagan's orders, American troops invaded the former British colony of Grenada, an island in the south Caribbean. On October 19, Marxist commandos overthrew the government, and there are fears that the new Grenadian leaders are aligned with Fidel Castro. The Cuban dictator has long sought to spread communism throughout the Western Hemisphere. Even as Reagan talks with Thatcher, there are civil wars under way in Nicaragua and El Salvador. Under the pretense that the lives of eight hundred Americans attending medical school in Grenada are at risk, eight thousand American marines, Navy SEALs, and Army Rangers have invaded the island.* Reagan's popularity among U.S. voters is soaring, and the president has bipartisan

* There is evidence that the invasion was planned long in advance of the coup. The overthrown regime was also pro-Cuban. Since 1979 the United States had sought to destabilize Grenada by discouraging U.S. tourism and offering little economic assistance. The Reagan administration escalated tensions by urging the World Bank to block funding to Grenada's government. In August 1981, U.S. troops rehearsed a mock invasion of Grenada on the Puerto Rican island of Vieques.

371

support in Congress for this bold move.

Unfortunately, Ronald Reagan never informed the Thatcher government. In fact, his advisers told Margaret Thatcher's foreign secretary there would be no attack. That information was then relayed to the British press. In the hours leading up to the American assault, Thatcher attempted to phone the president to warn him against military action but was told he was unavailable.

Ronald Reagan lied to the British, and now Thatcher wants an explanation.

"If I were there, Margaret, I'd throw my hat in the door before I came in," the president sheepishly apologizes.*

"There's no need to do that," Thatcher answers in a calm but firm voice. She knows not to antagonize the American president because there is too much at stake. Soviet president Leonid Brezhnev died almost a year ago, and since that time the Cold War has intensified. The threat level of nuclear

* Reagan is alluding to an old Irish custom of tossing a cap through a doorway before entering, to see if the visitor is welcome. It was later adapted in the American West as the habit of throwing a hat through a doorway to see if it would draw gunfire.

war between the United States and the Soviet Union, now led by former Soviet spymaster Yuri Andropov, is at its highest point in twenty years. U.S. nuclear missiles in West Germany are pointed at Moscow, even as Soviet mobile rockets in East Germany are aimed at America's allies in Europe, among them Great Britain. To combat this threat, Thatcher is currently lobbying for American Tomahawk cruise missiles to be based on her island nation. But public opinion in Britain is heavily against such a deployment. Now, at a time when the Reagan-Thatcher relationship needs to be stronger than ever to confront the new Soviet regime, the British are being treated like powerless American vassals.

"We very much regret the embarrassment caused you," says Reagan, his voice soothing, a trait learned from his radio years. "We were greatly concerned, because of a problem here — and not at your end at all — but here. We have had a nagging problem of a loose source, a leak here. At the same time we also had immediate surveillance problem [*sic*] — without their knowing it — of what was happening on Cuba to make sure that we could get ahead of them if they were moving — and indeed, they were making some tentative moves. They sent some kind of command personnel into Grenada."

"I know about sensitivity," Thatcher responds, alluding to her experience during the Falklands crisis. "The action is under way now, and we hope it will be successful."

"We're sure it is. It's going beautifully."

"Well, let's hope it's soon over, Ron, and you manage to get a democracy restored," she replies in a cold tone.

"We think the military part is going to end very shortly."

"That will be very, very good news. And if we return to democracy that will be marvelous."

"As I say, I'm very sorry for any embarrassment that we caused you."

"It was very kind of you to have rung, Ron."

"Well, my pleasure."

"I appreciate it. How is Nancy?"

"Just fine."

"Good. Give her my love."

"I shall."

"I must return to this debate in the House. It is a bit tricky." The debate, in fact, is a wholesale attack on Thatcher by her Labour Party enemies — all because of Grenada.

"All right. Go get 'em. Eat 'em alive."

"Good-bye."

President Ronald Reagan and British prime minister Margaret Thatcher share a private conversation.

■ ■ ■ ■

Ronald Reagan may have succeeded in calming Margaret Thatcher, but new problems continue to emerge all over the world. Even as U.S. forces wrest Grenada from the Marxists, the United States has fallen victim to a new form of warfare: terrorism.

It is 6:22 a.m. on October 23, 1983. This Sunday morning in Beirut, Lebanon, is quiet as the sun rises to the east of the Mediterranean Sea and the nearby Chouf Mountains. American soldiers are just waking up in their four-story barracks at the Beirut International Airport. The First Battalion, Eighth Marines, are part of a multinational peacekeeping force sent to this former "Paris of the Middle East" — a once-beautiful, cultured city now reduced to rubble after years of fighting. The antagonists are the Lebanese, Israelis, the Palestine Liberation Organization, and an Iranian-backed group known as Hezbollah. The sectarian struggle for power in Lebanon is chaotic and furious.

The U.S. Marine unit has a glorious past, having distinguished itself in combat on such famous battlefields as Guadalcanal and Saipan. But today they are not the aggressors.

Outside the barracks, a yellow Mercedes truck approaches the structure nicknamed the Beirut Hilton from a nearby access road. The truck turns into the parking lot in front of the building. At first, the vehicle appears harmless, even as it proceeds to make a single counterclockwise lap around the lot. A five-foot-high wall of concertina wire separates the truck from the marine compound. Beyond that, a six-foot wrought-iron fence also provides a barrier. Just inside that fence is a sentry shack, surrounded by sandbags, where armed marines guard the main barracks entrance.

Six months earlier, in the heart of downtown Beirut, an Iranian suicide bomber rammed a delivery truck loaded with explosives into the U.S. embassy. The blast killed sixty-three people, among them top intelligence agents.

The marine guards watch the Mercedes. They are expecting a supply truck full of fresh water this morning, so they are not on high alert. Their mission in Beirut is to help stabilize the Lebanese government after years of civil war. Several Christian and Muslim militant factions are fighting for control of Lebanon, and all see the United States as a roadblock to their success. Although the marines have engaged in several hellish firefights with armed insurgents, some so bad that the Vietnam veterans among them will claim they have never seen fighting so intense, they must maintain the pretense that firing their weapons is a last resort.

So under the rules of engagement, the sentries' weapons are unloaded this Sunday morning. In fact, they have to ask permission from their superiors if they wish to employ live ammunition.

The circling Mercedes is not, in fact, harmless. Rather, it is packed with the equivalent of twenty-one thousand pounds of dynamite. These are wrapped around butane cylinders to enhance the force of any blast.

Suddenly, without warning, the driver guns the Mercedes directly at the rolls of razor-sharp barbed wire at the compound's perimeter. The wire snaps as he blasts on through, aiming for a gate in the wrought-iron fence that has been kept open to allow vehicles to move freely. The young soldiers on guard duty frantically try to chamber rounds in their M16s — but the truck is coming too fast. Within seconds, the driver runs through the gate opening, past the sentry box, and toward the barracks lobby. One brave marine opens fire, while another throws his body in front of the vehicle — to no avail.

Then the "martyr," as Iran will one day proclaim this murderer, explodes his ordnance. An enormous fireball engulfs the barracks. A crater thirty feet wide and forty feet deep marks the site of the detonation. The entire Beirut Hilton collapses. Bodies fly through the air, some landing more than fifty yards from the building.*

It is an explosion so massive that the FBI will proclaim it to be the biggest nonnuclear bomb in history. The 241 American military killed is the worst single-day toll since the first day of the Tet Offensive, fifteen years ago. When rescue workers attempt to evacuate these wounded peacekeepers, terrorist snipers fire at them.

The violence in Beirut marks the first full-scale use of terror by Muslim factions against the United States. But it is hardly the last. Two months later, the U.S. embassy in Kuwait will be the target of a suicide-bomber attack. And six months from now, CIA Beirut station chief William Buckley will become the fourth of thirty key Americans kidnapped by Muslim extremists in Lebanon.

On March 16, 1984, the fifty-five-year-old Buckley rides the elevator from his tenth-floor Beirut apartment down to the parking garage of the Al-Manara building. It is minutes before 8:00 a.m. The career spy lives alone, and has just finished a breakfast

* A second suicide bomber strikes the nearby French military compound, killing fifty-eight French paratroopers and six civilians.

of coffee and cereal, accompanied by a recording of Dean Martin singing "Return to Me." Shackled to his wrist is a locked CIA burn bag containing top secret documents — and sandwiches he has prepared for lunch.

One floor down, a well-dressed man carrying a leather briefcase steps into the elevator, then rides wordlessly to the parking garage with Buckley. All at once, the CIA station chief feels a blow to the back of his skull. The assailant's briefcase is filled with rocks, and the American official crumples to the ground. A white Renault containing two men immediately pulls up to the elevator. Buckley is dragged into the backseat of the car, his captors sitting on top of him. The car speeds away in such a hurry that the back door is still open.

Within hours, the CIA is aware that the station chief is missing. Soon after, his captors round up his network of spies and informers within Lebanon and murder them one by one. This confirms to the CIA that Buckley was tortured, and has broken.

But it is not until May 7, almost seven weeks later, that American agents see the real horror. An anonymous videotape is delivered to the U.S. embassy in Athens, showing a naked Buckley being tortured.

Ligature marks on his wrists and neck indicate that he has been tied to a rope or chain. Analysts studying the tape note that his body is covered in puncture marks, showing that Buckley has been drugged repeatedly. CIA director William Casey will later remember of his viewing of the video. "I was close to tears. It was the most obscene thing I had ever witnessed. Bill was barely recognizable as the man I had known for years. They had done more than ruin his body. His eyes made it clear his mind had been played with. It was horrific, medieval and barbarous."

Three weeks later, another gruesome video arrives. This one is far more graphic than the last. Finally, after five more months of torture, a third and final video finds its way to the CIA. Buckley is clearly on the verge of insanity, a drooling mess uttering gibberish and rolling his eyes like a crazy man.

But his ordeal is not over. Bill Buckley must still endure almost another year of captivity before he is executed by Hezbollah. Although his Islamic jihadist captors announce the spy's death in 1985, his corpse will not be located until 1991.*

* Buckley was buried in Arlington National

■ ■ ■ ■

Ronald Reagan was powerless to help Buckley. But he exercised his power by bringing Grenada to its knees.* And while the tiny island nation may have been an easy target, Muslim extremists are not.

However, CIA station chief William Buckley does not die without consequence. Reagan will be tormented by his kidnapping and death. The result will be National Security Decision Directive 138, a bold, top secret decision to counter state-sponsored terrorism "by all legal means." Reagan affixes his signature to the directive on April 3, 1984.

But "legal means" will soon be set aside.

Cemetery with full military honors, Section 59, Lot 346.

* The United States captured Grenada at a cost of 19 American killed and 116 wounded in the seven-week war. Its primary opposition on the island came from a joint Grenadian and Cuban force, which suffered casualties of 70 dead and 417 wounded. They were aided by an additional contingent of Soviet, East German, Bulgarian, North Korean, and Libyan troops, which suffered no casualties.

Iran is currently engaged in a fierce war with its Middle East neighbor, Iraq, and has run out of military weapons. President Ronald Reagan will secretly authorize the sales of weapons to Iran, a sworn U.S. enemy and the nation responsible for killing hundreds of Americans. Reagan knows this, but he decides that liberating the American hostages is worth breaking the law. Under a plan masterminded by Marine Corps lieutenant colonel Oliver North, American funds will also be secretly funneled to the rebel Contras fighting communism in Nicaragua whom Reagan admires so much.*

* The scandal became known as Iran-Contra. The administration's actions were illegal for three reasons: the Boland Amendment of 1982 prohibited funding of the Contras beyond congressionally approved limits; the sale of arms to Iran was prohibited; and it is against U.S. national policy to pay ransom for hostages. Some thirty million dollars were transferred from Iran to the Contras. Eleven administration officials were ultimately indicted for their role in selling arms to Iran and funneling the money to the Contras, including Secretary of Defense Caspar Weinberger and CIA chief William Casey. Nobody went to prison, and George H. W. Bush pardoned many of

So it is that after three years in office, the president of the United States has had many successes: he has turned around the economy, bringing an end to the recession and reducing the level of unemployment; he has countered the Soviet threat in Europe by placing attack cruise missiles in Germany and England; and, simultaneously, he has begun urging the Soviets to join him in efforts to reduce the possibility of nuclear war through voluntary arms control.

But Ronald Reagan still faces problems all over the world. Despite his best efforts, there is growing tension with the Soviet Union. Reagan has invaded the Caribbean island of Grenada with U.S. troops. He has offended his greatest ally, Margaret Thatcher. And just a few days before that, America absorbed a horrific Muslim terrorist attack in Lebanon.

---

the perpetrators in the final days of his presidency. Although two key members of the conspiracy, U.S. Marine lieutenant colonel Oliver North and Secretary of Defense Weinberger, made it clear that Reagan knew what was happening, no charges were ever filed against the president. During the 1985–1987 investigations, Reagan's personal approval rating dropped from 67 to 46 percent but later rebounded.

And if all that isn't enough, Ronald Reagan must now begin another exhausting undertaking: getting reelected.

24

Rancho del Cielo
Santa Barbara, California
August 1, 1984
Noon

Ronald and Nancy Reagan stand before their round leather patio table under a blue California sky, gazing out at the oak-covered hills. Nancy is dressed in a cream plaid sweater vest over white denim pants. The president is even less formal in his blue jeans, boots, and open-necked cowboy shirt. The media form a tight scrum behind a rope line on the gravel parking lot in front of them, separated from the president and First Lady by less than ten feet.

This is a photo opportunity where the press isn't supposed to ask questions. Nevertheless, the president often indulges them with a response should they break protocol, though it is something Nancy and his advisers rarely allow. There is too big a risk he might slip up. Normally, the president's every public movement is stage-managed. He is given a daily set of scripted cards telling him what to say and where to stand for any formal occasion.

But today there are no cards. No notes. Just the president and the media throwing one-liners back and forth. The time for questions is limited to just five minutes. There is very little that can go wrong in such a short period of time — or so it seems.

As distasteful as it might be, Ronald Reagan knows he must talk to the media. This is an election year, and the Republican National Convention in Dallas is just three weeks away. After eight months pursuing a Rose Garden strategy, in which Nancy made sure that Reagan barely campaigned, talking to the media will be a nice little warm-up for the months of hard battle that lie ahead in his quest for reelection. The media have been exceptionally generous to him during his first term, leading editor Ben Bradlee of the *Washington Post,* the newspaper that brought down Richard Nixon during the Watergate scandal, to state, "We've been kinder to President Reagan than any president I can remember since I've been at the *Post.*"

This comment is made all the more

significant by the fact that not only has Bradlee been at the *Post* off and on since 1948, but he was also drinking buddies with President John F. Kennedy.

So Ronald Reagan is not worried about this impromptu news conference. The president is never more relaxed than when here at the ranch. Congress is not in session right now, and he and Nancy are taking advantage of the hiatus by spending two full weeks on this six-hundred-acre mountaintop property. Their ranch house is a one-hundred-year-old white Spanish adobe with faux-brick linoleum floors that Reagan laid himself. There is nothing lavish about this private retreat. It has the air of a summer camp bunkhouse, yet it restores Reagan's soul unlike any place else on earth. During his time in office, he will spend the equivalent of one full year on this mountaintop looking out over the Pacific.*

* Rancho del Cielo ("Ranch in the Sky") was originally developed in 1841 by Mexican landowner José Jésus Pico. He built the house in 1871. It remained in his family until 1941. Ronald Reagan bought the 688-acre ranch in 1974 for $527,000 from the family of Roy and Rosalie Cornelius. Their daughter, Glenda, had been Patti Reagan's roommate at boarding school. Glenda

Ronald Reagan works at the ranch, too, but guards his privacy very closely. He spends much of his time in the small living room, a private sanctuary to which not even his closest advisers are allowed regular access. Ever loyal, Reagan has filled the kitchen with GE appliances. The master bedroom is barely big enough to fit the two small twin frames pushed together to form one bed. The president is too tall for these mattresses, so a padded stool has been positioned at the end. He sleeps with his feet sticking out from under the covers, resting atop the stool.

Nevertheless, Ronald Reagan loves the place — Nancy, not so much. One popular legend is making the rounds among the press. Apparently, one day, while driving up the long, winding road from the main highway to the ranch, Nancy Reagan was whining nonstop about having to endure another vacation at the remote outpost. She would much rather be back in Los Angeles with her friends.

Cornelius was an accomplished rodeo rider, and her parents had intended for the home to be her inheritance. However, they sold the land after she was killed in a New Year's Eve head-on automobile collision.

At first Reagan put up with his wife's complaining, preferring to keep the peace. But this time, he snapped. He ordered his Secret Service driver to stop the limo. Turning to Nancy, he thundered, "Get out of this car."

Shocked, she did.

The president then commanded the driver to continue up the seven-mile road. In the rearview mirror, the Secret Service driver could see Nancy standing in the middle of nowhere, looking panicked. Finally, the president relented, ordering the driver to turn around to pick her up.

But on this afternoon, things are calm. Nancy's dominant protective streak is nowhere to be seen. The president is ready for the eight questions the press will be permitted this morning.

The first queries are softballs. Reagan fields them with ease.

Then ABC newsman Sam Donaldson strikes, posing a question about the Russians.

"Is there anything you can do to get them there?" Donaldson asks about a proposed nuclear arms meeting in Vienna, referring to the leaders of the Soviet Union.

"What?" Reagan asks, suddenly befuddled.

Donaldson smells blood.

He has been on the White House beat throughout the Reagan presidency and is no fan of the administration. He was an eyewitness to the assassination attempt, standing just five feet from John Hinckley when he pulled the trigger. Still, Donaldson feels little warmth for the president, and many members of the media share his disdain.

Donaldson doesn't even bother to speak to Reagan with a tone of civility. He is outwardly antagonistic, often shouting questions. He has publicly insulted Nancy Reagan by comparing her to a venomous snake, calling her a "smiling mamba."

Sam Donaldson is now in full confrontational mode.

"Is there anything you can do to get them to Vienna?" he bellows again.

The man who has spent his life speaking on cue, the entertainer who likes to tell a good joke, the politician who has dazzled millions with his rhetoric, has no answer.

Ronald Reagan is lost.

As journalists and television cameras record the moment, the president seems incapable of rendering an answer to Sam Donaldson.

Finally, Nancy Reagan leans over and

whispers into her husband's ear: "We're doing everything we can."

"We're doing everything we can," the president says to Sam Donaldson.*

With Nancy carefully controlling his every appearance, Ronald Reagan hits the campaign trail for real in September. The nation is riveted by his "Morning in America" commercials, which paint a patriotic picture of a country rising from the shambles Reagan inherited from Jimmy Carter. The president now enjoys a nineteen-point lead in the polls over Democratic challenger Walter Mondale, the fifty-six-year-old Minnesota native who served as Carter's vice president. At this point, Americans seem comfortable with Ronald Reagan as president. Many admire him — as a man and a patriot. They like his

* Nancy's words are picked up by microphones from the various network television cameras. Ten days later, while still at the ranch, Reagan himself will mistakenly speak into a live microphone, joking that he has outlawed Russia and that "we begin bombing in five minutes." As a result, Soviet military forces will go on war alert in preparation for an attack.

rock-solid belief in traditional values, and some voters see him as a father figure, putting their complete trust in his perceived paternal benevolence.

Yet there is also some unease. Relations between the United States and the Soviet Union are still very tense, and Reagan has exacerbated the situation by publicly calling the Soviet Union an "Evil Empire." Many Americans long for reassurance that their president will avoid nuclear war. They also crave relief from high unemployment and a skyrocketing national deficit that gives their dollar less buying power. Just as important, voters want to believe that their seventy-three-year-old leader is still vibrant.

But that reassurance does not come on September 19, when Reagan visits Hammonton, New Jersey. He wears a dark gray suit and crimson necktie. The small town, famous for its blueberries, has turned out in force to see the president. Thirty thousand people fill the town square. A large American flag looms over his left shoulder, accompanied by a sign reading, "America: Prouder, Stronger & Better."

Reagan's unlikely speech for today is based on the recent writings of two very prominent conservative voices. The first voice is that of columnist George Will, who behaves decades older than his forty-three years.

Surprisingly, Will has become a Bruce Springsteen fan. Wearing a bow tie, ears packed in cotton, he watched an entire four-hour show at the Capital Centre in Landover, Maryland, as a guest of Springsteen's drummer. Will comes away inspired by the artist's connection to Reagan. In the Boss, as Springsteen is known, Will sees a powerful believer in the American dream.

"An evening with Springsteen," Will writes admiringly in the *Washington Post* on September 13, "is vivid proof that the work ethic is alive and well."

Another guest at that concert is political correspondent Bernard Goldberg of CBS News, who reports that Springsteen's shows "are like old-time revivals with the same old-time message: If they work long enough and hard enough, like Springsteen himself, they can also make it to the promised land."

It is hard to imagine other 1980s pop icons with whom the aging president could identify. The toe-tapping boogie-woogie of his Hollywood days has been replaced by music that makes listeners swing their hips and shake their heads. Young voters listen to musical sensation Michael Jackson, not

Frank Sinatra. They like movies such as *Ghostbusters* and *Footloose* instead of Reagan's beloved Westerns, which hardly get made anymore. So it is only natural that Reagan's campaign staff attempts to make their boss look culturally relevant by cashing in on Springsteen's popularity during this visit to the singer's home state. At George Will's urging, deputy White House chief of staff Michael Deaver has invited Springsteen himself to the campaign event. But the rocker, while having an open date between performances in Philadelphia and Pittsburgh, declines.

Ronald Reagan invokes Springsteen's name anyway, his speechwriters mistakenly believing that the song "Born in the U.S.A." is a patriotic anthem. In reality, the opposite is true. "America's future rests in a thousand dreams inside your hearts," Reagan says to the crowd. "It rests in the message of hope in the words of songs so many young Americans admire: New Jersey's own Bruce Springsteen. And helping you make those dreams come true is what this job of mine is all about."

Chants of "U.S.A." sweep through the crowd, along with a number of incredulous gasps. Reagan's policies have been savaged on Springsteen's latest album, *Born in the*

U.S.A. Many of its songs vividly depict the loss of homes and jobs for the working poor. The title track, jingoistic in name only, attacks Reagan's economic policies through the eyes of a down-on-his-luck Vietnam vet. At a time when Ronald Reagan wants to appear as if he is in touch, his staff has succeeded in making him look completely clueless by misinterpreting Springsteen's lyrics.

Later, the singer himself responds directly: "You see the Reagan reelection ads on TV — you know: 'It's Morning in America,' " Springsteen tells *Rolling Stone* magazine. "And you say, well, it's not morning in Pittsburgh. It's not morning above 125th Street in New York. It's midnight, and, like, there's, a bad moon risin'."*

* Springsteen had been politically ambivalent until this incident, aligning himself with veterans' groups and local food banks but refusing to back political candidates from either party. However, as a result of the "Born in the U.S.A." incident, he will make it a point to openly endorse liberal causes. In 2004 he will endorse Sen. John Kerry for president, and in 2008 and 2012 Springsteen will make campaign appearances on behalf of Barack Obama. However, the misunderstood legacy of "Born in the U.S.A." lives on. Attendees at the 2014 Connecticut Republican Convention

Ronald Reagan's aides will later claim that his favorite Bruce Springsteen song is "Born to Run," but it is hard for even the most ardent Reagan supporter to imagine this might be true.

"If you believe that," Johnny Carson tells America during his *Tonight Show* monologue one evening, "I've got some tickets to the Mondale-Ferraro inaugural ball I'd like to sell you."★

Three weeks later, Ronald Reagan is confused when about to deliver his closing remarks in the first presidential debate with Walter Mondale. The location is the Kentucky Center for the Performing Arts, in Louisville, and television journalist Barbara Walters is the moderator. Walters has a history with the Reagans. In 1981 she paid a visit to the Reagan ranch for an interview, gripping her seat in Reagan's four-wheel-

---

were asked to name their favorite Springsteen song. "Born in the U.S.A." was the clear favorite. One delegate even compared it patriotically to "The Star-Spangled Banner."

★ Geraldine Ferraro is Walter Mondale's running mate. The forty-nine-year-old congresswoman from Queens, New York, is the first female vice presidential candidate from a major party.

drive jeep as he fearlessly drove it up and down the rugged dirt trails. But the fifty-five-year-old Walters is in her element now, pressing the president to begin his closing remarks. However, Reagan believes he is entitled to one more rebuttal to Walter Mondale's statements. Walters is having none of it and firmly tells the president to wrap it up.

The night has been a catastrophe for Reagan. Walter Mondale was the aggressor throughout the debate, commanding a quick grasp of domestic policy facts and appearing to be more physically robust than Reagan, despite being two inches shorter.

"I wanted to show presidential stature," Mondale will later remember. "I wanted to show mastery of the issues. I wanted to show that progressive dimension again, I wanted to show I was more alert than the president, without being negative. And I wanted the debate to build around that, that theme."

Mondale senses a mental weakness in Reagan, afterward telling an aide, "That guy is gone." Despite that, Mondale has refrained from attacking the president in a way that would make Reagan look foolish.

As Ronald Reagan begins his closing remarks, his rambling, disjointed speech does what Walter Mondale refuses to do. At a time when voters want reassurance of his vitality, the president looks visibly adrift on this very public national stage.

Looking into the camera, Reagan begins his soliloquy. "Four years ago, in similar circumstances to this, I asked you, the American people, a question. I asked, 'Are you better off than you were four years before?' "

Already, Reagan has lost his place. His eyes do not focus on the front row of the audience, as they should. Instead, they roll slowly from side to side as he struggles to recite the closing remarks that his speechwriters have prepared so carefully for this very moment.

Reagan continues: "The answer to that obviously was no, and as the result, I was elected to this office and promised a new beginning. Now, maybe I'm expected to ask that same question again."

To the discomfort of some, Reagan stutters. He appears a far cry from the man who improvised a brilliant speech within minutes of being called to the podium at the 1976 Republican National Convention.

He continues: "I'm not going to, because I think that all of you, or not everyone — those people that are in those pockets of poverty and haven't caught up, they couldn't answer the way I would want them to — but I think that most of the people in this country would say, yes, they are better off than they were four years ago.

"The question, I think," says Reagan, again stammering, "should be enlarged. Is America better off than it was four years ago? And I believe the answer to that has to also be yes."

There is little authority in Reagan's closing remarks. Walter Mondale beams.

"He seemed to lose his place," Lesley Stahl of CBS News will report. "He'd lose his thoughts. There were a couple of places where the words he was searching for wouldn't come to mind . . . [H]is closing statement didn't come together."

"I flopped," Reagan says to campaign adviser Stu Spencer immediately upon leaving the stage.

The president is correct. Polls show Walter Mondale winning the debate in a landslide. Two mornings later, the *Wall Street Journal* will publish a story stating that 10 percent of all people over the age of seventy-five are senile. Reagan is seventy-three years old.

Even worse, years later medical studies will link invasive surgeries like the one Reagan endured after the assassination attempt to the eventual onset of memory loss.*

"I didn't feel good about myself," Reagan will confide in his diary during a weekend at Camp David to recover from the debate. "The press has been calling him the winner for two days now."

But Ronald Reagan is not finished. He will have one last chance to convince Americans that he is still fit to be their leader.

That chance will come on October 21, in Kansas City.

---

* A 2001 Duke University medical study showed that 50 percent of individuals who underwent open heart surgery suffered immediate memory problems that were often still evident five years later.

25

Municipal Auditorium
Kansas City, Missouri
October 21, 1984
7:00 P.M.

The man who was nearly murdered three years ago is out for blood.

Ronald Reagan bounds onto the stage and takes his spot at the lectern, where he stands confident and poised. Despite it being evening, a time of day at which he often fades, the president looks crisp and attentive. As the contest gets under way, Walter Mondale stands on the opposite side of the stage, watching as Reagan fields a series of questions. The president does not like Mondale, thinking him a liar who has unfairly attacked his credibility. For Reagan, this second and last debate is personal. His answers now come easily. There is no sign of the stuttering or stammering from the first debate.

There is one question, however, that everyone in the audience knows is coming. Finally, after twenty minutes of debate, Henry Trewhitt of the *Baltimore Sun* gets to the heart of the matter: Is Ronald Reagan too old to be president?

Reagan stands ready to answer.

After the first debate, Nancy Reagan was livid — eager to apply blame on anyone but her Ronnie. "What have you done to my husband?" she screamed at Deputy Chief of Staff Michael Deaver. They were standing in the Presidential Suite at the Hyatt Regency in Louisville. "Whatever it was, don't do it again."

The problem, Nancy quickly decided, is that the president is being bullied in the pre-debate prep sessions. His advisers, notably budget director David Stockman, often interrupt Reagan when he makes a mistake. It is well known in the White House that the troika of Ed Meese, James Baker, and Michael Deaver have a method of slowing down Oval Office meetings if the president does not understand a complex issue. Without insulting him, they diplomatically reframe the discussion until Reagan comprehends.

But there is no time for niceties while

preparing for a presidential debate. Stockman is only doing his job, feeding the president facts so that he can easily rebut anything Walter Mondale might throw at him.

On October 17, during the initial debate prep for the final confrontation with Mondale, a newcomer observes the scene. From 2:06 to 4:36 in the afternoon, Reagan stands at a mock lectern in the Old Executive Office Building, fielding questions and arguing with Stockman, who stands at an opposite lectern playing the part of Walter Mondale. At one point, the normally polite Reagan barks "Shut up" at Stockman, filling the room with an embarrassing silence.

Tensions are high.

Clearly, something must change.

Afterward, Reagan returns to the White House, where he meets with the new observer. Roger Ailes is a stocky man with long sideburns. He is part of the so-called Tuesday Team, which has prepared the successful "Morning in America" commercials for Reagan. Ailes also worked for the Nixon administration and is known for his ability to stop chaos cold.

Michael Deaver makes the introduction. "Roger's here to help you with the debates."

"What kind of help do I need?" Reagan

responds. Though it is almost evening, Reagan shows no sign of fatigue, other than a slight hand and head tremor.

"You sort of wandered off the highway in the last debate. I'm gonna try and help you focus a little bit," Ailes answers.

"That's a pretty good idea," the president replies.

Roger Ailes agreed with Nancy Reagan that the president's debate problem had nothing to do with age or mental health. Instead, Reagan had been poorly prepared.

"You're giving him too many facts, too much bullshit that he can't use, you're interrupting him," Ailes tells Deaver. "Remember, he's a guy who's used to working with one director, who kind of lays out what the purpose of the thing is, and then he does it. Right now, you got five or six or eight guys interrupting him, all trying to prove they're smarter than he is."

So it is that Reagan's debate preparation is altered. Now it is just Ailes and Reagan, one on one. The president endures long bouts of "pepper sessions," in which he has to answer question after question without reaching for obscure facts or numbers. Instead, he simply speaks from the heart.

Now, with just four days left to the second debate, the strategy seems to be working.

The president is upbeat and optimistic. He works hard, rarely seeming to tire.

"When guys brief people for debates," Ailes will later remember, "they want them to memorize what they say 'cause they're the expert. . . . I shifted him back to staying in territory he knew and not trying to memorize a bunch of crap that nobody would remember."

Ailes's strategy has revitalized Reagan. "I can sum up the day in one sentence," he writes in his diary on Saturday, October 20, the night before facing Mondale. "I've been working my tail off to master the four minute closing statement I want to make in the debate tomorrow night."

On the same evening, the president and Ailes have a last-minute discussion about the debate.

"What are you gonna say if they ask you if you're too old for this job?" Ailes asks Reagan. The two men are standing in a White House hallway, walking to the elevator that will take Reagan back up to the second-floor residence.

Michael Deaver, Nancy Reagan, and all of the president's advisers have forbidden any talk about the age issue. But Reagan and Ailes are sure the question will be asked tomorrow night.

Reagan stops in his tracks. He blinks and looks hard at Ailes. "I have some ideas," the president begins.

Reagan tells Ailes what he intends to say. The words are rough and need a rhythm if they are to be effective, but Ailes likes the tone. Once upon a time, Ronald Reagan would have written the line for himself. Even now, he still makes elaborate changes in the margins of the scripts his speechwriters give him. But with his mind filled with debate minutiae, Ailes offers to write the entire response for Reagan.

"Whatever they bring up about age," he tells the president, "you go to this answer. You have to hit it specifically. Deliver it the way Bob Hope would. Don't move on the laugh line. If you want to get a drink of water or something and just stare at him, fine. But here's the line."

"I got it, coach," Reagan responds after hearing Ailes's retort.

As the final debate edges closer to a conclusion, the inevitable age question finally arrives.

Ronald Reagan is ready.

"Mr. President," the balding, bespectacled Henry Trewhitt says, "I want to raise an issue that I think has been lurking out there

407

for two or three weeks and cast it specifically in national security terms. You already are the oldest president in history. And some of your staff say you were tired after your most recent encounter with Mr. Mondale."

Reagan is smiling.

Trewhitt continues: "I recall that President Kennedy had to go for days on end with very little sleep during the Cuban missile crisis. Is there any doubt in your mind that you would be able to function in such circumstances?"

The president waits a beat, surveying the room. He appears to be fully in command of the situation.

"I want you to know that also I will not make age an issue of this campaign," Reagan says casually, allowing the moment to build, taking great care not to rush the punch line. "I am not going to exploit, for political purposes, my opponent's youth and inexperience."

The crowd erupts in laughter. Even Walter Mondale is laughing. Reagan looks down modestly. He knows that even though there are still forty-five minutes in the debate, he has already won.

Two weeks later, on November 6, in a

historic landslide, Ronald Reagan is reelected president of the United States.*

The next morning, Reagan celebrates the best way he knows how: with a four-day vacation at the ranch, Nancy in tow.

* Reagan wins forty-nine states. Mondale captures just his home state of Minnesota and the District of Columbia. The final Electoral College tally is 525 to 13.

26

Washington, DC
Christmas Day, 1986
6:00 A.M.

The would-be assassin will soon be a free man.

But only for today.

Escorted by the Secret Service, John Hinckley will spend the holiday at his parents' new home in Northern Virginia. Doctors here at St. Elizabeth's Hospital feel that Hinckley is making significant progress in dealing with his mental illness. They also believe that a day with his family will further the healing process. Jack and Jo Ann Hinckley have thrown themselves into their son's recovery, selling their Colorado home in order to move east. Each Tuesday afternoon, they attend therapy sessions with their son and a hospital psychiatrist. The Hinckleys are inspired by the advances John seems to be making. It appears that John Hinckley is "finding his voice," as his father describes it, even getting elected ward president by his fellow patients.

The Hinckleys and the hospital staff, however, are unaware that their son still secretly conceals pictures of Jodie Foster in his room, which is forbidden. Even more disturbing is that John Hinckley is cultivating friendships through the mail with murderers. He has secretly become pen pals with convicted serial killer Ted Bundy, now awaiting electrocution in Florida for murdering two Florida State University sorority sisters and a twelve-year-old girl.

Hinckley is also corresponding with Lynette "Squeaky" Fromme, imprisoned in California for attempting to assassinate Gerald Ford in 1975. Unbeknownst to his doctors or his parents, Hinckley asked Fromme to send him the address for the notorious murderer Charles Manson.*

* Fromme was a member of the Manson Family, members of which brutally murdered seven people on a two-day killing spree in 1969. On the second night, pregnant actress Sharon Tate was stabbed sixteen times, even as she pleaded to live long enough to give birth. Tate was married to director Roman Polanski, who was not present when the hideous crime took place.

Shortly after daybreak, John Hinckley is walked down from his fourth-floor hospital ward by an attendant. He then passes through the locked front doors of St. Elizabeth's and is rendered to his parents. Two Secret Service agents are in charge of supervising the visit.

But it is not his parents with whom Hinckley is eager to spend time. No, it is his girlfriend, forty-year-old Washington socialite Leslie deVeau. Today will be the first time they have the chance to be alone since they met four years ago.

Like John Hinckley, Leslie is a cold-blooded criminal. She was sentenced to St. Elizabeth's after murdering her ten-year-old daughter, Erin, in 1982. In an unconscionable act, deVeau placed a shotgun against the sleeping child's back and pulled the trigger. She then turned the gun on herself, but it misfired. Instead of killing her, the blast tore off deVeau's left arm. Like Hinckley, she was declared not guilty by reason of insanity and placed in the mental hospital.

At a hospital Halloween party in 1982, Hinckley sidled up to the petite brunette and began flirting. "I'd ask you to dance if I danced," he said. The two spent the rest of the party in deep conversation, sharing their life stories. Leslie deVeau, who comes from an old Washington, DC, family, did most of the talking. In vivid detail, she told Hinckley about how she'd murdered her daughter. When it came time for Hinckley to talk about his crime, he showed no remorse. Instead, he led deVeau to a hospital bulletin board where a newspaper clipping about his evil deed was posted.

"He was still operating under the delusion it made sense what he did," deVeau would later remember. "That he was supposed to do this to prove his love for Jodie Foster."

Although deVeau knew that Hinckley was still infatuated with the actress, her unlikely relationship with him blossomed. "I was lost until I met Leslie," Hinckley will later write. "Leslie made me want to live again, and she is the sunshine of my life."

Hinckley and deVeau resided on the same floor, but contact between them was restricted. Still, they found ways around the rules in order to communicate. They ate in the cafeteria at different times, but each furtively taped love letters underneath the dining table for the other to find. On the occasions that they actually saw each other in person, they used sign language to message "I love you."

In time, deVeau was granted the special privilege of being let outside to wander the hospital grounds. Hinckley, who had no such privilege, would shout to her from a window, and she'd answer back. In this way they conversed, not at all concerned that the whole hospital could hear them.

A year before, in mid-1985, deVeau was granted an even greater privilege: doctors decided she should be released from St. Elizabeth's and be treated on an outpatient basis. Thus, she no longer sees John Hinckley on a daily basis but returns to the hospital to visit him on weekends, where they can talk face-to-face. They sit across from each other at a glass table on visiting day, holding hands and kissing, ignoring the other patients and their guests all around them. During these visits, deVeau confides that she is still haunted by the night that she shotgunned her daughter to death.

In turn, Hinckley confessed that despite his outward bravado and trademark smirk, he had nightmares about the day he shot Reagan. He went on to tell Leslie that he sometimes dreamed that he was in a wheelchair, like James Brady.

In all the hours spent sitting sharing their

feelings, deVeau and Hinckley have always been supervised. All that will change this morning.

As two Secret Service agents stand guard outside, John Hinckley eats Christmas breakfast with his parents and Leslie de-Veau. They then spend two more hours in the living room, watching Hinckley home movies.

But as the clock strikes noon, the couple steals away.

Finding a secluded room, deVeau takes the initiative, pressing her body against Hinckley's and kissing him passionately. Normally demure, she is surprised and invigorated by her forward behavior.

Hinckley is flustered, unsure what to do. He has never had a girlfriend, and his few long-ago sexual experiences were limited to prostitutes. "I think he was startled," de-Veau will later recall. "What is this woman doing to me?"

Suddenly, a voice calls out from the kitchen. Jack Hinckley, suspecting what is going on, interrupts the couple, calling them back to the living room for Bible study.

By nightfall, a frustrated Hinckley is back in his hospital room alone. It has been an eventful Christmas.

415

If only Jodie Foster had been there to spend it with him.

27

White House Cabinet Room
Washington, DC
March 2, 1987
10:58 A.M.

Ronald Reagan is being watched very closely.

The president sits in his high-backed chair at the center of the mahogany table. His son Ron Jr. is a guest at today's Cabinet meeting, which has put Reagan in a jovial mood. Since their father's being reelected three years ago, the president's children have been cashing in on his fame. Ron Jr. has written articles for *Playboy* and even appeared in his underwear on *Saturday Night Live,* but he has always been loyal to his father. This is not the case with Reagan's other children. Daughter Patti has written a book savaging her father and the entire Reagan household. And soon, son Michael's painful tell-all is due in stores.

Meanwhile, the national press has begun a scathing series of broadsides against Nancy Reagan, blaming her for masterminding the recent firing of White House chief of staff Don Regan.

It was a battle so vicious and so public that *Saturday Night Live* lampooned the schism between the First Lady and Regan. All of this has led to growing criticism that the White House is out of control.*

That is why, in addition to Ron Jr., there are four other special guests at the morning's Cabinet meeting.

The new chief of staff, former Tennessee senator Howard Baker (no relation to James), is one of those in attendance. He has asked the White House counsel, A. B. Culvahouse, and director of communications Thomas Griscom to observe the

---

* Regan was secretary of the treasury during Ronald Reagan's first term in office. In an unusual move, he and James Baker switched jobs in early 1985 because Baker was exhausted from trying to keep the White House running independently of Nancy. The switch was orchestrated almost completely without the president's knowledge. He merely gave final approval to the plan when it was presented to him. The president did not seem to think it a big deal.

418

president. The final member of the group, sixty-nine-year-old Washington insider Jim Cannon, is the author of a recent report detailing the inner workings of the White House. Commissioned at Howard Baker's request, Cannon conducted formal interviews with employees throughout the West Wing.

He was shocked by what he learned.

The battle between Nancy Reagan and Don Regan is just the beginning. Cannon has uncovered evidence that the White House is in chaos at all levels. Ronald Reagan's aides are forging his initials to documents, Cabinet members are ignoring presidential policy to push their own agendas, and down in the White House basement, Marine lieutenant colonel Oliver North has spent years illegally selling arms to Iran and then diverting the cash to Contra fighters in Nicaragua. North knew he was breaking the law.

But Ronald Reagan is not engaged in many day-to-day White House activities. He delegates much power to Nancy. Occasionally, he avoids the Oval Office altogether, spending hours during the day watching television reruns in the upstairs residence. Even more troubling, it is no longer a given that the president will take the time to read important policy papers.

After reporting that information to Baker yesterday, Cannon went on to suggest that Ronald Reagan may no longer be fit to serve as president of the United States.

This bold statement is more than mere rhetoric.

The Twenty-Fifth Amendment to the Constitution states that if "the president is unable to discharge the powers and duties of his office, the vice president shall immediately assume the powers and duties of the office as acting president."

But Vice President Bush doesn't know anything about what's going on.

Only if the four observers decide that Ronald Reagan is impaired will Bush be told.

As radical as this might sound, the Twenty-Fifth Amendment has already been invoked during Reagan's presidency. On July 13, 1985, the president underwent a colonoscopy to remove a precancerous lesion. At 10:32 that morning, he signed a document handing the presidency over to George H. W. Bush. For eight hours, the vice president ran the country but ceded power back to Reagan as soon as the president emerged from the anesthesia.

But now Reagan seems to be in permanent

decline. In addition to the colon surgery and his hearing aids, Reagan recently underwent surgery for an enlarged prostate, which forces him to use the restroom frequently. He will soon undergo another procedure to have a cancerous melanoma removed from his nose. The president is now visibly frail, no longer the robust older gentleman who entered the White House six years ago. His energy level is lower. He naps frequently. His eyes often have a dull look, and he sometimes has trouble recognizing people that he has known for years.

Little does the president know it, but even loyal and uncritical Ron Jr. believes his father is suffering from Alzheimer's disease.

So it is that Howard Baker, Jim Cannon, A. B. Culvahouse, and Thomas Griscom sit along one wall scrutinizing the president's every action. Reagan does not know about Cannon's report, and the Cabinet meeting does not seem unusual to him.

But it is unusual. If the president shows signs of incoherence, he might not be president much longer.

Ronald Reagan's mental and physical woes, however, are not the greatest crisis of his presidency. The real test of his leadership began four months earlier, on November 3, 1986. An Iranian cleric leaked news that the United States was selling arms to Iran in exchange for the release of American hostages throughout the Middle East. Faced with the embarrassing report, Ronald Reagan appeared live on national television and explained that his administration has sold "small amounts of defensive weapons and spare parts" to Iran. But the president denied any knowledge of trading arms for hostages.

"Those charges are utterly false," he told the massive TV audience.

"We did not — repeat — did not trade weapons or anything else for hostages — nor will we."

But the people do not believe him. In a poll taken shortly after the appearance, 62 percent of Americans believe the president is lying.

One week later, Attorney General Edwin Meese confronted Reagan in the Oval Office. Meese knows that Lt. Col. Oliver North and his secretary, Fawn Hall, have destroyed hundreds of documents connected to the so-called Iran-Contra scandal. In fact, North and Hall shredded so many files that the machine jammed, forcing Hall to smuggle documents out of the office in her boots and panties.

But North and Hall were sloppy, overlooking one key memorandum linking the Reagan administration to the illegal arms sale.* In hushed tones, Meese informs Reagan of the smoking gun.

Edwin Meese is a Reagan loyalist. Along with Michael Deaver and James Baker, he has advised Reagan on almost every important issue confronting his presidency. Now serving as attorney general, Meese warned Reagan that he faced impeachment if he did not publicly acknowledge that America sold arms to Iran.

Reagan was stunned but admitted nothing. Instead, he convened a presidential commission to investigate Iran-Contra.†

Nancy Reagan was livid. She did not

---

* Hall was later given immunity from prosecution in return for her testimony against Oliver North.

† Known as the Tower Commission, it was named after its chairman, former Republican senator John Tower of Texas. The commission completed its three-month investigation in late February 1987. Its three-hundred-page report laid the blame for Iran-Contra on Ronald Reagan, demanding that he "take responsibility" for the illegality. The report also blamed his staff for shielding him from a number of key issues involving the sale of arms

blame her husband for the illegal scheme that took place with his permission.

She blamed Donald Regan.

The sixty-eight-year-old former marine is a tough Boston Irishman who rose to head the Merrill Lynch investment firm. From there, he became secretary of the treasury and eventually White House chief of staff. He likened his job to that of "a shovel brigade following a parade down Main Street." He said this because he was constantly fighting Nancy Reagan and the messes she created. Nancy's determination to control the president's schedule and her reliance on an astrologer to chart her husband's every move struck him as madness. But she had the president's full backing, so Regan was powerless to stop her.

Early in his White House tenure Don Regan discovered just how strong an adversary Nancy Reagan could be when she insisted that he fire Margaret Heckler, the secretary of health and human services. Heckler was one of only two women holding high positions in the Reagan administration. She was a timid person, but Nancy despised her, feeling she was an embarrass-

---

to Iran. "Yes, the president made mistakes," Tower told the press. "I think that's very plain English."

ment to her husband.* Yet neither the First Lady nor the chief of staff has the power to fire a Cabinet member, especially one who is sitting in a hospital undergoing a hysterectomy.

"I want her fired," Nancy told Regan in a call to his home one night. The president was completing his regular evening workout. This was her favorite time to call Regan, who got three times as many calls from Nancy as from her husband. Very often, Regan could hear the sound of the president's rowing machine in the background when he picked up the phone.

"But she's recuperating from a hysterectomy," Regan replied.

"I don't care. Fire her."

"I can't do it while she's in the hospital."

"I don't care. Fire the goddamned woman," Nancy Reagan said, seething.

Regan gave in, and Margaret Heckler suddenly became the ambassador to Ireland — far away from Nancy Reagan.

The same fate befell Secretary of Labor Ray Donovan, White House communica-

---

* Heckler's very public divorce was played out in the Washington newspapers. That drama, combined with what some considered her ineffective management skills, were factors in her ouster.

tions director Pat Buchanan, and CIA director William Casey. Nancy insisted that Casey be fired even as he lay in a hospital bed dying of a brain tumor. "He can't do his job," she argued with Regan, who once again questioned the humanity of the decision. "He's an embarrassment to Ronnie."

By January 1987, as the Iran-Contra scandal continued to erode Reagan's credibility, Nancy had taken complete control of the White House.

"The President's schedule is the single most potent tool in the White House," Regan will write, "because it determines what the most powerful man in the world is going to do and when he is going to do it. By humoring Mrs. Reagan we gave her this tool, or, more accurately, gave it to an unknown woman in San Francisco who believed that the zodiac controls events and human behavior and that she could read the secrets of the future in the movement of the planets."

Regan was referring to the astrologist Joan Quigley. Thanks to Nancy's intervention, Ronald Reagan now goes nowhere and does nothing without approval from Miss Quigley. Nancy is also receiving advice from a second stargazer, Jeane Dixon, but it is Quigley who has Nancy's ear and who is telling her the president should not appear in public until May because of "the malevolent movements of Uranus and Saturn."

Donald Regan was appalled. He insisted that the president needed to be seen in public. Hunkering down in the White House at the height of the Iran-Contra fiasco made it look as if he were hiding something. But other than his State of the Union address on January 27, 1987, and some other official business, Ronald Reagan does as Nancy tells him.

The president and Regan actually got along famously, often spending time alone together in the Oval Office, telling jokes. This only made Nancy Reagan more determined to edge out the chief of staff. The sniping between her and Don Regan soon seeped out into the public domain. Twice, Regan hung up on Nancy when she called to hector him. Her power continued to grow, and there was growing speculation that the president was dependent and weak.

"What is happening at the White House?" New Mexico Democrat William Richardson asked on the floor of the House of Representatives. "Who is in charge? A constituent of mine asked, 'How can the president deal with the Soviets if he cannot settle a dispute between his wife and his chief of staff?' "

As tensions rose, Nancy becomes so insistent on firing Don Regan that the president ordered her "to get off my goddam back."

This, too, seeped into the headlines. "Mrs. Reagan," ABC newsman Sam Donaldson asked Nancy on camera, "did the President ask you to get off his back about Donald Regan?"

"No," she replied curtly.

Donaldson immediately followed up with a different angle: "Have you been fighting over this?"

"No," she insisted.

Finally, as Nancy knew he would, Ronald Reagan gave in.

"Something has to be done," Ronald Reagan admitted to Nancy, who had already lined up former Tennessee senator Howard Baker to be Regan's replacement. The president did not deliver the news to his chief of staff in person. On February 27, Regan discovered he was out of a job when Nancy issued a statement to cable news outlet CNN.

Four days later, Nancy Reagan gave an address to the American Camp Association in which she viciously mocked Regan. "I don't think most people associate me with leeches," she told the audience of eighteen hundred, "but I know how to get them off. I'm an expert at it."

Soon the storm passes. As the president's staff likes to say, "He has his good days and he has his bad days." Today, March 2, 1987, is a good day for Ronald Reagan. Even though his chief of staff has been fired, and the Tower Commission has leveled blame for the Iran-Contra scandal on him, he is in a jovial mood and jokes his way through the Cabinet meeting that his son watches. To the four men observing Reagan, he possesses an easy command of facts while telling his usual anecdotes about his Hollywood days. At lunch, the president is even looser, swapping jokes with new chief of staff Howard Baker and looking every bit the most powerful man in the world.*

Without knowing that he has done so, Ronald Reagan has passed a test.

* Reagan loyalists insist that Reagan was firmly in control of the executive branch at all times. They reject any reportage to the contrary. It should be noted that Ronald Reagan retained his acting skills and rarely showed physical or mental distress to anyone but Nancy, whom he trusted implicitly.

There will be no invoking the Twenty-Fifth Amendment.

But another stern trial is just two days away.

28

White House Oval Office
Washington, DC
March 4, 1987
9:00 P.M.

Ronald Reagan is in trouble.

Wearing a dark blue suit and speckled blue tie, the president prepares to speak to the nation. His face is drawn and lined, with a red flush. His eyes look just to the left of the camera as he reads off a teleprompter.

"My fellow Americans:

"I've spoken to you from this historic office on many occasions and about many things. The power of the Presidency is often thought to reside within this Oval Office. Yet it doesn't rest here; it rests in you, the American people, and in your trust. Your trust is what gives a President his powers of leadership and his personal strength, and it's what I want to talk to you about this evening."

Since January, the president has testified before the Tower Commission twice. Both times he looked confused. During his second appearance Reagan was so lost that he made the blunder of reading from a top secret memo when asked what he knew about Iran-Contra.* The media, sensing that Reagan could soon be facing the same fate as Richard Nixon, are now on the attack. Ben Bradlee of the *Washington Post* openly compares Iran-Contra with Watergate.

"For the past three months, I've been silent on the revelations about Iran," the president continues. "And you must have been thinking: 'Well, why doesn't he tell us what's happening?'" He continues: "Others of you, I guess, were thinking: 'What's he doing hiding out in the White House?' Well, the reason I haven't spoken to you before now is this: You deserve the truth. And as frustrating as the waiting has been, I felt it was improper to come to you with sketchy reports, or possibly even erroneous statements, which would then have to be corrected, creating even more doubt and confusion."

* The memo concerned efforts to coach Reagan through the Iran-Contra affair.

Many watching the Reagan broadcast know the president has denied committing any illegal acts, but now he seems to be admitting his denial was false.

"A few months ago I told the American people I did not trade arms for hostages. My heart and my best intentions still tell me that's true, but the facts and the evidence tell me it is not."

These devastating words do not seem to affect Reagan very much. In fact, a paternal grin now crosses his face. For the first time in his presidency, he is about to admit some level of memory loss. This passage of the speech has been written very carefully — the message coming across is that the problem does not lie with him but with the people who work for him.

"One thing still upsetting me, however, is that no one kept proper records of meetings or decisions." He speaks into the camera. "This led to my failure to recollect whether I approved an arms shipment before or after the fact. I did approve it; I just can't say specifically when."

The speech is Reagan at his paternal best, letting the nation know that he is still in charge and is managing merely a clerical situation.

"You know, by the time you reach my age,

433

you've made plenty of mistakes. And if you've lived your life properly — so, you learn. You put things in perspective. You pull your energies together. You change. You go forward."

With that simple statement, Reagan is putting Iran-Contra behind him once and for all. He will move forward.

"Good night, and God bless you."*

Three weeks later, Ronald Reagan's political soul mate is trying to save her own skin. Margaret Thatcher is in Moscow for meetings with Soviet leader Mikhail Gorbachev. Thatcher, who is in the midst of a bitter reelection campaign, now sits with Gorbachev in the Kremlin, speaking to him

* Ronald Reagan was never held accountable for Iran-Contra. In 1990 he testified behind closed doors to Iran-Contra prosecutor Dan Webb, in the federal trial of former national security adviser John Poindexter. Reagan's defense was that he could not remember any details of illegalities. Poindexter and Oliver North were among the thirteen members of the Reagan administration indicted for Iran-Contra. Both men were found guilty of several felony charges, but their convictions were overturned. Not a single person went to jail for the Iran-Contra conspiracy.

about his recent capitulation to America in reducing his arsenal of nuclear missiles. It is the first time a British prime minister has come to Moscow in more than a decade.

Gorbachev has been in power two years. He is different from former Soviet leaders, more open to closer relations with America and Britain, simply because he has to be. The Soviet economy has been destroyed by years of military buildup and failed Communist economic policies. The Soviet Union is on its knees financially. Only by aligning himself with the West can Gorbachev ensure the viability of his country.

Mikhail Gorbachev is a bureaucrat. He worked his way up through the Politburo by holding positions such as secretary of agriculture and chairman of the Standing Commission on Youth Affairs. But his rise through the Soviet system has been an unlikely one, for he was born the son of peasants and once seemed destined to live out his life as a farmer. It was his father who encouraged him to attend Moscow State University, from which Gorbachev graduated cum laude with a law degree in 1955. As he went on to a career in politics, Gorbachev displayed a skill for organization and diplomacy that helped him move from unknown to general secretary within thirty years. Unlike his predecessors, the fifty-six-year-old Gorbachev is not a ruthless killer, nor is he a heavy drinker or womanizer. A balding man with a wine stain birthmark high on his forehead, he has enjoyed the favor of the Soviet people, who have rallied behind his youth and warmth. Even Ronald Reagan trusts him, believing "there is a moral dimension in Gorbachev" that was lacking in previous Soviet leaders.

Gorbachev is trying to find solutions to the problems his country faces. He has not given up on socialism, but he is introducing market reforms and individual freedoms through "glasnost" and "perestroika" — "openness" and "restructuring." But even openness has its limits. Gorbachev knows he cannot appear weak before Margaret Thatcher or Ronald Reagan. So the Soviet leader scolds Margaret Thatcher. He is angry that she has referred to his nation as evil, a phrase that Ronald Reagan has also used. Gorbachev thinks this makes him look weak.

"No, you can't have thought that!" Thatcher answers through her interpreter. Gorbachev and Thatcher each has a small number of advisers witnessing the conversation. "Nobody thinks that the Soviet Union is weak. The Soviet Union has enormous power. You have superior intermediate-range weapons and strategic offensive weapons, if we count warheads, as well as chemical and conventional arms. You are very powerful, not weak."

Gorbachev likes her tone. Just like Ronald Reagan, he has tremendous respect for Margaret Thatcher. Despite their ideological differences, he enjoys their verbal jousting.

"Once again I want to emphasize that the most important thing is to remain grounded in reality, otherwise we will all be in grave danger," he warns the prime minister.

She replies: "It is very important for us that you give up the doctrine of communist world domination."

"We never proclaimed such a doctrine," Gorbachev says. "There is the Truman Doctrine, the Eisenhower Doctrine, the neo-globalist Reagan Doctrine. All of these doctrines were publicly proclaimed by presidents. But you will not find our statements about 'planting the domination of communism' because they do not exist."

Six thousand miles away, Ronald Reagan pays little attention to the verbal duel. He has spent forty years battling communism, and doesn't much care what Mikhail Gorbachev has to say. That's because Ronald Reagan is already forming the words that will stun the world.

Two months after Margaret Thatcher and Mikhail Gorbachev meet in Moscow, she is reelected prime minister for the third time. On June 8, Thatcher spends time with President Reagan while both are attending a high-level economic summit in Venice. Both are in agreement that the time is right to strike a blow for freedom, and perhaps end communism throughout Europe forever.

So it is that Ronald Reagan stands before the Berlin Wall giving the speech that will define his presidency — if not his entire life. The date is June 12, 1987. Reagan is fully recovered from the Iran-Contra affair, and is standing in almost the exact same spot where the American general George S. Patton stood forty-two years ago. Back then, Patton warned that World War II would never truly be over until the United States defeated the Soviet Union militarily. The world did not listen to Patton. Not only did the Soviets remain in Eastern Europe, but they built a concrete barrier around West Berlin. The so-called Berlin Wall is a symbol of the Cold War. It divides the democratic West Berlin portion of the city from the

Soviet-occupied area known as East Berlin.*

In 1963, President John F. Kennedy traveled to Berlin and told the world that the Soviet Union was enslaving people. Now Ronald Reagan wants to build on Kennedy's historic speech.†

Flying from Venice to Berlin, Reagan arrived just before noon and traveled by motorcade through the heart of the city to the historic Brandenburg Gate, where a crowd numbering tens of thousands now awaits his words — "people stretching as far as I could see," he will write in his diary.

Reagan is theatrical, positioning the Berlin Wall behind him as he stands on an elevated platform. The weather is gray and overcast, with a light wind blowing. Reagan begins

* The wall was actually two walls, separated by 160 meters of open ground. This space was mined, contained trip-wired machine guns, and was patrolled by guard dogs. Watch towers overlooked this no-man's-land, and East German soldiers shot on sight all who tried to escape into West Berlin.

† John F. Kennedy spoke to the people of West Berlin on June 26, 1963. He expressed solidarity for their freedoms and disgust about the newly built Berlin Wall, telling the crowd, "Ich bin ein Berliner" ("I am a Berliner").

his speech at 2:00 p.m.

"Behind me stands a wall that encircles the free sectors of this city, part of a vast system of barriers that divides the entire continent of Europe," Reagan says. "From the Baltic, south, those barriers cut across Germany in a gash of barbed wire, concrete, dog runs, and guard towers. Farther south, there may be no visible, no obvious wall. But there remain armed guards and checkpoints all the same — still a restriction on the right to travel, still an instrument to impose upon ordinary men and women the will of a totalitarian state."

At least eighty people have died trying to escape from East Berlin into West Berlin. Communist authorities are ruthless and claim the wall exists to protect people by keeping out subversive capitalist influences.

The president continues: "Yet it is here in Berlin where the wall emerges most clearly; here, cutting across your city, where the news photo and the television screen have imprinted this brutal division of a continent upon the mind of the world. Standing before the Brandenburg Gate, every man is a German, separated from his fellow men. Every man is a Berliner, forced to look upon a scar."

The president, like Margaret Thatcher, has

enjoyed better relations with Soviet leader Gorbachev in the past year. But Reagan has taken a hard line in arms reduction talks, going so far as to walk out of one summit meeting when Gorbachev's terms of negotiation were not to his liking. The Russians respect toughness, not appeasement, and Reagan knows that backing down will be seen as a sign of weakness. He is not afraid of verbally scorching the Communist ideology.

"In the 1950s, Khrushchev predicted, 'We will bury you,' " Reagan says emphatically. "But in the West today, we see a free world that has achieved a level of prosperity and well-being unprecedented in all human history. In the Communist world, we see failure, technological backwardness, declining standards of health, even want of the most basic kind — too little food. Even today, the Soviet Union still cannot feed itself. After these four decades, then, there stands before the entire world one great and inescapable conclusion: Freedom leads to prosperity. Freedom replaces the ancient hatreds among the nations with comity and peace. Freedom is the victor."

Ronald Reagan is in complete control. There is no sign of weakness. His voice rises as he drives home his point. He was warned

Ronald Reagan standing before the Brandenburg Gate and Berlin Wall, June 12, 1987. With him are Chancellor Helmut Kohl (right) *and President of the Bundestag Philipp Jenninger* (left).

before the speech that by using the wall as a backdrop, his speech would automatically be "provocative."

But Ronald Reagan *wants* to be provocative. His message today is so powerful that he will be interrupted twenty-eight times by cheers and applause.

"Are these the beginnings of profound changes in the Soviet state? Or are they token gestures, intended to raise false hopes in the West, or to strengthen the Soviet system without changing it? We welcome change and openness; for we believe that freedom and security go together, that the advance of human liberty can only strengthen the cause of world peace.

"There is one sign the Soviets can make that would be unmistakable, that would advance dramatically the cause of freedom and peace." Reagan pauses, knowing the world is hanging on his words.

"General Secretary Gorbachev, if you seek peace, if you seek prosperity for the Soviet Union and Eastern Europe, if you seek liberalization:

"Come here to this gate! Mr. Gorbachev, open this gate!

"Mr. Gorbachev, tear down this wall!"*

* Reagan noted in May 1975 that "Communism is neither an economic or a political system — it is a form of insanity — a temporary aberration which will one day disappear from the earth because it is contrary to human nature. I wonder how much more misery it will cause before it disappears." By the time Reagan entered office it was clear that the Soviet Union was struggling economically and that its people were becoming unhappy with the ever-increasing hardships. Reagan's presidential foreign policy of "peace through strength" was a master plan to bankrupt the Soviet economy by building up America's military, forc-

ing the Russians to keep pace — knowing all the
while that they could not.

29

White House Oval Office
Washington, DC
January 20, 1989
10:00 A.M.

Two years after Ronald Reagan demanded the Berlin Wall be dismantled, it is still standing, and time has run out for Ronald Reagan. It is the last day of his presidency. He and Nancy have just said their final good-byes to the household staff at an emotional gathering in the State Room. Now Ronald Reagan takes a final walk along the Colonnade to the West Wing and his cherished office. Workers have already cleaned out his files, removing every vestige of the Reagan presidency from the Oval Office, right down to the jar of jellybeans he always keeps within arm's reach. At noon, new president George H. W. Bush will be sworn in at the Capitol.

President Reagan rose early, eating a final

White House breakfast in the residence with Nancy before getting dressed. At age seventy-eight, he is leaving political office for good. But Reagan is not retiring. Concerned about income, he is already planning to supplement his annual presidential pension of $99,500 by making paid speeches around the world.*

Reagan's last correspondence as president was a parting letter to Margaret Thatcher, reaffirming their deep friendship. She and her husband, Denis, visited Washington last month, fittingly making Thatcher the last foreign dignitary to meet with Reagan in the White House. "Our partnership has strengthened the ability and the resolve of the Western alliance to defend itself and the cause of freedom everywhere," Reagan would later write. "You have been an invaluable ally, but more than that, you are a great friend. It has been an honor to work with you."

* As an orator, Reagan is managed by the Washington Speakers Bureau and earns fifty thousand dollars per speech, minus a 20 percent agent commission. In addition to speaking with corporate groups in America, Reagan made $2 million on a ten-day speaking tour of Japan shortly after leaving office.

Thanks to the efforts of Reagan and Thatcher, global communism has been severely weakened. Before Reagan's election, it was almost unthinkable that the Soviet Union and its satellite countries in Eastern Europe would embrace democracy, but that process has already begun. Poland is just five months away from its first partially free elections since 1928. Emboldened, the people of East Germany will soon rise up and do as Ronald Reagan demanded of Mikhail Gorbachev: ten months from now, on November 9, 1989, the Berlin Wall will collapse.

None of this would have happened without Ronald Reagan's unswerving lifelong belief in freedom and America's exceptionalism. England's Iron Lady understands that: "Your beliefs, your convictions, your faith shone through everything you did," Thatcher responded to Reagan's letter. "You have been an example and inspiration to us all."

Ronald Reagan opens the top drawer of the empty *Resolute* desk and checks to make sure the workers did not remove a note he placed there yesterday. It is tradition for the outgoing president to leave a simple message for his successor in the Oval Office.

Reagan's handwritten letter wishes Bush good luck and reminds the new president that he will be in his prayers.

Despite the warm tone, there is tension between Reagan and Bush, stemming from the campaign. Ronald Reagan endorsed the candidacy of his former vice president but did very little campaigning on his behalf. Some believe Reagan was snubbing Bush, but the truth is the Bush campaign wanted the candidate to be his own man. A barnstorming Ronald Reagan could easily have overshadowed the less charismatic Bush.

The residence has become a beloved home to Ronald and Nancy. Reagan is a sentimental man and very much moved by the sense of history filling that space. The president is convinced that the ghost of Abraham Lincoln haunts the residence. He has stated that he can sometimes hear the creak of Franklin Roosevelt's wheelchair gliding from one room to another, and he once told a friend he could easily imagine the ghost of Teddy Roosevelt mumbling his trademark cheer of "Bully."

"We were familiar with every room and hallway," Reagan will later write, "and had the warmest memories of our life in that beautiful historic mansion."

But now it is time to go.

National Security Adviser Colin Powell steps into the Oval Office to give Reagan his last-ever daily briefing. "The world is quiet today, Mr. President," the former army general says succinctly.

Reagan reaches into the jacket pocket of his crisp blue suit. He pulls out the plastic card he has carried with him every day since taking office. It authenticates that he is president of the United States. In the event of a nuclear war he will present this to the military attaché who remains near him at all times, whereupon the special briefcase known as the "football" will be opened and the nuclear launch codes revealed.

"What do I do with this?" he asks Powell.

"Hang on to it," Powell replies. "You're still president."

Ronald Reagan's last official act as president of the United States takes place just before 11:00 a.m., as he hands the plastic authentication card to his air force military aide. Now, at 12:40 on a bitter cold Washington day, with George Bush already sworn in as the forty-first president of the United States, Ron and Nancy Reagan step aboard a government helicopter to begin the journey back to California. As he is no longer president, the call name Marine One no longer applies to the official aircraft. It is Nighthawk One that lifts off from the Capitol, taking the couple to Andrews Air Force Base.

The moment, in Nancy's words, is "wrenching." They have participated in a long list of "final" scenes in the past few weeks: final visit to Camp David, final dinner in the White House, and final moment with the press. This morning, at their goodbye reception, is when it hit Nancy the hardest that it was over. "We were supposed to have coffee, but I don't remember drinking any. Then it was time to leave for the inauguration," she will later write.

As she and Barbara Bush share a limousine to the swearing-in, Nancy gazes out the window at the White House Lawn, wondering if the magnolia trees she planted will survive long enough for her grandchildren to see them. "My heart ached as I looked at those beautiful grounds I was unlikely to see again."

Time and events have changed Nancy Reagan. Shortly after her return from Berlin in 1987, the First Lady was diagnosed with breast cancer and underwent a mastectomy to remove one breast. The procedure was a success, and Nancy's very public ordeal softened her in the eyes of many. With the end of her husband's presidency, whatever animosity may have existed between the Reagans and the media has now been replaced by nostalgic warmth. Walter Cronkite brought the Reagans onstage for a round of applause at the recent Kennedy Center Honors, leading the orchestra in a chorus of "Auld Lang Syne." And even Sam Donaldson, the ABC newsman who has been baiting the Reagans for eight years, approached Nancy recently to say that he would miss them.

As the helicopter lifts off, the Reagans take one last look at the White House. They push their faces against the windows, straining to see the glory of their former home. Below them sprawl the vast lawns, fountains, and famous columns they have come to know so well. Even as they look down, movers are hauling their furniture into trucks for transport back to their new home in Beverly Hills. The Bush family furniture, meanwhile, is being installed in its place.

"Look honey," says Reagan, not taking his eyes off the White House. "There's our little shack."

The pilot finally banks away, steering the VH-60N helicopter to Andrews — the Reagans vanishing into the clouds.

30

Mayo Clinic
Rochester, Minnesota
September 8, 1989
11:00 A.M.

Eight months later, the White House is the last thing on Ronald Reagan's mind.

A surgical drill hums as the former president lies flat on his back in an operating room. Fifty-nine-year-old brain surgeon Dr. Thoralf Sundt presses the bit against the right side of Reagan's skull and carefully opens a hole the size of a nickel in his cranium. Two months ago, Reagan was thrown from a horse while riding at a friend's ranch in Mexico, just south of the Arizona border.

The horses used during the ride were unshod and left to run wild when not saddled, leading Secret Service agent John Barletta to warn Reagan against the ride. Nancy took the advice, but the former

452

president did not. On the second day at the ranch, Reagan's horse was spooked by a wild bull. It began bucking wildly. At first, Reagan was able to hang on. But the frightened horse continued kicking its hind legs straight up into the air, and on the third buck, Reagan was hurled from the saddle. He flew so high that his entire body rose above the heads of those riding alongside him.

Reagan landed hard, slamming his head into the rocky soil, just missing a patch of cactus. "Rawhide down," Agent Barletta yelled into his radio, marking the first time those words had been uttered since the assassination attempt of eight years earlier.

Reagan lay unconscious, but he soon revived. At first he appeared uninjured. Nevertheless, he was flown by military helicopter to an army hospital in Arizona, where he was treated for scrapes and bruises, then brought back to the ranch to continue the vacation — albeit without any further horseback rides.

But unbeknownst to Reagan and his doctors, a blood vessel in his head ruptured during the fall. For two months fluid has been leaking into his skull, causing a clot that is slowly putting pressure on Reagan's brain. This condition, known as a subdural hematoma, alters mood and vision and elevates levels of dementia. Patients often complain of headaches or simply fall into a stupor before seeking treatment. But Reagan's hematoma is a silent killer, with no outward symptoms other than his usual forgetfulness. Were it not for his annual physical here at the Mayo Clinic, the former president's condition might never have been discovered. But a precautionary CAT scan located the clot, and Reagan was rushed into surgery.

Dr. Sundt removes the drill, then looks through the opening at Reagan's brain. In the course of his job, the esteemed surgeon glimpses the human brain on an almost daily basis. But this is the brain of a living president. Dr. Sundt has the unique opportunity to save Reagan's life.

Clinically, the procedure Reagan is undergoing is known as a burr. In many cases, it is necessary to drill a second and even third hole to ease the pressure, but the brain surgeon is satisfied that one burr is enough for Reagan.

And that, seemingly, is that. Less than an hour after being sedated, Ronald Reagan is wheeled into the recovery room. His doctors are satisfied that Reagan shows no signs of the stroke, nerve damage, or paralysis so common in elderly patients suffering from head trauma. But the truth is that despite the operation, the fall has accelerated Reagan's debilitating condition.

Nancy Reagan will one day sum it up best: "I've always had the feeling that the severe blow to his head in 1989 hastened the onset of Ronnie's Alzheimer's."

Four years later, Ronald Reagan is still functioning. The date is February 6, 1993, and the occasion is Reagan's eighty-second birthday. Reagan and Margaret Thatcher chat amiably about their lives since leaving office. Unlike Reagan, Thatcher did not go of her own accord. She was forced out by her own Conservative Party in 1990 and cried as she left 10 Downing Street for the last time.* Now, at age sixty-seven, she

* Thatcher's popularity was in such decline by the late 1980s that her reelection appeared all but impossible. A poll tax she advocated led to widespread rioting, and she was deeply mistrustful of Britain's participation in the European Union, thinking it eroded its power. Opinion polls showed her approval ratings to be below 40 percent at the time her party pushed her aside. Voters said that she had grown out of touch with the people.

makes her living giving speeches at fifty thousand dollars per appearance and works on her memoirs. The state of dementia in which she will spend her twilight years is still almost a decade away, and she is sharp as she stands next to Reagan in the "Oval Office."

The birthday fund-raiser is not at the White House but in Simi Valley, California. Tonight Reagan and Thatcher are standing in the exact replica of the Oval Office now on display here at the Ronald Reagan Presidential Library. Thatcher and a host of celebrities have gathered for this five-hundred-dollar-per-plate dinner to raise money for the library. Old Hollywood friends Jimmy Stewart and Merv Griffin and media mogul Rupert Murdoch are among the five hundred guests at the black-tie affair. The festive night sold out immediately.

Reagan and Thatcher move into the great white tent pitched on the library lawn, where dinner will be served. The menu is crab-stuffed fillet of sole, prime rib, and baby potatoes, all washed down with the California wines Ronald Reagan has long enjoyed. Dessert will be another longtime Reagan favorite, Häagen-Dazs ice cream topped with fudge sauce.

The night belongs to Ronald Reagan, and it is Margaret Thatcher who rises first to pay homage. She praises him for bringing "the Evil Empire crashing down."

"If Ronald Reagan's birthday is celebrated warmly in California," continues Thatcher, "it is celebrated even more warmly in Prague, Warsaw, Budapest and Moscow itself."

Then it's Reagan's turn to toast Thatcher. "Thank you, Margaret, for those very kind words," he begins. Reagan's toast continues at length. He wrote and memorized it beforehand. On paper, the speech fills four typewritten pages. "I don't think I really deserve such a fuss for my birthday. But as George Burns once said, 'I have arthritis and I don't deserve that, either,'" he says with a smile.

Reagan continues. "Margaret, you have always been a staunch ally and a very dear friend. For all of us, I say thank you for the immense role you have played in shaping a better world. And I personally thank you for the honor of your presence tonight."

As he finishes, the entire tent thunders with roars of "hear, hear" and the clinking of glasses.

Moments later, Reagan stands to deliver a second toast.

Anticipation grows as the former president stands erect, his blue eyes shining, his tuxedo perfectly fitted to his body, which looks a decade younger than his actual age of eighty-two. To the casual observer, Ronald Reagan appears to be fit and healthy.

Slowly, he turns to Margaret Thatcher and raises his glass once again. Mrs. Thatcher is beaming, and the audience eagerly awaits Reagan's next memorable line. Smiling, he begins to speak.

"Thank you, Margaret, for those very kind words," he says, raising his glass. "I don't think I really deserve such a fuss for my birthday. But as George Burns once said, 'I have arthritis and I don't deserve that, either,' " Reagan says with a chuckle.

Immediately, shock envelops the room as Ronald Reagan, word for word, delivers the same exact four-page toast to Margaret Thatcher that he uttered just a few moments ago.

Reagan continues for two excruciating minutes.

"And I personally thank you for the honor of your presence here tonight," the former president tells Margaret Thatcher, raising his glass once again.

Reagan's friends sit in stunned silence.

31

Los Angeles, California
June 1994
Morning

The man with ten years to live has been dealt a stunning blow.

His daughter, forty-one-year-old Patti Davis, is now fully exposed for the entire country to see. *Playboy* magazine is on newsstands everywhere, its cover promising a father's ultimate humiliation. Patti wears nothing but a smile as the hands of a muscular unseen man cup her bare breasts. The magazine's lurid headline promises that "Ronald Reagan's Renegade Daughter" will tell all.

As Patti Davis has intended, her father is deeply wounded by his estranged daughter's latest attempt to embarrass him. For years, Reagan has struggled to deal with his rebellious children. But Patti has always been the biggest problem. From her defiant liberal politics to her open use of marijuana, she has striven to be the polar opposite of Ronald and Nancy Reagan in every way.

Just two years ago, Patti published a tell-all memoir about life in the "dysfunctional" Reagan family. The book revealed Nancy's dependence on tranquilizers and diuretics, along with the fact that Patti was so afraid of becoming pregnant and parenting as her mother had that she had herself rendered infertile with a tubal ligation at the age of twenty-four. In addition, Patti openly led a lifestyle that flaunted a libertine attitude on social issues. One writer described her as "an angry daughter with scores still to settle."

Now, grinning on the cover of *Playboy*, she has humiliated her mother and father — and the whole world knows it.

Patti Davis publicly states that her rebellion is Nancy's fault, saying that her mother was physically and emotionally abusive, a chronic prescription drug user who slapped her daughter when she ate too much and even slapped her when she began menstruating at a very young age. When she told her father about the abuse, Davis alleged, Ronald Reagan called her a liar.

"Patti you are hurting us — your parents — but you are hurting yourself even more,"

Reagan wrote to his daughter in 1991, when word leaked that she was writing her tell-all memoir.

"We are not a dysfunctional family," Reagan's letter continues. "Patti, in our meeting at the office you said your mother didn't like you. That's not true. Yes, she's unhappy about the way things are but again I can show you photos in which the love between you is unmistakable. And these pictures are at almost every stage of your life. Pictures don't lie."

Reagan concludes: "Please Patti, don't take away our memories of a daughter we truly love and who we miss.

"With Love, Dad."

But Patti Davis did not listen, and her defiance is clear in each and every photo in *Playboy.* She looks straight into the camera, knowing that every click of the photographer's shutter publicly will humiliate the man whom she considers a failure as a father.

It is a stunning betrayal.

Two months earlier, Ronald Reagan experienced another episode of public embarrassment.

The date is April 27, 1994. Ronald and Nancy Reagan are attending the funeral of

Richard Nixon. Twenty years after the Watergate scandal brought him down, and less than a year after his beloved wife, Pat, succumbed to lung cancer, the thirty-seventh president of the United States is dead of a stroke at the age of eighty-one. Nixon is being laid to rest on the grounds of his birthplace and presidential library in Yorba Linda, California. Despite hitting afternoon traffic on the drive south from Beverly Hills, it takes the Reagans just a little over an hour to arrive for the 4:00 p.m. ceremony.*

There are four former presidents and the current chief executive, Bill Clinton, at the funeral. In addition, a crowd of four thousand sits in folding chairs, awaiting the

* Nixon's last residence was not in California, but in Park Ridge, New Jersey. His stroke occurred as he was sitting down to dinner on April 18. After his death four days later, his body was flown to California aboard the same Boeing VC-137C that transported the casket of John F. Kennedy back to Washington, DC, after his assassination in 1963. As with his departure from the nation's capital following his resignation in 1974, Nixon's plane landed at El Toro Marine Corps Base. Nixon's body was then transported by motorcade to his final resting place twenty miles north.

start of the ceremony. Among the last to be seated are the former presidents and their wives. There is no formal introduction, but as a Marine Corps band plays light triumphal music, each couple walks to their seats, to polite applause.

Gerald and Betty Ford, Jimmy and Rosalynn Carter, George and Barbara Bush, and President Clinton and wife Hillary all take their seats.

But it is the arrival of Ronald and Nancy Reagan that steals the show. As the television audience and those in attendance look on, Reagan's confusion is apparent. Making their way down the steps after Ford and before Carter, the former president holds tight to Nancy's hand. She leads him like a child, walking in front and pulling him along. Reagan looks bewildered and frequently swivels his head. He wears a fascinated smile, as if not sure what all the hoopla is about. As the audience breaks into applause, Nancy whispers to her husband, telling him to wave to the crowd.

He dutifully obliges.

As the Reagans take their seats between the Carters and Bushes, Ronald Reagan's physical decline is clear as well. Compared to Gerald Ford, who at age eighty is just two and a half years younger, Reagan looks

Ronald and Nancy Reagan at President Richard Nixon's funeral

frail and wrinkled. Ford thinks he looks "hollowed out," and Bush is telling friends that he is deeply worried about Reagan. Carter, for his part, thinks that Reagan's responses to everyday questions are "not right."

But even as these former presidents are well aware of Reagan's decline, there is a general consensus among the media that the matter must be kept hushed until the Reagan family chooses to make it public.

Nixon's funeral is Ronald Reagan's last major appearance. After a lifetime of performing, the actor has now left the stage.

Four months after the Nixon funeral, Ronald Reagan is back at the Mayo Clinic for his annual physical. It is August 1994. Southern Minnesota is humid and hot this time of year, but it is cool and comfortable in the small examination room in which Ronald Reagan now sits. His hair is turning silver in a show of his advanced age. As he does every year, the former president is having his blood pressure checked as a doctor listens to his heart.

But at Nancy Reagan's behest, the esteemed physicians of the Mayo Clinic are also conducting a different sort of test today.

"What did you have for breakfast?" Ronald Reagan is asked.

It is a simple question, something anyone with a memory could answer immediately.

Reagan stammers. He smiles as he racks his brain. He does not know what he had for breakfast. In fact, it is not clear if he knows what breakfast is.

The doctors take notes. The truth is the former president is now totally dependent on Nancy. Reagan has begun asking Nancy questions such as "What do I do next?" and observing aloud, "I'm not sure where I am." He no longer recognizes old friends. Nancy

Reagan listens in on his phone calls to prompt him when he experiences memory failure. When asked by *Time* magazine journalist Hugh Sidey about Watergate shortly after Richard Nixon's death, Reagan cannot even recall the scandal.

"Forgive me," Reagan finally admitted to Sidey, "but at my age, my memory is just not as good as it used to be."

Now, at the Mayo Clinic, Reagan fails to answer the breakfast question. He also cannot recite a short three-item list after it is presented to him. The situation is clear.

"Over the past twelve months we began to notice from President Reagan's test results symptoms indicating the possibility of early stage Alzheimer's Disease," reads the diagnosis. "Additional testing and an extensive observation over the past few weeks have led us to conclude that President Reagan is entering the early stages of this disease.

"Although his health is otherwise good, it is expected that as the years go on it will begin to deteriorate. Unfortunately, at this time there is no cure for Alzheimer's Disease and no effective treatment exists that arrests its progression."

Three months after his Mayo Clinic physical, Ronald Reagan joins past presidents and First Ladies who have made public their health woes. It was Franklin Roosevelt whose frank admission about polio in 1938 launched the charity known as the March of Dimes. Betty Ford's honesty about her breast cancer, and later her battle with alcoholism, helped make those two emotional topics open for public discussion.

Now, despite his growing confusion and forgetfulness, Ronald Reagan is still alert enough to be aware of the fate that has befallen him. On good days, he understands he is helpless to stop the advance of Alzheimer's. The disease is fatal, killing its victims in four to twelve years. The only drug currently on the market, Tacrine, is not a cure but a stopgap to improve memory temporarily.

The world is still learning about Alzheimer's. They lump it together with terms such as *senility* and *dementia.* The date is November 5, 1994, as Ronald Reagan takes pen to paper to tell the world.

My Fellow Americans,

I have recently been told that I am one of the millions of Americans who will be afflicted with Alzheimer's Disease. Upon learning this news, Nancy & I had to decide whether as private citizens we keep this a private matter or whether we would make this news known in a public way. In the past Nancy suffered from breast cancer and I had my cancer surgeries. We found through our open disclosures we were able to raise public awareness. We were happy that as a result many more people underwent testing. They were treated in early stages and able to return to normal, healthy lives.

So now, we feel it is important to share it with you. In opening our hearts, we hope this might promote greater awareness of this condition. Perhaps it will encourage a clearer understanding of the individuals and families who are affected by it.

At the moment I feel just fine. I intend to live the remainder of the years God gives me on this earth doing the things I have always done. I will continue to share life's journey with my beloved Nancy and my family. I plan to enjoy the great outdoors and stay in touch with my friends and supporters.

Unfortunately, as Alzheimer's Disease progresses, the family often bears a heavy burden. I only wish there was some way I could spare Nancy from this painful experience. When the time comes I am confident that with your help she will face it with faith and courage.

In closing let me thank you, the American people, for giving me the great honor of allowing me to serve as your President. When the Lord calls me home, whenever that may be, I will leave with the greatest love for this country of ours and eternal optimism for its future.

I now begin the journey that will lead me into the sunset of my life. I know that for America there will always be a bright dawn ahead.

Thank you, my friends. May God always bless you.

Sincerely,
Ronald Reagan

With his fate sealed, Ronald Reagan sits in a pew at the Bel Air Presbyterian Church. A tall wooden cross rises from behind the pulpit as senior pastor Michael Wenning leads the congregation in the Lord's Prayer. "Our Father," says Reagan, in words he memorized as a child. He fixes his eyes on the cross. "Who art in Heaven, hallowed be thy name . . ."

Next to Reagan sits Nancy, who also prays aloud.

And next to Nancy is Patti Davis. After years of bitter isolation and estrangement, Ronald Reagan's Alzheimer's diagnosis has finally brought his daughter back. Incredibly, she is about to move home, mending a lifetime of wounds to be near her father in his last days. Patti Davis's turnaround is amazing.

Like her siblings, she has set aside the past. Gone are the days of angrily mocking her father's politics. Her aim is now reconciliation instead of rebellion.

"Amen."

It is a February afternoon in 1996, a day of cool sunshine and clear skies in Southern California. George Shultz sips tea with Ronald and Nancy Reagan at their Bel-Air home. The azaleas along the driveway are just beginning to bloom. The former secretary of state has come to say hello to his former boss, a man whom he served for six and a half years. Together, they spent countless hours crafting the foreign policy that would come to define the Reagan administration, ending the Cold War and bringing an end to Communist influence around the world. They traveled together aboard Air Force One and sat together at the bargaining table as Reagan coolly negotiated a new arms treaty with Soviet leader Mikhail Gorbachev.

But Ronald Reagan remembers none of that. He has even begun to forget that he was once president of the United States. And although he keeps regular hours at his nearby office in Century City, his time is spent mostly reading the comics and sitting in the nearby Armand Hammer Park, watching children at play.

On the outside, Reagan still looks healthy. On the inside, he is dying. Sometimes Reagan wakes up in the middle of the night thinking it is time for breakfast. He can still dress himself, sometimes tying a neat Windsor knot. His handshake is still firm. And when he ventures out to the Los Angeles Country Club to play golf, he is very much like other golfers on the course, exulting in good shots and swearing angrily when his drives go astray. But Reagan's round is limited to one or two holes instead of eighteen.

Perhaps the most telling sign that the end is near is that Reagan's beloved Rancho del Cielo is for sale. No longer able to ride a horse or clear brush, Reagan never goes to the ranch. It is now up for sale to the highest bidder.

Of this, Ronald Reagan has no idea.

As George Shultz and Nancy Reagan continue to visit on this warm winter afternoon, Reagan finally stands and leaves the room, followed by a nurse.

"Who is that man sitting on the couch with Nancy?" the former president asks the nurse. "I know him. He is a very famous man."

32

St. John's Health Center
Santa Monica, California
January 20, 2001
9:05 A.M.

Nancy Reagan sits in a chair next to her husband's hospital bed, watching a new president being sworn in.

"I, George Walker Bush, do solemnly swear . . ."

Ronald Reagan also watches the ceremony, completely unaware that he took that same oath twenty years ago today. There is a faraway look in his eyes as he gazes at the television. It is now seven years since the Alzheimer's diagnosis. Reagan will turn ninety in two weeks. Eight days ago, he broke his hip in a fall at home, and upon his release from the hospital he will be bedridden for the rest of his life. The former president's rugged physique has grown frail, his daily workouts a thing of the past. His once-broad shoulders are shrunken; the bones in his back are clearly visible, pressing through his thin flesh.

But Ronald Reagan is unaware of his physical condition. He also does not even recognize his own wife. "My mother speaks of the loneliness of her life now," daughter Patti writes in her journal. "He's here, but in so many ways he's not. She feels the loneliness in small ways — he used to put lotion on her back. Now he doesn't. And in the huge, overwhelming ways — a future that will be spent missing him."

Nancy knows that her unswerving devotion to her husband made her a target of scorn in their White House days, and for that she makes no apologies. "I'm the one who knows him best, and I was the only person in the White House who had absolutely no agenda of her own — except helping him," she stated in her autobiography.

The Reagans' good friend Jimmy Stewart once noted that if "Nancy had been Ron's first wife instead of his second, he would have been a real star in Hollywood, with a couple Oscars to show for it."

Instead, Nancy guided him to the presidency. "As much as I love Ronnie," she writes, "I'll admit he does have at least one fault: He can be naive about the people around him. Ronnie only tends to think well of people. While that's a fine quality in a friend, it can get you into trouble in politics."

In this way, Nancy Reagan had a hand in changing the world. Now, as she and her Ronnie watch the presidential inauguration just hours before Reagan will be released from the hospital, her commitment to him continues. Since the fall, he never leaves the house anymore, other than on those occasions when he is placed in a wheelchair and rolled outside to the patio.

"My father is the only man in the house these days, except for members of his Secret Service detail who occasionally come in," Patti Davis will write. "It's a house of women now — the nurses, my mother, the housekeepers."*

It is a tedious life for Nancy. She remains at her husband's side night and day, leaving

* Ronald Reagan's home is watched over by a Secret Service detail. There is also a day nurse and night nurse, along with a full cooking and housekeeping staff. There are bedrooms for two servants, a wine cellar, an exercise room, and a hothouse for growing flowers outside near the pool.

only occasionally to have a Cobb salad and chocolate chip cookies with friends at the nearby Hotel Bel-Air. The relief is needed because Ronald Reagan can no longer do anything for himself. His home office has been turned into a bedroom. There, next to the desk on which he once wrote so many letters and speeches, he spends his days on a hospital bed, tended to by his staff and Nancy. He cannot feed himself or even speak.

He is simply waiting to die.

"I christen thee United States Ship *Ronald Reagan,* and God bless all those who sail on her," says Nancy Reagan on March 4, 2001, standing before a crowd of thousands in Newport News, Virginia. She swings the traditional bottle of champagne, shattering it against the ship's steel hull. Nancy smiles as the audience of naval personnel and dockyard employees breaks into applause. Her husband would love knowing that a nuclear-powered aircraft carrier is being commissioned in his honor.

On this day, she and Ronald have been married forty-nine years. But Ronald Reagan does not know this as he lies almost still, day after day, in California.

"It's lonely," Nancy will tell Mike Wallace

in a rare televised interview for *60 Minutes.* "When you come right down to it, you're in it alone. And there's nothing that anybody can do for you."

So it is that one year after the USS *Ronald Reagan* is launched, the Reagans' landmark fiftieth wedding anniversary comes and goes without fanfare. "There were times I had to catch myself," Nancy will recall of March 4, 2002. "Because I'd reach out and start to say, 'Honey, remember when . . .' "

Two years later, it is clear that Nancy Reagan's lonely vigil will soon come to an end.

Ronald Reagan, asleep, is struggling to breathe, unaware that his daughter Patti sits atop his old desk, watching him slip away. Ron Jr. has cut short a Hawaiian vacation and is on his way to California. "We are witnesses to the end of a life," Patti will write, "and even though we have known this is coming for years, it feels as if we have never considered it as a reality."

But Nancy Reagan will not say good-bye to her husband. Throughout his decade of decline, she has tended to him as if he were still sound of body and mind. Nancy still sleeps in their bed, keeping as many traditions alive as possible.

From the day they met in 1949, she made it her mission to marry Ronald Reagan and then mold him into the man she thought he could be. She has endured years of scathing attacks, all because of her loyalty to her husband.

Even now, in the midst of what doctors are calling "continual neurological degradation," Nancy protects the former president. No outsiders are allowed to see him, other than family. Right to the end, she is managing the legacy of Ronald Reagan, even as she struggles to imagine life without him.

"He's there," she once told an interviewer, explaining why she could not say good-bye to this man with whom she'd shared a wondrous lifelong journey. "He's there."

Two days later, on June 5, 2004, a sobbing Nancy finally acknowledges the reality.

Ronald Reagan is gone.

33

National Cathedral
Washington, DC
June 11, 2004
Noon

The whole world is watching.

"We have lost a great president, a great American, and a great man, and I have lost a dear friend," says Margaret Thatcher, her face appearing on the big-screen monitors arrayed throughout the cathedral. "In his lifetime, Ronald Reagan was such a cheerful and invigorating presence that it was easy to forget what daunting historic tasks he set himself."

Nearly four thousand mourners fill this century-old Episcopal church, watching as Thatcher praises her dear friend on videotape. Among the crowd are the Reagan family, President George W. Bush, and former presidents Ford, Carter, Bush, and Clinton. Thatcher herself is in attendance, dressed all in black with an enormous hat, seated up front next to Mikhail Gorbachev. She is frail and hunched, her doctors having ordered her not to travel. Thatcher has ignored them out of respect for her longtime friend. However, fearing that she might embarrass herself by speaking live at the service, Baroness Thatcher videotaped her anticipated eulogy for Reagan months ago in London.

But not everyone is giving tribute. In Communist Cuba, the government greets Reagan's death with a proclamation attacking his conservative policies, stating, "He should never have been born."

And in America, the far left's opinion of Reagan's passing is summarized in *Slate* magazine: "He was as dumb as a stump," writes Christopher Hitchens. "I could not believe that such a man had even been a poor governor of California in a bad year, let alone that such a smart country would put up with such an obvious phony and loon."

Reagan's funeral is the largest in America since that of President John F. Kennedy more than forty years ago. Security is extremely tight, as this is the first major national event since the September 11, 2001, terrorist attacks on New York City and Washington, DC. But once Reagan's body rests inside the Capitol Rotunda and the doors are opened to the public on the evening of June 9, a wave of humanity arrives to pay their respects. Many have been waiting two days for this opportunity. All through the night and the next day, five thousand visitors per hour walk past the casket of Ronald Reagan.

On the morning of June 11, which President George W. Bush has declared a national day of mourning, the body of Ronald Reagan is delivered to the National Cathedral for the first state funeral since that of Lyndon Johnson in 1973.

With a global television audience looking on, and 3,700 mourners in the pews, Margaret Thatcher's taped eulogy concludes.

"Ronald Reagan's life was rich not only in public achievement, but also in private happiness. Indeed, his public achievements were rooted in his private happiness.

"The great turning point of his life was his meeting and marriage with Nancy. On that, we have the plain testimony of a loving and grateful husband. 'Nancy came along and saved my soul.'"

Television cameras and all within view

Nancy Reagan kisses her husband's coffin.

turn to Nancy. Despite the ten long years of Reagan's decline, and the ample time she has had to prepare for this moment, she is consumed by grief.

"We share her grief today," Thatcher continues. "For the final years of his life, Ronnie's mind was clouded by illness.

"That cloud has now lifted. He is himself again, more himself than at any time on this Earth, for we may be sure that the Big Fellow upstairs never forgets those who remember him. And as the last journey of this faithful pilgrim took him beyond the sunset, and as heaven's morning broke, I like to think, in the words of John Bunyan, that 'all the trumpets sounded on the other side.' "

A subtle smile creases Thatcher's lips on the screen as she ends her eulogy. As she does so, it is possible to see the slight facial paralysis from her recent series of strokes, and yet her voice is clear and deliberate.

"We here still move in twilight, but we have one beacon to guide us that Ronald Reagan never had.

"We have his example."

That evening, the body of Ronald Reagan is buried in California. Margaret Thatcher is there. So is Jane Wyman. Nancy Reagan kisses the coffin and whispers, "I love you," before stepping away for good. Nancy, clutching the American flag that once draped her husband's coffin, dissolves in tears. She looks pale, fragile, and frightened.

Four F-18 fighter jets thunder overhead while a military band plays "America the Beautiful." Symbolically, one of the jets suddenly peels away, leaving the other three to fly on in the "missing man" formation.

"I know in my heart that man is good," the inscription on Reagan's tombstone reads, "that what is right will always eventually triumph, and there is purpose and worth to each and every life."

AFTERWORD

In January 2015, the *Journal of Alzheimer's Disease* published a study examining the press conferences of Ronald Reagan's presidency. Researchers were looking for changes in his vocabulary that might have signaled an early onset of dementia. They found three specific symptoms: Reagan's use of repetitive words increased, as did his habit of substituting "it" or "thing" for specific nouns. Meanwhile, use of unique words declined. The study's authors also noted that trauma and the use of anesthesia can hasten dementia. They specifically mentioned that the 1981 assassination attempt could also have played a pivotal role in Ronald Reagan's decline.

The man who shot Reagan, **John Hinckley Jr.**, remains at St. Elizabeth's Hospital in Washington, DC, to this day. More than thirty years after being found not guilty of attempting to assassinate the president by reason of insanity, Hinckley may not remain in custody much longer. In December 2013 a federal judge declared he was "not a danger" and authorized unsupervised visits of up to seventeen days at his mother's home in Williamsburg, Virginia. Hinckley is allowed to drive a car but not to talk to the media. The judge requires that he carry a GPS-enabled cell phone in order that they can track his movements. In time, he may become a completely free man, following in the footsteps of attempted presidential assassins Squeaky Fromme and Sara Jane Moore, who were released in 2009 and 2007, respectively. Both women served more than three decades in prison for attempting to kill President Gerald Ford.

In January 2015, prosecutors declined to press additional murder charges in the August 2014 death of Reagan press secretary **James Brady** — despite the fact that Hinckley's bullets were directly responsible for the wounds that ultimately killed Brady at age seventy-three. Brady never fully recovered from the ordeal, spending the second half of his life dealing with constant pain, slurred speech, paralysis, and short-term memory loss. As a result, his wife, Sarah, who sat with Nancy Reagan in the hospital chapel on the day of the assassination attempt, became a ferocious advocate for gun control. **Sarah Brady** died of pneumonia at the age of seventy-three in April 2015, less than a year after her husband passed away.

Tim McCarthy, the only man in Secret Service history to take a bullet for a president, currently serves as the chief of police in the Chicago suburb of Orland Park. "I'm glad I got to do it," he told the *Chicago Tribune* in 2011. "I'm glad to do what I was trained to do."

District of Columbia policeman **Thomas K. Delahanty**, Hinckley's final victim, sued the gun manufacturer whose bullet ended his police career. He also sued John Hinckley, though the courts ruled against him in both cases. Delahanty made cameo appearances in two movies about the assassination attempt but never returned to police work.

As of this writing in August 2015, **Nancy Reagan** still lives in the Bel-Air, California, home she once shared with Ronald Reagan. The former First Lady, who in the words of one reporter "rescued the Reagan presidency," laid a wreath on his tomb in 2011 to celebrate the hundredth anniversary of his birth. She has endured her own health problems, including a fractured pelvis in 2008 and broken ribs sustained in a fall four years later. Yet while often confined to a wheelchair and in declining health, Nancy Reagan continues to be an advocate for Alzheimer's research.

The Reagan children remain in the public eye. **Patti Davis** once again posed nude, this time for *More* magazine in 2011, at the age of fifty-eight, and continues to make a living as a freelance writer.

Ron Reagan Jr. lives in Seattle, where he currently works as an advocate for atheism and for stem cell research. In March 2014, he lost his wife of thirty-three years, Doria Palmieri Reagan, to a progressive neuromuscular disease. Ron Reagan continues to be a liberal advocate, often appearing on cable news programs.

Michael Reagan is a longtime conservative radio talk show host. He called his adoptive half brother, Ron, an "embarrassment" for suggesting in a book that their father suffered from Alzheimer's disease while serving as president. Michael Reagan's life has not been easy, as he has been involved in a variety of civil lawsuits.

The only child of Ronald Reagan to attempt a political career, **Maureen**, died of melanoma in 2001 at the age of sixty. She is buried at Calvary Catholic Cemetery in Sacramento.

Jodie Foster not only survived the media scrutiny that came with the Reagan assassination attempt but has thrived. After graduating from Yale in 1985, she went on to a distinguished Hollywood career as an actor, director, and producer. Foster has won two Academy Awards for Best Actress, the first in 1989 for her role in *The Accused* and the second in 1992 for her signature lead role in *The Silence of the Lambs.* John Hinckley was reportedly outraged when Jodie Foster came out as a lesbian in 2013.

Two thousand thirteen was also the year **Margaret Thatcher** died, at age eighty-seven. The former British prime minister was elevated to baroness in 1992 and made a member of the House of Lords after a lifetime as a commoner. Her memory began to fail her in 2000, but it was a series of small strokes in 2002 that led her to withdraw from public life. Her taping of Ronald Reagan's eulogy was the last public speech she ever gave. The ashes of Margaret Hilda Thatcher are interred on the grounds of the Royal Hospital Chelsea in London, next to those of her husband, Denis, who died in 2003.

James Baker III, Ronald Reagan's chief of staff during his first term in office, is still active as a political adviser at the age of eighty-five, as is his fellow member of the Reagan troika, **Edwin Meese**. At age eighty-three, Meese lives in Virginia, where he serves on a number of educational boards and public policy think tanks.

Reagan's third adviser, **Michael Deaver**, fell prey to pancreatic cancer on August 18, 2007. Deaver left the Reagan White House after the first term, opening a successful Washington lobbying agency. On March 18, 1987, he was convicted of five counts of perjury during an investigation into his use of insider influence and power with his new firm. His crime was perjuring himself to Congress and a federal grand jury. For that, Deaver was sentenced to three years' probation and fined one hundred thousand dollars. Despite Deaver's request, Ronald Reagan did not extend the offer of a pardon before leaving office. Nancy Reagan did not attend Deaver's funeral, but she issued a statement saying that Deaver was "like a son." Michael Deaver was sixty-nine years old when he passed away.

Nancy's feelings were obviously not as warm toward **Don Regan**. After the White House chief was fired because of her, Regan turned to landscape painting as a way to pass his days. He was content in his artistic endeavors, often spending as much as ten hours a day painting. Don Regan died of cancer on June 10, 2003. He is buried in Arlington National Cemetery.

Ronald Reagan's first wife, **Jane Wyman**, lived to be ninety years old. After divorcing Reagan, Wyman went on to have one more husband, bandleader Fred Karger, whom she married and divorced twice. By the time of her death in 2007, she had become such a devout Catholic that she was laid to rest in the habit of the Dominican Sisters religious order. Jane Wyman is buried in Forest Lawn Cemetery in Los Angeles, California.

Ronald Reagan's mother, **Nelle Reagan**,

died on July 25, 1962. She was seventy-nine years old. Her husband, the hard-drinking Jack Reagan, died in 1941 at age fifty-seven. Both are buried at the Calvary Cemetery in East Los Angeles. Ronald Reagan's lone sibling, his older brother Neil, died in 1996 of heart failure. His body was cremated.

Ronald Reagan's beloved **Rancho del Cielo** was sold in 1998. But the property has not been developed or subdivided, nor has the white adobe ranch house been torn down. Rather, the property remains exactly as it was during the time Ronald and Nancy Reagan owned it. A conservative group known as the Young America's Foundation purchased the land from Nancy Reagan, who lowered her asking price significantly to make the sale possible. A museum in Santa Barbara, California, recounts the history of the ranch, while also displaying a number of items of Reagan memorabilia. There are a limited number of tours of the property, allowing visitors to comprehend firsthand exactly why Ronald Reagan knew such contentment at this mountaintop retreat.

To this day, there are those who contend that the ghost of Ronald Reagan is present on the property.

LAST WORD

In researching and writing this book, Martin Dugard and I were extremely careful to use only material we could confirm through at least two sources, and even then we tried to be very fair in presenting facts that might put certain individuals in a bad light.

In the last year of his presidency, Ronald Reagan was aware that some close to him were questioning the way he was running his administration. Critical books by daughter Patti, Donald Regan, former spokesman Larry Speakes, and others apparently wounded Reagan, who valued loyalty. The president, however, kept his own counsel, rarely saying anything in public.

On May 16, 1988, he finally let loose in a private letter to his friend and adviser John Koehler. That letter is now owned by me and so it is fitting to publish it in this book, thereby giving Ronald Wilson Reagan the last word.

He deserves it.

BILL O'REILLY
Long Island
New York

THE WHITE HOUSE

WASHINGTON

May 16, 1988

Dear John:

Thank you very much for your May 10 letter.
You were more than kind, and Nancy and I
thank you from the bottom of our hearts.
You know, John, one of the hardest things to
bear in all of this are the outright falsehoods.
Nancy never opened her mouth about Casey,
Donovan or Heckler, and she certainly didn't
fire Don. Truth is, he'd told me several months
earlier he wanted to get back to private life,
and I left it to him to name the day. And,
of course, we haven't been charting our course
by the stars.

Nancy sends her thanks, and from both of us to
Dorothy; and again we deeply appreciate your
words and your prayers.

Sincerely,

Ronald Reagan

Mr. John O. Koehler
One Strawberry Hill Avenue
Stamford, Connecticut 06902

SOURCES

Ronald Reagan lived his entire adult life in the public eye. This media scrutiny could be burdensome to him at times, but it worked very well for our purposes, greatly assisting our research process. One particular advantage is the enormous supply of video documenting his acting and political careers. The reader is encouraged to look at the many press conferences, inaugurations, speeches, presidential debates, and myriad other public appearances, and even *Saturday Night Live* sketches, available online.

And while this book is about Ronald Reagan, the powerful historical moments that defined the careers of Richard Nixon, Gerald Ford, Jimmy Carter, Alexander Haig, Margaret Thatcher, and so many other towering figures are also available for all to see. Video does not go as deep as letters and diaries, but it does allow the researcher to see the anguish or joy on an individual's face (Margaret Thatcher's eulogy of Reagan is heartbreaking in this regard), to hear the rhythm of spoken words, and to know the context in which those words were delivered. Reagan's "Tear Down This Wall" speech is all the more powerful when watching him deliver those words.

As with the other books in the *Killing* series, we consulted a wide variety of sources to tell Ronald Reagan's story in vivid detail. In addition to video, sources included books, magazine articles, archives, newspapers, FBI and CIA files, online databases, presidential libraries, and transcripts of interviews with people who worked with him in a personal and professional capacity. The Zillow website, for instance, allowed us a tour of the Reagan home in Pacific Palisades, which was recently on the market. It was also very helpful that the Margaret Thatcher Foundation (margaretthatcher.org) and the Ronald Reagan Presidential Library (reaganlibrary .gov and reaganfoundation.org) have catalogued not only the letters of these great leaders but also the transcripts and even audiotapes of their discussions, allowing us to listen in.

The Miller Center at the University of

Virginia (millercenter.org) is a treasure trove of information about all things presidential. Reagan's diary entries and daily White House schedule can be found online at reaganfoundation.org. On a different note, the White House Museum (whitehouse museum.org) takes readers throughout the entire building, with behind-the-scenes photos of the West Wing and the residence through the years.

Travel, as always, was vital to adding great descriptive detail, sending us to locations in the United States and around the world that were pivotal to Reagan's personal and political life. Most pivotal was the day spent at Rancho del Cielo, just north of Santa Barbara. Thanks to Andrew Coffin of the Young America's Foundation for the lengthy and engaging private tour.

What follows is a brief list of the many books, magazines, and newspapers that we used in the writing of this book. Much thanks to the world of Google Books, which allows writers to research a library's worth of great reference works without leaving the home office. These meanderings drew in a number of other historical figures and unchronicled events. Hundreds of books, magazine articles, and newspaper stories were bookmarked and cross-referenced as we wrote. We have chosen to list the ones most crucial to this research. The books include: All the works of Kiron K. Skinner, Annelise Andersen, and Martin Anderson, particularly *Reagan: A Life in Letters* and *Reagan, In His Own Hand: The Writings of Ronald Reagan that Reveal His Revolutionary Vision for America;* Edmund Morris, *Dutch: A Memoir of Ronald Reagan;* Kitty Kelley, *Nancy Reagan: The Unauthorized Biography;* Jane Mayer and Doyle McManus, *Landslide: The Unmaking of the President, 1984–1988;* Nancy Reagan, *My Turn: The Memoirs of Nancy Reagan;* John R. Barletta, *Riding with Reagan: From the White House to the Ranch;* Del Quentin Wilber, *Rawhide Down: The Near Assassination of Ronald Reagan;* James W. Clarke, *Defining Danger: American Assassins and the New Domestic Terrorists;* Peter Schweizer, *Reagan's War: The Epic Story of His Forty-Year Struggle and Final Triumph over Communism;* Stephen Vaughn, *Ronald Reagan in Hollywood: Movies and Politics;* Jimmy Carter, *White House Diary;* Lou Cannon, *President Reagan: The Role of a Lifetime;* Michelangelo Capua, *William Holden: A Biography;* Marc Eliot, *Reagan: The Hollywood Years;* David Gergen, *Eyewitness to Power: The Essence of Leadership;*

Jonathan Aitken, *Margaret Thatcher: Power and Personality;* Patti Davis, *The Long Goodbye: Memories of My Father;* and the very emotional *Breaking Points,* by Jack and Jo Ann Hinckley.

We also consulted a broad number of magazines and newspapers marking the passage of Reagan's life and career through the many stories published in their pages. Listing each of the hundreds of articles would have been unwieldy; instead we've given the publications upon which we relied most: the *Los Angeles Times,* the *New York Times, Vanity Fair, Time,* the *National Review,* the *Washington Post,* the *Daily Mail* (London), the *Daily Telegraph* (London), the *Philadelphia Inquirer,* the *Boston Globe,* the *Atlantic, Billboard, Variety, Forbes,* and the *Pittsburgh Press.*

The authors would also like to thank Roger Ailes, Pat Caddell, Lou Cannon, and Lesley Stahl for their personal insights. In addition, Dr. Jimmy Byron at the Richard Nixon Foundation was particularly helpful.

ACKNOWLEDGMENTS

The usual suspects helped me get it all down on paper: my assistant for more than twenty years Makeda Wubneh, literary agent to the stars Eric Simonoff, perspicacious publisher Steve Rubin, wise editor Gillian Blake, and my TV boss Roger Ailes. Thank you, guys!

— BILL O'REILLY

Thanks to Eric Simonoff, the world's greatest agent and the man who made the O'Reilly/Dugard team a reality. To the calm and very organized Makeda Wubneh. To Steve Rubin and Gillian Blake at Holt, for their wit, insight, and quick reads. To Al and Rosemary Dugard. To my boys: Devin, Connor, and Liam. And as always to Calene, who makes me a better man.

— MARTIN DUGARD

ILLUSTRATION CREDITS

Maps by Gene Thorp
Page 16: © Bettmann/CORBIS
Page 37: SNAP/REX Shutterstock
Page 43: John Kobal Foundation/ Moviepix/ Getty Images
Page 45: mptvimages.com
Page 52: Warner Bros./Photofest
Page 64: © Everett Collection/age fotostock
Page 75: Photofest
Page 89: Everett Collection/Newscom
Page 124: Universal Pictures/Photofest © Universal Pictures
Page 127: CSU Archives/Everett Collection
Page 174: PA Archive/ABACAUSA.com/ Newscom
Page 214: Columbia/Kobal/Art Resource
Page 256: Archivio GBB/Contrasto/Redux
Page 278: akg-images/Universal Images Group/Tass
Page 305: AP Photo/Ron Edmonds

ABOUT THE AUTHORS

Bill O'Reilly is the anchor of *The O'Reilly Factor,* the highest-rated cable news show in the country. He is the author of many number-one bestselling books, including *Killing Lincoln, Killing Kennedy, Killing Jesus,* and *Killing Patton.*

Martin Dugard is the *New York Times* bestselling author of several books of history. He and his wife live in Southern California with their three sons.